The Scottish Parliament

BRIAN TAYLOR

POLYGON

AT EDINBURGH

328.411

1297364

Polygon at Edinburgh
An imprint of Edinburgh University Press Ltd
22, George Square, Edinburgh

Typeset in Bembo
by Pioneer Associates, Perthshire, and
Printed and bound in Great Britain by
The Cromwell Press, Trowbridge

A CIP Record for this book is available from the British Library

ISBN 1 902930 12 6 (paperback)

Contents

Introduction

Slowly, up the steps of Bute House in Edinburgh, they saunter. Donald Dewar, the First Minister of Scotland, and John Reid, the Secretary of State for Scotland, pause briefly for the persistent demands of the cameras. Just one more, Mr Dewar. This way please, Mr Reid. Into the house itself, a government residence, an elegant Georgian dwelling in Charlotte Square, the kernel of the New Town. Welcomed by eager staff who are delighted that the old mansion will still have a role to play in the new politics of Scotland.

Donald Dewar, turning to his friend and colleague, says comfortingly: 'Just make yourself at home, John. Whatever you need.' Reid looks at him with a wry grin and replies: 'Funny thing, Donald, but I was just going to say exactly the same to you.'

It was Friday, 22 May 1999, and Scotland was still experiencing transitional power. The new Parliament had not yet taken full responsibility; that happened on 1 July, with the royal opening. Donald Dewar had not yet assumed executive power.

Before the election, the splendid terraced house had been Dewar's to command as Secretary of State at Westminster. It became his again as fully-fledged First Minister in the Scottish Parliament. However, this was during the handover – that curious period of political limbo which followed the tension of the May contest and the coalition talks. John Reid, as the new Secretary of State, was the political boss of Scotland, and, strictly speaking, the host at Bute House.

Scottish politicians have had to get accustomed to a lot more than an amusing quibble about property rights. There may be more uncertainty yet before Scotland adapts to her new political structure.

From being a participant in a Westminster Parliament, elected by the traditional first-past-the-post system, and with a landslide majority Labour Government, Scotland has been transformed. Alongside that Westminster link, Scotland now has her own Parliament – the first since the Act of Union with England in 1707. That Parliament was elected by a proportional voting system. In addition, those elections produced, ultimately, a coalition government between Labour and the Liberal Democrats.

My purpose in this book is to trace the steps leading to that remarkable development. Not the history, not an arid incantation of dates and statistics, but the key underlying developments and motivations. I intend also to look at the problems which will confront the Parliament: not day-to-day policy issues but elemental questions

Getting down to business: Scotland's new Cabinet Ministers take up their posts,
17 May 1999. (Kindly supplied by *The Scotsman* Publications Ltd.)

like finance, relations with Europe, the future of Westminster after devolution.

Before plunging into the background, however, a quick reminder of the basics. Scotland went to the polls on 6 May 1999. On the same day, there were elections to the National Assembly of Wales and local elections throughout Britain.

The contest in Scotland was fascinating, if relatively tame on occasion. Partly that was because the positions of the various parties had been well established over a period of years. They were like chess players who have contested each other so often that they can generally guess the next move. For all that, the end game – the election of a hung parliament – was enthralling.

Partly, also, the election campaign was somewhat understated by contrast with an atmosphere of violence elsewhere. Predominantly, there was the conflict in Yugoslavia: the bombing campaign launched by NATO in an effort to prevent Serbian aggression against Kosovo.

The campaign was accompanied by other shocking events: the killing of broadcaster Jill Dando in London on 26 April, the nail bomb in a Soho pub on 30 April which followed earlier bombs in London's Brixton and Brick Lane, violence at the Old Firm football match on 2 May. With events like these to the forefront of everyone's consciousness – and especially the Kosovo conflict – it was perhaps understandable that partisan politics became apparently a little less strident.

Still, there was much to intrigue the media and the voting public. There were the party manifestos: no longer simply regional versions of UK policy pledges, but distinct programmes for government, deserving the closest scrutiny.

There were the policy controversies – the Private Finance Initiative, student tuition fees, the tax powers of a Scottish Parliament, drugs sentencing, the prospects for independence. There was speculation over the Liberal Democrat stance on coalition, gossip over problems in the SNP campaign, rumours of tension in Labour ranks, question marks over Scottish Tory efforts to return to elected parliamentary politics. I intend to look at each of these later.

Above all, there was the culmination: election night and the coalition talks. Inside BBC Scotland, whenever we discussed the campaign, I constantly stressed that the election on Thursday, 6 May was not necessarily the core news event. It was almost certain that there would have to be subsequent political haggling to resolve Scotland's government. 'Friday's the story,' I would insist. At one point, I gently threatened to emblazon a banner with that slogan and suspend it over the newsroom.

Friday, indeed, proved to be the story. And Saturday, Sunday, Monday. . . The coalition talks stretched out, tense, awkward, hampered by a Liberal Democrat pledge to scrap tuition fees and Labour's determination to keep them in place.

On Saturday, 8 May, the new Liberal Democrat MSPs gathered at the Dome in Edinburgh's George Street, financial offices elegantly converted into a smart restaurant and rooms. The LibDems looked like entrants for the political equivalent of the Eurovision Song Contest, eager, fresh and perpetually smiling. Still grinning, they endorsed the opening of negotiations with Labour.

The talks were needed because the election had left a hung parliament. There were 129 seats on offer: seventy-three of them in traditional first-past-the-post constituencies and fifty-six from top-up party lists, counted in eight regions around Scotland. Labour had

Smiles before the hard bargaining: Jim Wallace and Liberal Democrat MSPs meet in Edinburgh on the Saturday after the election, 8 May 1999. (Kindly supplied by PA News Ltd.)

won fifty-six seats in total (including three from the lists), the Scottish National Party had taken thirty-five (with no fewer than twenty-eight coming from the lists), the Conservatives eighteen (all list) and the Liberal Democrats seventeen (including five list).

Dennis Canavan – the long-serving Westminster MP ruled out by Labour as a potential Scottish parliamentary candidate – had delighted most observers (except, of course, Labour loyalists) by winning Falkirk West on his own initiative. The PR voting system had given Tommy Sheridan of the Scottish Socialist Party a seat in Glasgow and Robin Harper of the Greens a seat in Lothian.

In the event of a hung parliament, the LibDems had pledged to open talks with the largest party. So on Monday, 10 May, after the weekend endorsement from their parliamentary group and executive, the Liberal Democrats despatched their negotiating team to begin the task.

The first initiative had come on the Friday, the day after the election, when Labour's Scottish leader had telephoned his Liberal Democrat counterpart, Jim Wallace, to suggest talks. Dewar had made plain from the outset that he was interested in a formal partnership, a coalition, rather than any looser arrangement.

In truth, this was enforced by the election result. Labour were nine seats short of an overall majority. They needed a stable pact. Equally, though, Dewar was stamping his mark on the process. Other senior Labour figures, including, it was claimed, the Chancellor Gordon Brown, had argued internally for the party to keep open the options of a loose accommodation or a minority government, steering clear of a formal deal. With the tone of his call to Jim Wallace, Dewar was signalling that he was driving the talks.

The argument for a formal pact was strong. Unlike in Wales, the Scottish Parliament has primary powers to make and reform laws. Without the assurance of a coalition, Labour would be entering the Scottish chamber each day uncertain as to whether it could get its legislation through. Uncertainty, indeed, would be the hallmark of Scottish governance. Further, the Liberal Democrats had repeatedly stressed that they were not interested in anything short of a full partnership administration.

On Monday, 10 May, then, the Liberal Democrat team set off in a taxi from party headquarters to the new Parliament's temporary home on the Mound in Edinburgh. At party HQ opposite Haymarket

Station, the champagne corks still lay on the ground and the steadily deflating party balloons clung to the ironwork gates: the remnants of a celebration – not, understandably, for coming fourth but for coming within sight of government, the party's dream for generations.

The Liberal Democrat team was headed by Wallace and included MSPs Nicol Stephen, Ross Finnie and Iain Smith plus the party convener Iain Yuill and two members elected by the executive, Andy Myles and Dennis Sullivan. Of these, Myles was perhaps the most sceptical about links with Labour – and had been inserted by the executive as a counterbalance to the varying degrees of enthusiasm among the others.

The Labour team for these talks included Dewar and his ministerial colleagues from the Scottish Office, Henry McLeish and Sam Galbraith, plus group business manager Tom McCabe and one of the younger MSPs, Sarah Boyack. Prior to these formal talks, there had been three hours of informal discussion between Wallace and Dewar the night before. Both sides fielded teams of back-up advisers.

Monday's extended session ends in stalemate. Indeed, one Liberal Democrat source told me the entire process 'looked dead' at various points that day. The two sides were working from separate statements of their key aims and policies. It was possible to match elements from each – but both sides knew that there was an obstacle in waiting, the rather bizarre issue of student tuition fees.

I say bizarre because – although important to those directly affected – the issue could scarcely be compared with taxation or the condition of the health service in terms of universal public interest. Yet tuition fees had emerged as a totem of Liberal Democrat credibility.

As a Westminster government, Labour had introduced student fees of £1000 per year with exemptions and tapers for those from lower-income families. The policy was defended as a method of expanding the higher education system. It was vigorously condemned by critics as a prohibitive tax on learning, a further erosion of the supposedly free education system. In their election manifesto, the Liberal Democrats – along with the Nationalists and the Tories – had pledged to abolish fees.

The talks trudge on in the fifth floor ministerial suite in the starkly ugly former local government building, close to the Royal Mile, which has been fitted out as the administrative headquarters for the Parliament. The parliamentary chamber is in the Church of Scotland's Assembly Hall, accessed by MSPs via one of Edinburgh's ancient closes at the other side of the Royal Mile.

There are head-to-head talks, with Dewar and Wallace taking the lead. There are internal party discussions – with sessions reporting back to the parliamentary groups. Civil servants play a key role: Muir Russell, the Permanent Secretary, Robert Gordon, head of the executive secretariat, Ken Thomson, Dewar's private secretary, and others. Individual civil service experts, like Gerry Wilson, who heads the education department, are brought in to help with detail. They produce draft wordings, they help identify the scope for potential agreement and narrow the areas of dispute.

The talks go on into Tuesday. Still no deal – with Labour insiders privately muttering that the Liberal Democrats do not appear to know what they want. Indeed, one particularly acerbic Labour source tells me at one point that it is like 'negotiating with children'. The LibDem interpretation of this is that the Labour team is not getting its own way – and does not like the experience. It seems likely, however, that any apparent vacillation on the LibDem side is caused by apprehension as to what the wider party will tolerate.

Wednesday comes and the Parliament is called to order by Winnie Ewing of the SNP, as the oldest member. With dignity and evident pride, she announces that 'the Scottish Parliament which adjourned on 25 March in the year 1707 is hereby reconvened.' The link is made to the ancient, independent legislature which suspended proceedings on completion of the Union with England.

The 129 Members of the new, devolved Scottish Parliament take their oaths of allegiance to the sovereign, some prefacing their legally required statement with a declaration that their true loyalty is to the Scottish people. Tommy Sheridan replaces the customary raised open palm with a clenched fist as he mouths the words of the obligatory oath. Donald Dewar looks on in evident irritation, like a form teacher with an errant class.

In the afternoon, Sir David Steel is elected as the Presiding Officer in the very chamber where he first co-chaired the Constitutional Convention which led, ultimately, to this new Parliament. Although entitled to be called Lord Steel as a member of the Upper House at Westminster, he has chosen to be nothing more than a knight in the new Scottish politics.

Still the coalition talks continue – and still the stumbling block is the issue of tuition fees or rather the issue of the credibility of the Liberal Democrats. Labour orchestrate a series of demands from the education sector for the question of student finance to be placed before a wider review. The Liberal Democrats are initially reluctant. Would this be seen as serious by the voters – or as a fudge?

Finally, in the early hours of Thursday morning, the negotiating teams finalise a deal. They have a partnership agreement. The issue of tuition fees is indeed to be subject to a review – but, crucially from a LibDem standpoint, it is to be placed in a separate category from other elements of the deal. Wallace insists privately that this was his suggestion.

The deal has yet to be ratified by the party groups. Later that day, Thursday, 13 May, Donald Dewar is elected First Minister with seventy-one votes: his own Labour group plus the Liberal Democrats – apart from Keith Raffan, who has voiced anger at what he believes is a climbdown on tuition fees. The LibDems explain their vote for Dewar by saying the leader of the largest party is entitled to lead the Parliament. The partnership pact is still in the balance.

The First Minister's post is also contested by SNP leader Alex Salmond, Tory leader David McLetchie and Dennis Canavan. Canavan ignores parliamentary procedure, crossing the floor to offer the hand of friendship to Dewar after the vote.

Thursday afternoon and the Liberal Democrat parliamentary group meets. It is a decidedly difficult occasion. Some say the party has sold out its independent standpoint for very little in terms of concrete concessions from Labour. Several MSPs warn that the deal on tuition fees will be misrepresented by the party's rivals and misunderstood by the voters. As the talks reach a crisis, onlooking officials calculate that it is fifty/fifty – that roughly half the members of the group are opposed to ratifying the deal.

The MSPs continue to pore over the details. From London, Paddy Ashdown – then the party's federal leader and a keen advocate of closer links with Labour – frantically pages Wallace and senior Scottish officials in an effort to discover progress. Andy Myles and Dennis Sullivan from the negotiation team leave the MSPs to head to the Dome in an effort to placate the party's executive. They are next in line for consultation – but they cannot begin until the MSPs decide.

Jim Wallace knows that he cannot bully his group into submission. Liberal Democrats can be instinctively anarchic, distrusting overarching authority. Wallace must allow the critics to voice their concerns. Equally, he knows that his leadership cannot continue if the deal which he has negotiated with Dewar is rejected by the group. He opts finally to confront the critics with the consequences of rejection.

He challenges those who say that the deal risks shedding party principle. What, he asks, will we tell the voters at the next election? Vote for us – but we don't have the faintest intention of putting even a proportion of our policies into practice if given a chance? Vote for us – we are the party of consensus politics but don't expect us to compromise a single thing in order to achieve a consensus government? Do we want, in short, to be a party of protest or power?

Steadily, his arguments win over the critics – along with the consideration that Liberal Democrats may end up voting for many of the policies in the partnership document in any event. The deal is endorsed by the group – with three, Keith Raffan, Donald Gorrie and John Farquhar Munro, voting against. Finally, late at night, the

Donald Dewar and Jim Wallace seal their partnership pact with a handshake, 14 May 1999.
(Kindly supplied by *The Scotsman* Publications Ltd.)

coalition is backed by the Liberal Democrat executive. Labour's ratification has come, almost unnoticed, much earlier in the day.

Friday, 14 May, half-past eight in the morning. Donald Dewar and Jim Wallace arrive at the Museum of Scotland for a news conference to unveil the details of their deal. The twenty-four-page document promises stable, cooperative, innovative and integrated government, arguing that 'these prizes mean more to the people of Scotland than party differences.'

It tracks priorities, from extra money to hire more teachers, more support for students in financial difficulties, new targets for health care, firm backing for the enterprise economy, action on drugs, rural initiatives, a clear move towards PR voting in local government.

Yet other key Liberal Democrat demands are shelved or reduced in scope. Skye Bridge tolls are to be frozen, not scrapped. The ban on beef-on-the-bone is to be reviewed, not ended. Above all, tuition fees are to be examined as part of a wider scrutiny, not abolished. Liberal Democrat manifesto plans to use the Parliament's tax-varying powers 'if necessary' are quietly dropped by a single, brief sentence in the partnership document.

The media questions are all about tuition fees. Will the Liberal Democrats have a free vote on the outcome of the inquiry? LibDem critics say they were promised one in the internal talks. Will they get one? Wallace indicates he hopes it will not come to that – that it may be possible to reach a consensus position, that the inquiry may recommend the abolition of fees. Dewar indicates he expects a coordinated decision by the partnership government – and the operation of collective responsibility.

The controversy continues. Critics of the deal within the Liberal Democrats persist with their claim that they were explicitly offered a free vote on fees. They would not have endorsed the deal otherwise, they say. Party officials say privately the pledge was only that the Liberal Democrats as a group would be 'free to make up their own minds' on the question. Privately it is accepted that LibDem Ministers might have to back a collective line.

The eleven-member Cabinet is formed. Jim Wallace joins as deputy First Minister, grinning broadly as he enters Bute House for the first talks with his new colleagues. Accusations that he has compromised his party principles for a 'Ministerial Mondeo' turn out to be false; he has a Rover. Ross Finnie is the other Liberal Democrat in the Cabinet, with the rest Labour. A second eleven of junior Ministers, including a further two LibDems, is announced.

Scotland has a new Parliament, a new style of coalition government, a new Cabinet: new politics entirely. For the remainder of this book, I intend to examine how Scotland arrived at that point.

1 Identity – What Makes a Scot?

Do you remember the first meeting of the Scottish Convention to draw up a scheme of devolution? It was on 15 November 1924. Or the further Convention after World War II? If not those, perhaps you are more familiar with the body formed in 1989 when the Labour Party, the Liberal Democrats, the Greens, the trades unions, the local authorities, the churches and various civic groups combined in the Constitutional Convention and ultimately drafted the scheme which led to the recent reforms in the governance of Scotland.

Do you remember when the Scottish Tories produced a strategy paper advocating increased administrative devolution to Scotland? No, not under the former Scottish Secretary Sir Michael Forsyth. But on 3 November 1949.

Do you remember the House of Commons carrying a Scottish Home Rule motion? No, not in the 1990s or even the 1970s. But on 3 April 1894.

Dipping into history, of course, can be a troublesome business for political journalists and indeed for politicians. While in office as Secretary of State, Sir Michael Forsyth delivered a lecture at Stirling University attempting to place in context the modern Scottish Conservative preoccupation with the Union. In the course of the lecture, he reflected upon the centuries during which Scotland had vigorously and physically asserted her independence. In passing, he queried why Scots apparently preferred the gallant – but ultimately unsuccessful – patriotism of William Wallace to the victorious independence campaign of Robert the Bruce. The result? Headlines to the effect that the Scottish Secretary had condemned Wallace as a loser.

Although more than a mite apprehensive about deploying historical lessons to contemporary politics, I would stress that it is important at least to bear in mind that Home Rule, even post-Union, is a long-running story in Scotland.

That brings a potential upside in that politicians have a fund of earlier analysis upon which to draw. They can attempt to avoid initiatives which, while bright and shining at the time, were later seen to contain errors. Specifically and most obviously, the Labour Government learned a lot from the problems which dogged the devolution efforts of their 1970s predecessors.

The longevity of the devolution debate, however, has had a clear downside for the advocates of change. There is a risk that the public become cynical over promises, even subjects for discussion, which they feel they have heard before. Additionally, the peculiarly protracted nature of the controversy meant that the debate over Labour's latest scheme was pursued by rival party cynicism, most notably from the Nationalists but also sporadically from others.

The SNP famously declared that they 'wouldn't trust Labour to deliver a pizza – let alone a Parliament'. Labour leaders would scarcely be human if they didn't permit themselves a statesperson-like chuckle over that one in the light of subsequent developments. The Nationalists would argue, however, that they were pursuing an understandable political tactic while Labour were in opposition: essentially, warning that devolution couldn't be guaranteed in the light of history and urging the electorate to underwrite Home Rule with SNP support.

The common factor is that those who advocated devolution were aware that there was a crust of history and potential public cynicism to pierce before the dish could be presented to the voters. Before we examine the main dish – Scotland's new Parliament – let us pick a little at the piecrust of history.

The standing political joke – regularly deployed by those in search of a wry, knowing laugh – is that devolution is like evolution, only it takes longer. In various forms, the campaign to restore at least a measure of Scottish Home Rule has been around since the Scottish and English Parliaments both voted to end their separate identities and to merge in 1707.

That clinical description of the Act of Union between Scotland and England, of course, masks a persistent concern among sections of the Scottish public that the partnership was unequal, that the English Parliament regarded itself as simply continuing in the supposedly merged Westminster, that the previously independent Scotland was absorbed.

Such concerns were vigorously voiced by opponents of the Union when the measure was debated by the Scottish Parliament. These concerns were counteracted by the offer of guarantees for established Scottish civic and religious institutions plus promises of general economic advancement plus, it would appear, offers of patronage to key individuals.

Historians commonly attribute the apparent decline of such overt anti-Union sentiment to a combination of economic growth in Scotland after the middle of the eighteenth century and direct or indirect efforts to play down Scottish cultural identity and foster British links.

Equally, it should be stressed that many Scots saw clear advantages in the Union. British attachment was built upon a range of motivations: the trading and colonial opportunities presented by the Empire, the maintenance of the Protestant religion, the perception of a common foreign enemy in France.

Whether voluntarily or under subtle duress, Scotland in the nineteenth century showed some signs of surrendering at least the public manifestations of national identity.

Giving a lecture on St Andrews Day in 1998,[1] the Scottish Secretary Donald Dewar reflected this element. He depicted Victorian Scotland – or at least its wealthier segment – as 'aping polite London society'. Further, he cited the concerns of Lord Cockburn, whom he described as 'the great recorder of nineteenth-century Scotland'. Cockburn, said Dewar, had voiced fears in the 1850s that Scotland was destined to become 'but an English county'.

Certainly, this was the era of North Britain, the North British railway, the palatial North British Hotel in Edinburgh. This was the era of partial assimilation, the era of a common role for Scots in the creation and maintenance of the Empire. But still a sense of Scottish identity survived to the present day and it is that sense which has informed and underpinned the political initiative to devolve power to Scotland.

One argument is that civic Scotland persisted while political Scotland decamped to Westminster – that the 'high politics' of London, with its concern for foreign and defence matters, bore little relation to and had little influence over the 'low politics' of everyday Scottish life, with its concern for the church, the courts, parish education and the like.

While accepting that analysis, I believe that the persistence of a sense of Scottish identity is, in many ways, a simpler, less scientific matter. As noted above, the impulse towards a sense of being British was strong and welcomed by many, including many in Scotland. Had that sense been all-pervasive, the totems of Scottish identity evident in civic society might have lost their impact or their importance.

It is important, however, to distinguish between national identity and state identity. They may be coterminous – or they may not.

It was possible to welcome the political arrangement represented by the Union, to welcome the structural or economic impact, while retaining a sense, even a keen sense, of Scottish national identity. The people of Scotland have simply chosen, often without assertion or demonstration, to remain Scottish.

Not, it should be stressed, exclusively or incontestably Scottish. A typical profile in Scotland might blend a sense of Scottish national identity with perhaps a weaker sense of British national identity allied to at least a recognition of the British state. Identity in this sense resembles a spectrum graph or spreadsheet. For Nationalists, the dominant or peak points will focus around Scottish national identity. For the more Unionist-inclined, there will be key clusters around the British end of the spectrum.

The balance would appear to be tilting towards the Scottish identity end of the spectrum, either because that has grown in importance, or because the British state or national ties have weakened, or from a combination of factors.

Devolution is a political, state recognition of that apparently strengthened Scottish national identity. One key question for the proponents of devolution is whether the state identity of Britain will be weakened or strengthened by the project.

Those who are hardy enough to ascend the steps arising from

Waverley Station in Edinburgh will find an entertaining icon of Scottish identity. As they surmount the final step, defying the attendant hurricane-force wind which seeks to cast them back down again, they will find that the hotel at the top is no longer named the North British. It is now the Balmoral. North Britain, it would seem, has lost something of its force as a marketing tool.

But what is that Scottish identity? Is it clear-cut or confused? How does it impact on daily politics? Is it shared with other identities?

There are obvious institutional examples of the perseverance of Scottish identity: the Church of Scotland, deliberately protected in the Act of Union and now providing temporary shelter to Scotland's new Parliamentarians in the General Assembly building on the Mound in Edinburgh; Scottish education, which has remained distinct; the Scottish legal system; Scottish banks and banknotes; Scottish sporting teams.

But institutions can only ultimately reflect identity. They cannot forge it where no genuine, popular attachment exists. Think, for example, of restructured local government past and present, north and south of the Border. You cannot make a person talk lovingly of returning to Cleveland. You cannot persuade someone that their roots are in Strathclyde when they know they come from Ayrshire.

Equally, it is futile to fix Scottish identity on a generic basis. Scotland, as others have commented, is a cheerfully mongrel nation: an ancient blend of Highland and Lowland, Celtic, Anglian, Viking and Roman – with just a tangy hint of Pict. There are Scots of Irish birth or descent, those who might claim a comparable attachment to England, Wales, continental Europe or elsewhere. Then there are the more recent arrivals, notably from Asia.

Clearly, there is a strong cultural element to identity. People may express their Scottish identity through an interest in Scottish artists or, more commonly, writers. They may find that a particular author matches their sense of identity, perhaps through insightful description of their environment or empathy with their problems and challenges.

Frequently, Scots express their identity through the poems and songs of Robert Burns or more accurately through the accretion of national sentiment, both genuine and misplaced, which has been added down the years to the image of Ayrshire's finest.

Incidentally, too much is expected of Rabbie. He has been annually required at Suppers in his name to encompass the national feelings of a people who for three hundred years lacked the political and constitutional machinery to share that burden. He has occasionally, as his fellow poet Hugh McDiarmid wickedly explained, been asked to replace the experience of actually living in Scotland. I find I still grin knowingly at the line in *A Drunk Man Looks at the Thistle* which describes 'croose London Scotties wi' their braw shirt fronts' enjoying a Burns Supper.

Writers can sum up the identity of a nation although it is unfair to expect them to bear this task alone or to be circumscribed in their work by considerations of national origin. The best writers, perhaps, contrive to relate experiences drawn from their own identity to the wider world or to more fundamental human characteristics.

Other cultural forms, too, have exemplified an increase in attention paid to matters Scottish. The reawakening over the past few decades of the interest in Scottish folk and popular song comes into this category. Most strikingly, this element has moved far beyond a self-conscious revival of culture. The key factor is that those enjoying Scottish-derived music no longer feel the need to see it almost entirely as an act of cultural solidarity or defiance.

I am very far from an expert but it strikes me there is a welcome maturity too in the Scottish music field. Bands will make their base or their recordings in Scotland and think it no big deal. People will dance themselves silly to ceilidh music because they like the Eightsome Reel, not because they are making a cultural statement. Formal Highland dress, once obligatory, often gives way to a relaxed kilt, rough socks and boots.

Again, though identity can be expressed through popular culture, it is not defined by it. Neither can language be relied upon as the defining characteristic.

Gaelic is an extremely important element in Scotland's cultural mix and I share the concerns of those who advocate its requirements for support. Indeed, youthful enthusiasm at university prompted me to attempt a couple of lessons in the language. The only phrase which I confess I can recall is: *Ha an cu aig an doruis.* I may well have got this wrong but, as I remember, this means 'there is a dog at the door.' Scarcely the path to linguistic fluency, but handy all the same if one is in a pub in Stornoway and there is a noise of barking outside.

Then, keeping it personal, I am fond of employing Scots words familiar from the area around my native Dundee. As a correspondent at the House of Commons, I was occasionally called upon by bemused colleagues from Hansard and the Press Association to translate Scots words and phrases which diligent MPs, notably Donald Dewar, had managed to slip past the linguistic restraints of a chamber which insists on pure and frequently stilted English.

An anguished cry of 'gey dreich', I would assure them, implied nothing more than that the Honourable Member found the proceedings 'somewhat dull'. An inadequate rendering, I know, but linguistically legal as far as Westminster was concerned.

On certain occasions, nothing – not even the imprecations of concerned friends – can prevent me from singing *Nicky Tams* or *The Road and the Miles to Dundee*, hand clasped firmly to my right ear, nostrils working furiously.

Those preparing for the new Scottish Parliament recognised Scotland's linguistic diversity.

The Consultative Steering Group provided that members may repeat the oath of allegiance in a language other than English. More generally, the group recommended that members should be facilitated to speak in Gaelic if they gave prior notice to allow arrangements for interpretation facilities. I was intrigued to note, incidentally, that occasional 'clarification' may be required for the Scots language. Perhaps my old Westminster role will return.

In addition, the Steering Group recommended that public information from the Parliament should be made available in Gaelic and in other languages, such as Urdu, which are spoken in Scotland.

However, it was the underlying view of the steering group that the Parliament must not become over-absorbed in such matters, that the Parliament must be defined by its workaday efforts on behalf of the entire Scottish people rather than through any linguistic expression of Scotland's distinctiveness.

Viewed more generally, it can be argued that Scotland's identity cannot simply be defined in terms of language. Naturally, I am aware that the history of attempted suppression of the Gaelic language and the discouragement of Scots speech were linked to efforts to mute Scottish identity. Both were to be deplored.

However, there can be hazards in over-reliance on any linguistic definition of identity. Those who do not speak the specified language – be it Gaelic, Scots, Welsh or Breton – can feel set apart from an identity which they would otherwise profess. The hope must be that Scotland's new politics will be linguistically – and ideologically – tolerant.

Then there is the Scottish identity which arises from sporting allegiance: the 'ninety-minute nationalists' of Jim Sillars' famous phrase. I yield to no one in my passion for Scotland's national football and rugby squads. Even the most polished and urbane Scot can turn into a typhoon of patriotic fervour at Hampden or Murrayfield. I once attended a rugby match in the company, among others, of a highly intelligent, sophisticated Scottish MP who had the good grace to warn us in advance that he intended to behave like an extra from *Braveheart* for the following eighty minutes. He was as good as his word.

Is it only my impression, though, or has the nature of that sporting patriotism changed? Scots want their national squads to win as much as ever but that seems to be tinged now with a whimsical recognition of Scotland's sporting flaws. The Tartan Army of football fans seems, thankfully, in search of a good time and a good reputation, perhaps more even than a good victory. They seem less likely to be 'on the march with Ally's Army' as in the past and more inclined to be in a conga line with the local *gendarmerie*.

Perhaps, just perhaps, this phenomenon is a reflection of a growing maturity in the debate over Scottish national identity and its outward expression.

In this consideration of Scottish identity, it should of course be stressed again that there are many advocates of British identity, that there are many physical and psychological ties which bind Scots to the UK.

There are many people who, quite clearly, consider themselves British first and foremost. Writing in *The Scotsman* on 15 August 1998, in an essay repeated from *The Spectator*, Andrew Neil complained that 'those of us who are proud to be Scottish and British have become strangers in our own land.'

There will be many who identify with that blend of Scottish and British while not, perhaps, accepting the analysis of estrangement from Scotland. Scots work in England in their thousands. Many who live in Scotland are employed by UK-wide companies or concerns. Many will have other daily connections with London or other English centres.

None of that, however, precludes the adoption of 'Scottish' as someone's prime identity, just as contacts with the European Union or America need not undermine a sense of being British or English.

Scottish identity is more than, or perhaps other than, language, culture, sporting links and the rest. It is vague, imprecise, emotive: an issue which cannot be determined mechanistically or scientifically. Despite the theatrical caricatures, there is no list of personal facets which, added up, comprises a Scot. Again, the only conclusion I can draw, aware that it will be unsatisfactory to those who like matters neat and tidy, is that people are Scottish by choice.

During the run-up to the 1997 general election, I was commissioned by the BBC's 'Nine o'clock News' programme to prepare a substantial feature item on the campaign in Scotland. The BBC, of course, covered the Scottish political contest thoroughly. The parties were far from neglected. But this was to be different.

We opted to examine the nature of Scottish identity and to feature a range of opinions and analyses including voices from Scotland's academic and cultural sectors. I was most struck, however, by the day we spent filming in Coldstream, a small Scottish community on the Border, as close to England as it is possible to be.

Virtually everyone we spoke to stressed their Scottish identity, some in the most vigorous tones. I recall the man, serving behind a bar, who dropped his voice slightly as he talked of 'over there', referring to neighbouring England a few hundred yards away as if to some form of uncharted, dangerous territory. No one had anything against England or the English. People were simply stating that they lived in Scotland and were Scottish.

Now I can understand that, psychologically, people on a border may be the most assertive in defining their geographical identity. I can believe that there are Scots more generally who define their identity in negative terms, who start from the presumption that they are 'not English'. For the most part, however, it is my experience that people north of the Border are content increasingly to label themselves Scottish or predominantly Scottish, without rancour and without question.

I have regularly had occasion to pursue this issue through 'vox pops' or interviews conducted in the streets of Scotland. (My eternal gratitude, incidentally, to those many people kind enough to stop for a shivering reporter and camera crew.) When I raise the topic of identity, the most common and unhesitating response is 'Scottish'. Indeed, the answer is often given in a tone which suggests that the respondent wonders why I feel the need to ask.

The history of devolution is that of a people who increasingly believed they had a particular national identity and wanted that identity expressed in political form. It is a history of political response, not political initiative.

The Scottish people, I believe, were not crying out for a particular form of political expression. It is a familiar anecdote of canvassers from a range of parties that voters are far less inclined than the politicians to make sharp distinctions between devolution, independence and federalism.

That does not mean they are unconcerned about such matters. They are simply not the starting point for the electors. The factor which motivates Home Rule is an imprecise feeling of Scottishness, an attachment by choice to Scottish identity. It is, if you like, Scottish patriotism.

It is the feeling which formed the Scottish National Party and contributed to the obliteration of the Scottish Tories at the 1997 general election through their popular identification as an English party. It is the feeling which has driven Labour's devolution reform package.

The same feeling, note. I do not believe there is a rigidly defined core of devolution supporters and an entirely distinct cadre of independence advocates, with occasional seepage at the edges. If that were so, there would be a relatively precise match between those who tell opinion pollsters that they favour independence and those who declare for the SNP.

By contrast, opinion polls regularly find that constitutional opinion varies across the parties – that there are, for example, Labour supporters who favour independence and SNP supporters who opt for devolution among the range of views offered to the pollsters.

I would not wish to overstate this. Self-evidently, there are party activists and voters who do make a sharp distinction between the various constitutional options. There are people who support devolution but fear independence. There are people who support independence but regard devolution as a sideshow or a Unionist trap.

However, my impression – and it is first and foremost an impression – is that the starting point is identity rather than the particular constitutional options on offer from the parties. The constitutional gap is frequently less precise than politicians fretting about their party's future would perhaps wish. People begin by saying: we are Scottish. Then they implicitly challenge the political parties to offer a response. Electoral success is partly determined by that response.

Again, that feeling of Scottish identity brought the SNP into being. It has prompted the Labour and Liberal (or Liberal Democrat) parties to promise devolution in various forms over a century or more. It damaged the Tory Party, which was most obviously identified with British or English identity. Above all, it is the driving force behind the latest reforms. Scotland's new governance has a popular engine, not a party political one.

As we shall examine later, that has implications for the stability of the present settlement and for the future strategy of the political parties. It will be enough for now simply to register the existence and impact of Scottish identity.

In a multicultural and interdependent society, people can obviously have a range of attachments. Someone living in Glasgow can feel Scottish, British and European with perhaps an added allegiance to ancestral origins in Ireland or elsewhere. It is the balance of those allegiances which is important and which can have political significance.

This question of balance was addressed among many other issues in the analysis of data from the 'Scottish Election Survey' and the 'Scottish Referendum Survey' of 1997. These were relatively substantial surveys aimed at uncovering the attitudes which underpinned the behaviour of the Scottish electorate in the general election and referendum during that year.

Many of the findings were tracked by three prominent academics, Alice Brown, David McCrone and Lindsay Paterson, in the updated second edition of their book, *Politics and Society in Scotland*.[2]

The 1997 election survey suggested that a majority of Scots considered themselves either Scottish and NOT British or Scottish more than British. The authors note that this tendency to state a Scottish identity was more marked among working-class voters than among the middle classes. Overall, the authors noted, some 23 per cent of respondents felt Scottish and not British, 38 per cent felt Scottish more than British, 27 per cent felt equally Scottish and British while 4 per cent each felt British more than Scottish, British and not Scottish or none of these.

In his book *Strategies for Self-government*,[3] Professor James Mitchell notes that the maintenance of Scottish identity has run alongside a phenomenon which he identifies as British nationalism: a blend of emphasis on the United Kingdom dimension to culture and politics allied to a denial or downplaying of distinctively Scottish elements. Mitchell traces the apparent re-emergence of Scottish, as distinct from British, identity and links this to a range of motivations including the Scottish cultural revival and the decline of binding British institutions like the empire.

These thorough and valuable studies serve to reinforce what is anecdotally obvious to anyone living and working in Scotland. People feel increasingly Scottish more than British or even rather than British.

Importantly, there is no automatic cross-matching between a feeling of Scottish identity and support for Scottish independence. Almost by definition, those who support independence will be basing that view substantially on a sense of Scottish identity. But the reverse is not necessarily true. As Labour, the Liberal Democrats and the Tories repeatedly point out, a sense of being Scottish does not of itself engender backing for an independent Scotland.

However, that sense of identity has had an enormous and lasting impact on political and constitutional developments in Scotland. A common mistake among observers has been to observe that constitutional matters have not customarily been accorded high priority by Scots in opinion polls and to conclude that, consequently, the issue does not matter to Scots.

During their years of fervent opposition to devolution, most notably in the early 1980s, the Conservatives were inclined to answer challenges on the topic by stating that they saw no evidence that the Scots were urgently seeking a change in their status. It became almost a mantra for Ministers.

From a Labour perspective during those same years, visiting Labour Shadow Ministers would frequently voice exasperation that the Scottish media seemed obsessed with the constitutional issue and did not want to ask questions on whatever pet project they had come north to market.

Certainly the Scottish media have doggedly pursued the constitutional story – but not, I would submit, to the exclusion of other topics. They did so because it was the defining issue in Scotland, underpinning the cross-party debates over education, health, public spending and the rest. It was the big story.

Almost by definition, constitutional relationships are essentially a second-order question for most people. This is simply the same as saying that politics should not be an end in itself but rather a means to an end. It is not, however, remotely the same as saying that constitutional relationships do not matter.

I believe that in Scotland the constitutional issue – what one might call in shorthand 'the Scottish Question' – has underpinned the political choices of the electorate. They have factored it into their opinions of the various parties' policies on the first-order issues: jobs, education and the rest.

People vote the way they do for a range of reasons. Some will be single-minded, casting their vote either for or against a single policy of a political party or even a single individual. Mostly, however, people opt for a blend, an amalgam of policy and personality, a composite impression of their empathy with a particular party's approach.

In Scotland, a key element of that composite is Scottish identity, or perceived political association with that identity. The Nationalists, naturally, play that card strongly and hope to thrive, consequently, when the Scottish Question is to the fore in the minds of the electorate. Labour and the Liberal Democrats both take pains to project their own Scottish identification alongside their raft of policies.

In recent history, it has been the Conservatives who have suffered most from the Scottish Question. From choice, they identified themselves with the Union. From their party's majority inclination, they opposed Scottish Home Rule. The consequence, which they now acknowledge, is that they were depicted as a predominantly English party.

As we shall examine later, they suffered electorally as a result. It will be sufficient for now to note that the party which previously stood so vigorously against Scottish devolution lost every seat in Scotland at the 1997 general election. Their stance on devolution was not the only issue but it scarcely helped the party's prospects.

In addition, it may be helpful to point out to those who would play down the importance of the constitutional question that the United Kingdom as a corporate state entity has been all too aware of the potency of the Scottish identity issue.

There have been, as we have noted, sporadic attempts to subsume Scottish cultural and national identity within a wider UK or British allegiance. However, since the Union in 1707, Westminster policy has broadly aimed at a quiescent Scotland: not in itself an unworthy objective.

Devolution within the UK may be seen as an enhancement of that policy. That is not, I stress, to assert that devolution is necessarily a Unionist trick or anything of the sort, merely to note that the establishment of a Parliament for Scotland follows a series of previous efforts to answer the Scottish Question.

Intriguingly, many if not most of those previous efforts came from Conservative administrations anxious to offer an answer which fell short of the devolution of legislative power.

When a feeling grew towards the end of the nineteenth century that legislation affecting Scotland was receiving insufficient attention, Westminster responded. A Scotch Education Department, as it was called, was formed in 1872. A Secretary for Scotland – with an office in Dover House in Whitehall – was appointed, although the first incumbent reportedly thought the measure 'quite unnecessary'.

That post was occupied by a full Secretary of State from 1926. The Scottish Office progressively developed, opening headquarters in Edinburgh and steadily taking over the powers of the Boards (or quangos) which had administered Scotland since the Union.

Immediately before the establishment of the new Parliament, the Scottish Office was responsible for virtually the full range of Scottish domestic issues including health, education and the rest.

Throughout this period of administrative change, the campaign for political change remained in place – sometimes flourishing, occasionally subsiding. That is because, I believe, the core argument could not be addressed by administrative changes, however inherently worthy or valuable. The core argument has been that Scottish governance should not be dependent on political control created by a Commons majority in which Scotland – with a numerically small presence at Westminster – inevitably could play only a minor role.

The case is that Scotland's priorities as expressed through the democratic system should be directly reflected in the political structure responsible for enacting those priorities. It is not enough, this argument runs, that Scotland's priorities may coincide for a time with those of England, meriting similar or identical treatment.

Scotland's political structure should be capable of responding to changes in Scottish voters' priorities, quite distinctly from developments in England.

That core argument, critically, is logically untouched by the presence of so many powerful Scots in the Labour Cabinet. Certainly, that presence is substantial. Even excluding the Edinburgh-educated Prime Minister, the general election of 1997 left the UK's economy, diplomacy and defence in the hands of Scottish MPs. In addition, that election left the English legal system to be supervised by a Scottish Lord Chancellor.

English friends, acquaintances and colleagues have regularly asked me – sometimes in bewilderment, sometimes in irritation – what the motivation for Scottish devolution was when the Scots were already running the show.

Deploying such skills as I have picked up from politicians, I reply by turning the question round: that the case against devolution to Scotland should not lie with the make-up of a particular Cabinet generated by a UK mandate, whatever the constituency of the members.

The longer-term argument for Scottish devolution would not have been strengthened had English MPs been placed in charge of the Treasury, Foreign Office and Ministry of Defence. Indeed, the surrounding arguments for and against would not have been altered.

It may well be helpful, even very helpful, to Scotland to have influential Scottish accents in the Cabinet. Scotland may feel psychologically boosted as a consequence. But in practical terms such Ministers are obliged, entirely reasonably, to take their decisions on a UK basis, as dictated by UK government considerations.

Certainly there are potential consequences for Westminster from the devolution settlement – and I shall look at those later – but the core devolution argument should not hinge on the personal background of the UK Labour Cabinet.

Nor equally should the case FOR Scottish devolution rest solely or even principally upon any resentment engendered by the years when Scots were governed by a party, the Conservatives, they had palpably refused to support.

That argument grew in strength or at least in volume during the years of the Conservative administrations from 1979 to 1997. In individual circumstances, it may have been a useful campaigning tool. The argument was voiced particularly with regard to policies such as the poll tax, which was introduced in Scotland a year before its implementation in England.

In vain did the Conservatives protest that they were responding to Scottish or, more accurately, Scottish Tory Conference pressure. Scotland, critics said, had suffered the imposition of a policy inimical to her own wishes and priorities. The case for Home Rule, it was claimed, was self-evident.

It is, to say the least, unlikely that a devolved Scottish administration will in future seek to reinstate the poll tax. In that respect, it may be argued that the Conservatives previously went against the grain of Scottish thinking in implementing the tax.

Some politicians went further, however, and claimed that the Conservatives had no mandate to govern Scotland at all. That particular argument was even tentatively deployed by Donald Dewar as Labour's Shadow Scottish Secretary in the immediate aftermath of the bitter disappointment experienced by his party over their defeat by John Major in the 1992 general election.

In truth, however, that particular claim sits more comfortably with a Nationalist interpretation.

Scottish Nationalists set out to challenge the legitimacy of all Westminster governance in Scotland. It was not genuinely open to politicians who endorse the Union between Scotland and England to argue that a Westminster majority was an insufficient mandate to govern Scotland, a constituent part of that Union.

By the same logic, it could be argued that the Labour Governments of 1964 and February 1974 had no 'mandate' to govern England in that the Conservatives held more seats south of the border while Labour had a UK lead. Again, that is not an argument which admits of a strictly Unionist interpretation although it is being revived in a modern form now that Scottish devolution has happened and there is a focus on the Westminster impact.

It may be claimed that alleged Conservative insensitivities in handling Scottish affairs backed up the Labour case for devolved self-government within the Union. Labour supporters of that Union, however, could not legitimately set limits on the extent of the mandate provided by a UK general election under the rules operating at the time.

Critics of the Conservative Party had played by those rules and sought to win under those rules. Labour Governments had been content to govern in the past under those rules. It was scarcely consistent to complain that the rules had produced the 'wrong' result for Scotland.

So the core argument embracing devolution does not hinge on the individual make-up of the UK Cabinet nor the perceived lack of a UK mandate to govern Scotland.

Perhaps the classic error in observing devolution is to consider it as self-contained: as a constitutional reform driven by the desire to produce the specific plan enacted by the present UK Labour Government and implemented in the May elections.

Tony Blair in particular and Labour leaders in general are understandably keen to describe their reforms as part of a construct. Governing parties naturally like to talk in terms of controlled developments, to sustain the notion that the reins of political power are firmly and incontestably grasped.

Consequently, Labour leaders consistently list Scottish devolution within the substantial body of constitutional change promoted by the party and Government at various points. Scottish Home Rule, we are told, sits alongside devolution to Wales and Northern Ireland, the development of an English regional dimension, reform of the House of Lords, the arguments surrounding freedom of information legislation.

By contrast, I believe (and some Ministers privately confess they agree) that a Parliament for Scotland is one thing, an Assembly for Wales is something else and reform of the House of Lords is entirely something else again. Each has a range of different motivations, some popular, some partisan.

I hope not to labour this point but the example of Northern Ireland may help to clarify the question. Why was the previous Conservative Government willing to consider devolution to Northern Ireland but not to Scotland? Why did John Smith as leader of the Labour Party warn against drawing parallels between Scotland and Northern Ireland? Because Northern Ireland is different, because of the history of conflict.

Accepting that point – and who would not who wishes success to efforts to sustain peace – it can perhaps be gently noted that Scotland too is different in the constitutional canon. Different from Wales because of history and popular pressure, distinctly different from English regions despite occasional ill-informed comparisons. Scotland is a signatory of the Treaty of Union, not a county or region. The Scottish Question represents a different issue, also, from the arguments surrounding potential reform at Westminster.

Reform in Scotland is motivated by the popular will. The Labour Government's devolution package is their mechanism for responding to that popular will: not, first and foremost, a self-starting initiative which can be placed in the constitution section of the manifesto. That is not in itself to criticise the package, simply to analyse its nature. It implies, also, that Scotland's constitutional future is not in the hands of Labour or any other single political party.

The essential argument advanced by those who support either devolution or independence rests upon the same premise: Scottish self-determination. In other words, if the Scots demonstrably want devolved self-government, they must have it. If they demonstrably want independence, they must have that.

Notes

1. St Andrew's Day lecture by Donald Dewar in St Andrews, Monday, 30 November 1998.
2. Brown, A., McCrone, D., Paterson, L. (1998) *Politics and Society in Scotland*, Basingstoke: Macmillan, pp. 209–10.
3. Mitchell, J. (1996) *Strategies for Self-government*, Edinburgh: Polygon.

2 The Route to the Convention

The Glasgow Central by-election in June 1989 was a curious affair, far less vibrant than the contest for Glasgow Govan the previous year. The voters seemed somewhat disengaged in a constituency which was later to disappear under boundary changes.

The candidates adopted a range of challenging postures. Union official Mike Watson for Labour successfully stonewalled on tricky questions, aware that his Govan predecessor Bob Gillespie had landed himself and the party in trouble with frank, if occasionally confused, answers. Watson knew this was a by-election to be survived rather than fought.

For the SNP, Alex Neil faced a difficult task, battling to replicate the success of Jim Sillars in Govan: a different seat and different circumstances. High expectations and relatively low returns produced a Nationalist campaign which, occasionally, became irritable in the later stages. This culminated in the news conference where the candidate answered every question on whatever topic with a single, identical sentence designed to present his core independence message.

Then there was the Liberal Democrat candidate Robert McCreadie, an intellectual Edinburgh lawyer, who told an intrigued media that he was the only contender with 'street credibility' in this inner city Glasgow seat. He was affectionately labelled 'Street Cred McCreadie' by some of the more irreverent hacks. Finally, among the major parties there was the spectacle of Allan Hogarth, now an official at the Confederation of British Industry (CBI), gamely offering his brand of free-market, libertarian Toryism to indulgent but decidedly sceptical Glaswegians.

All in all, a source of innocent merriment to the pursuing press-pack. However, the night of the count brought a tiny cameo incident which I have never forgotten.

I was standing in the balcony at the counting centre, the customary speculation buzzing around my head. The ballot papers were stacking up for Labour. Mike Watson (later to be ennobled as Lord Watson and later still to gain a seat in the new Scottish Parliament) won comfortably with more than half the popular vote. As the returning officer announced the result, a senior Labour MP who was also spectating from the gallery leaned over to me and whispered: 'Well, that's the end of that Convention nonsense.'

The words have stuck in my mind for two reasons. Firstly, they are a blunt reminder that some within the Labour Party regarded the cross-party Constitutional Convention – and devolution more generally – as a tactic to undermine the SNP, a strategy to be dusted down only when the Nationalists threatened. When the Nationalists waned – as they did in Glasgow Central – it was back to partisan Labour politics. My Labour confidant on this occasion was ostensibly a supporter of Home Rule.

Secondly, that whispered exchange reminds me that the Labour leadership and the wider party contrived to set aside such cynicism. Labour's victory in the Glasgow Central by-election was not, as it turned out, anything like the end of 'that Convention nonsense'. That says much about the attitudes adopted by the Labour leadership but also about the various forces which kept Labour to its task.

The work of the Scottish Constitutional Convention broadly fell into two periods: one leading up to the 1990 publication of *Towards Scotland's Parliament*, which formed the devolution framework presented to the voters at the 1992 general election; then a further phase which produced the far more detailed blueprint of *Scotland's Parliament, Scotland's Right* in 1995.

That later publication was the basis for Labour's White Paper in government and for the subsequent Act legislating for devolution. It is worth stating at the outset of this section that there is, as the Scottish Office repeatedly pointed out, a clear progression from

Convention to White Paper to law. The detailed core of what has now become Scotland's Parliament can be traced through the three documents although, as I shall examine, there are significant changes in content and emphasis between Convention One and Convention Two.

The Convention is perhaps best remembered for the role of the political parties: for efforts by Labour and the Liberal Democrats to strike a deal, for the decision by the Scottish Nationalists to stay out, for the derision heaped upon the project by the Conservatives. It began, however, as an initiative outside the formal party structure.

The Campaign for a Scottish Assembly had been set up in 1979 following the collapse of Labour's devolution scheme of that period. Inevitably, many of its members and supporters were politically aligned to those parties which had most favoured devolution. However, the CSA attempted, in its own words, 'to unite the widest possible spectrum of pro-Home Rule opinion around a self-government plan for Scotland'.

It sought, in other words, to keep the issue alive in a period of vigorous condemnation of devolution by the new Conservative Government under Margaret Thatcher and newly resurgent hostility to any midway solution short of independence from the thwarted ranks of the SNP.

Little happened, frankly, in the policy area of devolution while politics concentrated on the new Tory Government, on the conflict within the Labour Party, on the formation of the Social Democratic Party, on the turmoil within the post-1979 SNP.

Labour persevered with its support for devolution policy – but it became increasingly difficult to market the electoral route to Scottish reform. Although the party in Scotland continued to pile up votes, the British Labour Party – politically divided and facing a challenge from the SDP/Liberal Alliance – looked frankly incapable of winning power at Westminster. That created a particular problem for Scottish Labour.

As a democratic party, Labour had to acknowledge that devolution would only be implemented in practice through obtaining a Westminster majority. At the same time, Scottish Labour knew it could not simply shrug its shoulders in the face of continuing Westminster defeat. It feared – it has always feared – that its Scottish power base might start to slip towards the Nationalists if Labour weakness or vacillation at the British level left it incapable of delivering for Scotland.

Through the 1983 general election, this Scottish Labour dilemma was eased by the relative political incapacity of the Nationalists, who were facing their own internal conflict in the aftermath of the 1979 referendum, when Scotland had voted, narrowly, for devolution but had failed to provide the required support of 40 per cent of the total electorate. Many in the SNP felt the party had been damaged by its association with Labour's thwarted devolution scheme. The Nationalists were agonising over the search for a new strategy to advance the case for independence.

Labour, however, feared that this relative weakness of the SNP might not last indefinitely. Labour knew it must at least give the appearance of advancing the self-government cause in Scotland – while, of course, facing the reality that it was prevented by the Tory majority at Westminster from implementing change. It was a political bind for Labour: the frustration of UK opposition linked to the need to 'do something' or, more accurately, appear to do something with their substantial popular support in Scotland.

Onlooking Home Rule supporters watched this quandary for Labour – and strategic debate within the SNP – and concluded that a new initiative was needed. After Labour's defeat in the 1987 general election, the Campaign for a Scottish Assembly (CSA) decided that the devolution campaign needed more broadly based support.

This was not a direct challenge to Labour but it was scarcely a tribute to the party. It was a recollection of the devolution failure in 1979 alongside an analysis that Labour could not be relied upon solely to deliver the change which the CSA adherents sought. That should be stated to stress that Labour support for this emerging initiative was far from guaranteed. In some respects, the CSA move was an embarrassing reminder of failure for Labour.

No doubt aware of these sensitivities, the CSA initiative at first seemed deliberately quiet and unassuming. That was certainly the tone adopted by its gently spoken and smartly besuited convener, Alan Armstrong. It was the approach followed by Professor Sir Robert Grieve who was invited to chair 'a committee of prominent Scots' to investigate the way forward. They conducted their investigations between January and June 1988, leading to a report in July of that year.

I remember discussing the initiative with Sir Robert in his comfortable if slightly gloomy flat on the edge of the New Town in Edinburgh. Those who, like Sir Robert, have spent a lifetime in public service tend to follow one of two routes: they become deeply cynical, even bitter, or they develop a calm perspective on the realities which confront those seeking to make progress in an imperfect world, contorted by politics, prejudice and mishap.

Sir Robert Grieve was definitely in the calm camp. He smiled gently and knowingly as I questioned him eagerly about the challenges which would undoubtedly beset his endeavour. He shared with me a few anecdotes about political and personality problems which he had encountered in his previous progress through Scotland's quangocracy. It was plain, however, that he was determined to rescue the devolution debate from its torpor.

To assist him in this task, he had Jim Ross, a former Scottish Office senior civil servant who had helped prepare the devolution initiative of the 1970s Labour Government. Ross had a store of detailed practical knowledge about the machinery of government and, as it turned out, a passionate commitment to change. As Secretary, his efforts were unceasing.

The members of the committee included church leaders, union leaders, Nationalist thinkers, Liberal Democrat adherents, figures from the arts and others. If the genesis of this initiative had seemed unassuming, their final document, *A Claim of Right for Scotland*, was demanding and, in parts, uncompromising.

To understand the extent of the dilemma which confronted Labour in particular over this development, it is important to recall the tone of this document, largely drafted by Ross and Grieve. It opens with a prologue deliberately placing Scotland's contemporary situation in the context of previous constitutional upheavals in 1689 and 1842.

The challenge to the UK Conservative Government is quite explicit. It states: 'We hold ourselves fully justified in registering a general Claim of Right on behalf of Scotland, namely that Scotland has the right to insist on articulating its own demands and grievances, rather than have them articulated for it by a Government utterly unrepresentative of Scots.'

Self-evidently, this is not to be a bland public document. The above wording is, of course, easily open to a Nationalist interpretation. It could form the prelude to a declaration of independence. The point of the exercise, after all, was to attempt to find common preliminary ground in rebuilding support for Home Rule, however subsequently defined.

Such an approach, however, can present problems for a party like Labour which avowedly supports the Union. It is one thing to demand devolution. It is quite another to challenge the legitimacy of the Conservatives to govern Scotland as part of the United Kingdom when Labour had similarly sought to govern the UK under precisely the same rules which returned the Tories.

That is not, by any means, to say that the Claim of Right committee were inherently misguided in the approach which they adopted. It was entirely consistent with their own remit. It is, however, instructive to recall the potential challenge which greeted Labour in particular in ultimately pursuing this approach. Labour leaders had to swallow hard before pursuing this road to reform.

The committee's document continues in like vein. It sets out 'the essential facts of Scottish history', declaring that 'although the government of the United Kingdom rests nominally with a "British" Parliament, it is impossible to trace in the history or procedures of that Parliament any constitutional influence other than an English one.'

It tackles the political identity question abruptly: 'Much ink is wasted on the question of whether the Scots are a nation. Of course they are.'

By contrast with these quasi-nationalist prefacing sentiments, the bulk of the document deals with the case for a devolved Assembly, as it was still then described, carrying echoes of 1979. As with the challenge confronting Labour above, it might be noted that the inherently devolutionary tone of the core content presented a potential problem for the SNP and their programme of independence, although the document notes that Scotland's ultimate future will be determined by Scots.

It then proceeds to dismiss or challenge the various objections raised to an Assembly. The complaint of over-government, the West Lothian question concerning the impact on Westminster, the issue of cost, the economic impact: all are tackled and contested.

This is the work of Scots embroiled in public service, who have heard all the arguments before and dismissed them. Alongside the meticulous detail of the document, there is a note of impatience that the case still has to be made at all, a note of anger with the Conservative Government.

Finally, the document proposes the establishment of an indirectly elected Constitutional Convention with three specific tasks: to draw up a scheme for a Scottish Assembly, to mobilise Scottish opinion behind that scheme and to deal with the Government in securing approval of that scheme.

The scene then inevitably shifts to the political parties. Pressed by the CSA, they then had to say whether they would join such a Convention or not. After the summer break, the talking continued into the autumn and the winter, leading to a key cross-party meeting in January 1989.

For the Conservatives, a relatively easy decision. They were formally invited to join the putative Convention with, of course, no expectation that they would do so. The Tories dismissed the initiative as a pointless talking shop, arguing that Scotland's interests were well served within the United Kingdom and that devolution would jeopardise that.

Ian Lang, then Minister of State at the Scottish Office, took the point a little further in a statement issued on 25 January 1989, as the other three parties were preparing for talks. 'How much further', he asked, 'will Labour go down the dead-end road of separatism in seeking to outflank the Nationalists?' Mr Lang added: 'The Convention is a pretentious piece of nonsense that can only do Scotland harm.' He compared Labour in particular to sulking schoolchildren, taking their ball away from the real political forum of Westminster to play in a different game under rules of their own making. Political rhetoric, certainly – but with a key theme: a deliberate challenge to Labour to reject the argument, explicit in the *Claim of Right*, that the Tories had no mandate or a questionable mandate to govern Scotland.

For the Liberal Democrats, a relatively easy decision. They had argued for Home Rule in one form or another for more than a century, they professed support for consensual politics, they were eagerly seeking a role after the early promise of the Alliance had turned to disappointment. They were on board.

Difficult decisions for different reasons faced Labour and the SNP. Labour's core concern was where the Convention, with its founding quasi-nationalist rhetoric, might lead. Would the party be forced into commitments beyond its policy programme? Was there an exit strategy?

The Nationalists' underlying worry lay in parallel to that concern: would the SNP be signing up to an inherently devolutionary exercise? Had not the party suffered enough from the devolution backwash in 1979 when it lost all but two of its Westminster seats? Was it all, despite the rhetoric, a Unionist trap?

Labour's attitude was inherently and understandably cautious. After all, it had to believe that if devolution ever happened, it would come about through a Labour government at Westminster, not through cross-party negotiations in Scotland, however well intentioned. That had to remain the perspective of a party seeking UK power.

So Donald Dewar as Shadow Scottish Secretary and Murray Elder as Secretary of the party in Scotland proceeded with the watchful care which has always been their trademark, occasionally to the irritation of more rumbustious colleagues. They opted ultimately to go ahead – but in a manner which provided safeguards for the party and boxed in the SNP, potentially their most serious opponents.

To understand the attitude, it is necessary to recall the atmosphere of the time. Labour had lost three UK general elections in a row while maintaining substantial numbers of seats in Scotland. Nationalist rivals and indeed figures inside the party were taunting the Scottish leadership, challenging them to exercise their 'mandate', to act on behalf of the people of Scotland. As discussed above, no such mandate existed nor could reasonably be claimed by a UK party.

In addition, throughout much of the 1980s there had been questions raised as to whether Labour would ever govern again. The party faced Westminster attacks from the Right in the shape of the governing Conservative Party and Scottish attacks from the Left in the shape of Socialist and Nationalist demands for Labour to resist policies such as the poll tax.

At the same time, the Campaign for a Scottish Assembly was gently assembling support for a consensual approach, urging that the path to change lay in reasonable people working together. Nothing is more difficult for a politician to reject than polite reason, particularly when accompanied by phrases like 'the will of the people'.

The prime motivation for Labour was to be seen to be doing something, to be taking action, particularly over the Scottish

Question. I discussed Labour's motives of that time in an interview with Donald Dewar.[1]

He acknowledged that Labour appreciated the need to assemble a consensus which would allow the debate to go beyond 1970s devolution. Labour, however, saw a potential political gain. He told me: 'There were genuine wishes to strengthen the base, to strengthen the coalition and at the same time pushing the SNP to the extremes, out of the mainstream of Scottish politics.'

Adding swiftly that he did not wish to sound too cynical, he stressed: 'I would have been perfectly happy to go ahead if they [the SNP] had gone in although it would have been a difficult bus to steer. But the invitation was there.'

Labour, however, set conditions on the talks. There could be no question of direct elections, inviting voters to pick Convention delegates. That would have been too time-consuming and divisive, as the *Claim of Right* document had recognised. Instead, the political membership of the Convention would largely be drawn from elected MPs, MEPs and Scottish local authorities, giving Labour an inbuilt advantage which reflected its historical strength.

As Donald Dewar told me, the party was interested only in devolution, not in devolution followed, possibly, by independence at a subsequent date. In talks at the time, Labour also ruled out the notion of following the Convention with a multi-option referendum which would have invited voters to choose between devolution, independence or the status quo. Labour argued, with some justice, that it would be unreasonable to expect the Convention to draft one constitutional option then invite the electorate to consider others. That would indicate a lack of confidence in whatever scheme emerged.

Labour's objective, plainly, was to make it very difficult if not impossible for the SNP to join. Remember too that the detailed negotiations on this issue coincided with a new collision between the two parties. Jim Sillars of the SNP had taken Glasgow Govan from Labour in a by-election on 10 November 1988.

Donald Dewar stresses that he had endorsed the Convention in principle before the Govan defeat. In a speech at Stirling University in October 1988, the month before Govan, he had spoken in favour of the Convention route and noted: 'Scots are going to have to learn to live dangerously for a while.'

At the very least, however, Govan concentrated Labour's mind on the need to address the Scottish Question in a practical fashion. Labour followed its support in principle by taking the initiative.

Donald Dewar wrote to Margaret Ewing, the parliamentary leader of the Nationalists, on 15 December 1988 to suggest preliminary private talks aimed at addressing any problems which might arise in the full negotiations over the Convention scheme. He despatched a similar letter to Malcolm Bruce, the leader of the Scottish Liberal Democrats.

Then came the day of the first cross-party talks on 27 January 1988 at the headquarters of the Convention of Scottish Local Authorities (COSLA) next to Haymarket Station in Edinburgh. The Nationalists were represented by their leader Gordon Wilson, by Margaret Ewing and by Jim Sillars, the victor of Govan.

Gordon Wilson provided the context for me when I spoke to him at his Dundee home.[2] The Nationalists, he recalled, 'went mad during the early 80s' in the aftermath of the 1979 referendum and general election. Policies on devolution, on Europe and NATO were altered. Wilson says the party which he led had become 'anti-everything'.

In an effort to re-engage the party and attract media attention, he had responded by drafting a plan for an elected Convention. It was, he freely concedes, to be seen to be doing something, to get people to look at things from a different angle.

It meant, however, that the SNP was on record as supporting a Convention, although a very different beast from the indirectly elected body under discussion on 27 January 1988. It was still going to be difficult for the SNP to say no, to appear to be going against the consensus carefully assembled by the CSA. Like Labour, but in a different fashion, the SNP faced a quandary.

Thinking back to that day, Wilson recalls: 'During the course of the day's discussions, it became apparent to everyone that it [the Convention] was going to be dominated by Labour. They would have a two-thirds majority – with MPs, councillors, trades unions. The rest of us were going to be purely decorative.'

According to Wilson, those who signed up to the Convention would be obliged to adhere to the decisions which emerged from the prevailing consensus, from the Labour majority in short. Dewar and Dundee West MP Ernie Ross, he said, made plain that those would be the terms of membership. The SNP, according to Wilson, would have ended up 'campaigning for the Labour Party's policy'.

Such marginalisation of the SNP, of course, was Labour's objective. Arguably, Labour's approach was understandable from a party which had a controlling interest in Scottish Westminster seats and Scottish local authorities. If the SNP would have been uncomfortable campaigning for Labour policy, it was surely no more reasonable for the Labour Party to offer an avenue of opportunity to a detested rival advocating a policy, independence, in which Labour did not believe.

As I recall from covering the event, Wilson, Ewing and Sillars emerged from the talks at COSLA looking ill at ease. Wilson himself concedes that he was obliged to fend off media questions in a cagey fashion. The party, he said, would consider its position. That consideration took place over the weekend.

On Monday, 31 January, the SNP leadership announced that they would take no part in 'Labour's rigged Convention'. In a statement, Wilson disclosed that he had offered to give some ground, to moderate the party's formal policy of a directly elected Convention.

The SNP, he said, had been willing to adjust Convention membership to take account of the voting pattern at the European elections which were due on 15 June. Labour's approach, he said, would give the SNP just 8 per cent of the Convention's membership, 'a travesty of political reality'.

The condemnation was bold and accompanied by an attack on Labour for refusing to sanction a multi-option referendum. However, as Wilson privately knew then and acknowledged in the interview with me, the SNP leadership had been out-manœuvred. He told me Labour had 'succeeded with their maximum objective, which was to freeze us out into an extreme position'.

Wilson also knew there was a substantial section of the SNP membership which favoured the devolutionary, gradualist approach. Isobel Lindsay, then a prominent SNP activist and a member of the Grieve Committee, had warned in advance that if the SNP rejected the Convention it would have 'alienated the very sections in Scottish politics and society which have been moving towards us'. She recalled that, on winning Govan, Jim Sillars had suggested cooperation and consensus as the way forward.

Wilson says he was able to fill two files with the letters of critical attack upon the decision to stay out of the Convention, including letters from party members who felt that the spirit of the original support for the notion had been betrayed.

He also told me: 'Tactically at the time it was bad. Tactically it blunted us. It brought down our support in the opinion polls. It held us back for about a year. We had been out-manœuvred – and I had to take responsibility for it.'

Wilson, however, remains adamant that the underlying reasoning was sound, that the SNP would have suffered in the long term from Convention membership. He told me: 'For us, strategically, it would have been a trap because we would have been mandated to fight for devolution. If we did go in, then for the next three or four years we would have been obliged to support devolution.'

The Nationalists, he said, had to remain in the vanguard of Scottish politics, 'riding point', as he put it. Their primary role was to stride ahead of the pack, 'creating a vacuum by our forward movement'. Beyond the apparent consensus, in other words.

Whatever the motivation, that weekend decision in January 1988 meant the SNP were out: out of the Convention and, if the Labour Party could contrive it, out of the mainstream of Scottish politics. The nature of the decision angered Alex Salmond, then a key party office-bearer, later to succeed Wilson as leader of the SNP.

I discussed the issue with Salmond when I interviewed him at SNP headquarters in Edinburgh.[3] He told me that the move to remain remote from the Convention was 'the right decision at the wrong time'. He added: 'It was the right decision because I don't think it would have been possible for the SNP to run into the 1992 election on the same platform, effectively, as the Labour and Liberal parties. The wrong timing because if you are going to make a decision like that you have got to be able to demonstrate your case and you can't do that if you apparently, in terms of public percep-tion, flounce out within forty-eight hours of the talks taking place. So it was badly handled in that sense but the decision strategically was the right one.'

The Nationalists have taken a lot of criticism for their decision to remain out of the Convention. Non-partisan Home Rulers, the genus which inspired the Campaign for a Scottish Assembly, found the decision or, in some cases, affected to find the decision incom-prehensible. Labour, naturally and understandably, made considerable political capital from the SNP's decision to 'walk away' from the apparent Scottish consensus.

I believe some of the criticism underplays the nature of the division between the SNP and Labour or, more generally, between Nationalist and Unionist politics. The most beguiling plea cast in the direction of politicians is: why can you not simply all sit down together and settle your differences? The blunt answer in this case and in many others is that those differences are irreconcilable.

The Nationalists want to end the Union with England, to establish an independent Scotland. Labour and the Liberal Democrats believe a devolved Parliament will cement Scotland into the Union. The Tories now tolerate devolution, while stressing their Unionist credentials. These political positions can, in certain circumstances, be covered by the catch-all phrases 'self-government' or 'Home Rule' but they are in practice mutually contradictory.

It will be argued that the Nationalists campaigned for a Yes/Yes vote in the devolution referendum of 11 September 1997, that they implicitly accepted a devolution settlement which they had played no direct part in shaping.

The circumstances of 1997, however, were very different from those of 1989. For one thing, gradualism had become more ingrained in the SNP leadership psyche. In more concrete terms, by the time of the devolution referendum in 1997, the Nationalists were faced with an active legislative programme to implement devolution.

Their choice was to attempt to block that programme or to attempt to advance it. In 1989, they faced no such clear choice. Labour and the Liberal Democrats were operating in opposition. The SNP had to frame a strategy which covered the possibility of a further general election victory for the Conservatives, as indeed subsequently happened.

They would have been entering the Convention on apparently comparable terms with Labour and the Liberal Democrats. Yet what was the Nationalist exit strategy? The Convention was plainly predisposed towards devolution. At some point – perhaps not the first week or the first month, but eventually – the Nationalists would have had to confront the fact that the Convention was not going to support independence or even offer it as an option in a subsequent referendum.

Some may argue that the SNP should, in such circumstances,

have accepted the apparently prevailing view. That is asking the SNP to shed its core belief. It is to misunderstand the realities of partisan politics. To take part under the emerging Convention rules, the SNP would either have had to abandon independence as an objective or, more realistically, to put it on hold. How then to face the electorate with a distinctive choice at the general election, with a reason to vote SNP?

Yet there was still, at minimum, presentational pressure on the SNP to give the Convention serious consideration. This was a difficult decision for the SNP, with no clear and obvious route. One Labour MP told me whimsically at the time there were moments when they became worried that the Nationalists were going to spoil the game and join the Convention after all.

In practice, strictly from a Convention perspective, the absence of the SNP made a deal easier to obtain although that meant, of course, that agreement was reached partly through the exclusion of the independence perspective. In other words, the deal was assisted by narrowing the scope of the participants.

This made it arguably less 'consensual'. However, as I have indicated above, I believe there can be a decidedly bogus air to the plea for consensus. It is like asking the chicken and the fox to settle their differences amicably. Both cannot win. One must give ground. Success for the fox is, inevitably, bad news for the chicken, however consensually the outcome is presented.

In precise terms, there is no consensus possible between devolution and independence. They may not be diametrically opposed but they are forces pulling in different directions. To remain in the Convention, the SNP would have had to drop their core aim of independence. Had they initially joined, I think it certain they would have subsequently pulled out, proclaiming that their interests were being blocked.

The Liberal Democrats forged a 'consensus' with Labour only by sidelining their own constitutional preference for a federal Britain. Only in that context can it be authentically argued that the Convention turned the available 'consensus' – between Labour and the relatively compliant Liberal Democrats – into a detailed plan.

In one of the neater twists of politics, the SNP, of course, subsequently campaigned for that plan in the 1997 referendum. However, I think two comments might usefully be made to conclude this rather tangled tale. Firstly, I think the SNP decision to remain out of the Convention was, at least, understandable at the time given the implicit challenge to independence, their core reason for existing.

Secondly, I think it likely that the Convention arrived, intentionally or accidentally, at the only process which enabled the three parties – Labour, Liberal Democrat and SNP – to join the Yes camp in the referendum. It would not, I believe, have been possible to get the three parties to agree a detailed Home Rule policy in a single forum. Devolution would always have conflicted with independence.

It was, however, possible for Labour and the Liberal Democrats to settle their practical differences over devolution and for the SNP, subsequently, to accept that the scheme drafted by others was better than the status quo. Politics can be a complex business.

Notes

1. Interview with Donald Dewar, 16 January 1999.
2. Interview with Gordon Wilson, 28 November 1998.
3. Interview with Alex Salmond, 4 December 1998.

3 Politics and Pomposity – the Convention in Operation

Full Convention meetings, once they got under way, frequently oscillated enticingly between politics and pomposity. The quandary was obvious. Those taking part felt obliged to reflect a little of the spirit of the *Claim of Right*, to propagate a sense that they were reclaiming Scotland's destiny. At the same time, the down-to-earth longed to tackle detailed questions of policy while the more literate fretted that pageantry belonged properly in the pages of *Alice in Wonderland*.

For the most part, the Convention steered around this potential trap. There was the odd sententious speech to endure but more commonly the participants would stick to the practicalities of building and sustaining agreement.

The Convention went ahead with Labour, the Liberal Democrats, the Greens, the Communist Party (later Democratic Left), the Scottish TUC, most local authorities, the main Scottish churches, the Federation of Small Businesses, the Scottish Convention of Women, cultural and Gaelic language groups and representatives of ethnic minority organisations. In attendance as observers were representatives from various bodies such as the Scottish Council for Development and Industry, the Committee of University Principals – and the Campaign for a Scottish Assembly which had prompted the initiative.

The first full meeting was held on 30 March 1989 in the Kirk's Assembly Hall on the Mound, now with neat symmetry the temporary home of the Scottish Parliament. Despite the qualms outlined at the start of this chapter, it was an impressive occasion. With the former Liberal leader Sir David Steel and the former Labour Minister Harry Ewing jointly taking the chair, speakers set out their intentions seriously – but without overmuch solemnity.

Part of the occasion obliged the MPs and others present to file forward and sign the declaration presented to the meeting. This was known as the *Claim of Right*, carrying on the title of the original Grieve committee report. This declaration read:

> We gathered as the Scottish Constitutional Convention do hereby acknowledge the sovereign right of the Scottish people to determine the form of Government best suited to their needs and do hereby declare and pledge that in all our actions and deliberations their interests shall be paramount.
>
> We further declare and pledge that our actions and deliberations shall be directed to the following ends:
>> To agree a scheme for an Assembly or Parliament for Scotland;
>> To mobilise Scottish opinion and ensure the approval of the Scottish people for that scheme; and
>> To assert the right of the Scottish people to secure the implementation of that scheme.

If any Labour or Liberal Democrat signatories felt uncomfortable with the quasi-nationalist tone of this declaration, with its reminder of the Scottish constitutional doctrine of popular sovereignty, with its implicit challenge to the supposed sovereignty of Westminster, they kept their feelings to themselves. Labour MP Tam Dalyell, a persistent critic of devolution since the 1970s, did not sign.

Certainly there were no such qualms for the star of the day, Kenyon Wright, the Scottish churchman with the Anglican title of Canon from his days at Coventry Cathedral. He had been chosen to chair the Convention's Executive Committee.

In a rousing speech, he invited the audience to reflect on the likely reaction from a familiar voice, that of the Prime Minister Margaret Thatcher, who had herself addressed the General Assembly of the Church of Scotland in a 1988 speech which came to be known as the Sermon on the Mound.

'What', he noted, 'if that other single voice we know so well responds by saying, 'We say No and we are the State.' Well, we say Yes and we are the People!' It was brilliantly delivered with the necessary minimum of mockery and a closing declaratory flourish. Again, it represented an overt if politely delivered challenge to Westminster sovereignty: a challenge impossible to sustain in reality for UK political parties.

There were seven full meetings of the Convention during this early phase in the run-up to the 1992 election. They culminated in the session in Glasgow's Royal Concert Hall on 30 November 1990, St Andrew's Day, which witnessed the presentation of the report *Towards Scotland's Parliament*.

Many involved now privately accept that the report was drafted too soon, that it left too many gaps to be exposed by political opponents, that it left too many questions unanswered, that it lessened the Convention's impetus in the period immediately before the election. At the time, however, it often seemed remarkable that agreement was reached at all.

The detailed negotiations took place in the Convention Executive. As a journalist covering these events, it frequently seemed to me that there was zero progress to report and yet the participants, the Conventioneers, insisted that everything was on course.

This is, of course, the familiar stuff of political reporting everywhere, with the journalists wickedly insisting on asking awkward questions about matters of detail and the politicians urging us to focus on the main objective, the fabled 'big picture'.

Every politician up against it becomes, if necessary, a 'big picture' person. Every journalist is or should be a nit-picker. Politicians complain that the media focus on minute matters, on relative trivia. Journalists retort that politicians dodge their questions. That is the way things are and the way they should be.

Even in the absence of the Nationalists, it was extremely difficult for the parties in the Convention Executive to strike a deal. Canon Kenyon Wright reflects this in his book about the period, *The People Say Yes*.[1] He writes: 'God knows it has been difficult enough as it is with the broad spectrum of politics and social concern which existed in the Convention. With a nationalist view present, consensus might have been impossible.'

The non-party representatives – or 'civic groups' as they came to be known – played a substantial role. But it was recognised that any practical programme for devolution would have to be processed through Westminster, would have to be brought about by elected political leaders.

That meant a deal between Labour and the Liberal Democrats. In this early phase of the Convention, that meant a deal between the Shadow Scottish Secretary Donald Dewar and the leader of the Scottish Liberal Democrats Malcolm Bruce. Dewar and Bruce did not get on with each other.

They were political rivals, certainly, but friendship is common across party lines. Politics is less personally partisan than those who glean their analysis from observation of Prime Minister's Questions in the Commons might suspect. But Dewar and Bruce did not get on.

Bruce says now:[2] 'I would not have said we were the closest of friends. I certainly respect him but I think he is a different kind of personality from me.' Bruce speculates that Dewar was happier with legally trained Liberals like Menzies Campbell or Jim Wallace. Without adopting that analysis, Dewar confirms that he and Malcolm Bruce were scarcely soul-mates.

Malcolm Bruce's retrospective view of the Convention is almost certainly coloured by his own fate at the 1992 general election. Diligent local effort over several years had finally brought him the prize of taking the Gordon constituency from the Tories in 1983. By 1987, he had a majority of 9519.

In the 1992 contest, that majority slumped to 274 as Bruce was nearly ousted by a prominent local Tory councillor. Malcolm Bruce blamed the impression fostered by his participation in the Convention that he was too close to Labour, that he was in Labour's pocket. Tory-inclined voters in the North-east did not apparently like this.

Those MPs who make it back to the Commons frequently swap campaign and election stories with each other. On returning in 1992, Donald Dewar politely inquired of Malcolm Bruce what had happened to his majority, what had gone wrong. Bruce retorted: 'I spent too much time with you!'

However, the Executive meetings in Phase One of the Convention drew their tension from more than personality, however important that is in political life. There were issues of substance to address with regard to the proposed Scottish Parliament, as it was now commonly called, with the earlier term 'Assembly' consigned to history.

They had to determine the powers of the Parliament. Broadly, they eventually opted in *Towards Scotland's Parliament* to give the new body full legislative control over those matters already administratively devolved to the Scottish Office.

This is devolution almost by simple definition and no great surprise. There was, however, more emphasis in this first Convention phase upon the potential economic powers of the Parliament than is evident later. Convention One was more socialist.

The 1990 document *Towards Scotland's Parliament* specifies the need for strategic economic planning powers in key industries like whisky, steel, offshore engineering, textiles and agriculture. It also demands the power to negotiate the terms of inward investment with multinationals, responsibility for monopolies and mergers policy and the power to build an international trade organisation. Finally, it specifies that the Scottish Parliament should have 'the power to initiate some form of public ownership or control in the public interest'.

In the eventual government White Paper of 1997, the Scottish Parliament is still given 'responsibility for the economic development of Scotland'. But the document is notably less prescriptive and notably less detailed, no doubt in parallel with a changing emphasis on such matters as social ownership within the governing Labour Party over the years but perhaps also reflecting a durable concern within the Liberal Democrats.

In a document from 4 April 1989, Malcolm Bruce set out his key aims. He said the Liberal Democrats' 'role in the convention will be to ensure that it does not come up with a vehicle for imposing "Socialism in one country"'. The Scottish Parliament, he said, 'should seek a partnership with business, not tired old counter-productive intervention'.

By contrast with that declaration of intent, the 1990 Convention document had an avowedly interventionist spirit – fostered partly by influential trades unions and some local authorities, but chiefly reflecting a traditional Labour approach, an approach which even at the time of the document was facing substantial challenge.

There were, certainly, important caveats such as the insistence that the Scottish Parliament's economic powers could only be of use 'working with Westminster and within the guidelines of national policy'. It is the sentiment in the caveat which has tended to survive, while the main theme of a powerful interventionist Scottish Parliament has largely evaporated.

The Convention Executive in this first phase worked hard to agree a detailed scheme for financing the Parliament. Again, this was substantially changed in later years.

The model which emerged in the phase up to 1992 featured a system known as 'assigned revenues'. Under this, the Scottish Parliament would have gathered the Scottish product of a particular levy such as income tax or VAT. In other words, if you earned your keep in Scotland, your income tax would go to Edinburgh and not to the UK Treasury. It was claimed there was no technical problem in doing this with income tax although it was conceded that VAT revenue might have to be based on Treasury estimates.

The claimed advantage of this scheme was that the Scottish Parliament would have had an incentive to operate responsibly and to keep the Scottish economy buoyant. A booming economy would mean a greater tax take for the Scottish Parliament. This would, in the words of the 1990 Convention document, 'underline the independence of the Parliament'.

However, it was stressed that the principle of equalisation of resources across the UK would still apply. In other words if, as the Conventioneers expected, the cash available to the Scottish Parliament from assigned taxation fell short of the money needed, then there would be a top-up grant. If, on the other hand, Scotland had particularly prospered then money might flow in the other direction, benefiting the UK Treasury. It was further pointed out that Scotland would continue to pay her share in other ways – for example, through North Sea oil revenues.

The advocates of this scheme said it would bring greater transparency into public finances. It was that very aspect which later brought it down. Labour grew increasingly nervous after the 1992 general election over Conservative taunting at the claimed cost of devolution. The block grant from the Treasury was resurrected and assigned revenues ditched.

It was argued in that later period that the assigned revenues system was far too complex and costly. That was ultimately accepted by the Convention although Liberal Democrat leaders still hankered after such an approach.

One financial element which has survived through both phases of the Convention and into law is the power for the Scottish Parliament to vary income tax. Under this power, the Scottish Parliament can, if it chooses, raise or lower the standard rate of income tax by a maximum of 3 per cent for those defined as Scottish resident tax-payers.

Any additional cash raised by such an imposition on the people of Scotland would, naturally, accrue to the Scottish Parliament. Any cash foregone by a reduction in Scottish income tax would be returned to the UK Treasury. There would, it has been repeatedly stressed, be no question of England overtly subsidising Scottish tax cuts.

This tax power has been hugely controversial over the years. In the Scottish parliamentary elections in May, it formed a core element when the Nationalists pledged to use the power to reverse a UK penny tax cut. Prior to the 1997 general election, it was of course the basis of the Tories' persistent complaint that Scotland would face a 'Tartan Tax'. That complaint partly produced Labour's devolution referendum with its second question specifically on tax powers.

The tax plan arose largely in response to fear: anxiety that the problems which had beset the devolution efforts of the 1970s would return. Then, a key complaint had been that the proposed Assembly would have been utterly dependent on Treasury support.

It was argued that it was irresponsible to establish a tier of government which had no power to raise even a proportion of its spending by its own decisions.

Local authorities, it was pointed out, levied a share of their income from local residents and, in theory at least, took the consequences at the ballot box. Devolution, 1970s-style, had, however, side-stepped the complaints. The Scottish Assembly would have had no revenue-raising power.

However, the tax plan which was formulated to answer old anxieties ended up prompting new concerns: fears that Scottish business would face damaging extra costs. As with the economic powers, the tax pledge was steadily surrounded by back-up assurances which became more varied down the years. The power would only affect spending at the margin. It might only be used for specific projects, rather than current spending. It would even – in a plan which Labour temporarily endorsed – be subject to a further popular referendum before it was actually used.

In a party pledge, Labour ultimately ruled out any early use of the tax power. The whole issue of tax had become embarrassing to a political party which was desperate to project a new image, to shed its 'tax and spend' label. There were repeated rumours that the power was to be dropped altogether. Yet it survived to become Scotland's mirror-image political principle: there could be no representation without taxation powers.

It can occasionally appear that Labour's reluctance to use the tax power lies deeper than transient political advantage. During the Scottish parliamentary election campaign, Labour sought to contrast its stand on tax with that of the SNP. The Nationalists had declared their readiness to use the tax power to reverse – for Scotland only – Labour's UK pledge of a penny cut in the standard rate of income tax. Labour depicted that as irresponsible, as unpicking a central element of the 1999 Budget, as making a fair financial settlement unfair.

But Labour went further, attacking the impact of such a variation in the standard rate as particularly iniquitous for the low-paid, for pensioners and for small businesses who pay income tax rather than corporation tax. These, however, may be said to be structural objections rather than passing political complaints.

The Scottish Parliament cannot alter tax bands. It cannot touch the upper or lower rates of income tax. If it seeks additional revenue, consequently, it is left with no option under Labour's own legislation. It must increase the standard rate. Equally, it lacks the power – under Labour's legislation – to take any steps which might lessen or vary the impact upon the low-paid. If we pursue the logic of Labour's objections to the SNP tax policy, it would appear difficult if not impossible for Labour ever to use the tax power unless the UK Chancellor somehow provided a framework which met those objections.

I intend to look in detail at the issue of finance later. For now, it will be sufficient to note that the Convention reached agreement on making the tax power available to the Scottish Parliament, by contrast with the approach taken in the 1970s.

There was a protracted debate in the Convention over 'entrenching' the Scottish Parliament. This meant in effect protecting the Edinburgh Parliament from subsequent tampering with its powers – or even from outright abolition by Westminster.

The early-phase Convention considered endless options, all of which tended to run smack into the fact that this was devolution, not independence. This would involve the sovereign Westminster Parliament volunteering to devolve power. There was no getting round the fact that the sovereign Westminster Parliament could, technically, opt later to resume that devolved power.

I covered this debate attentively, although I always felt it was utterly specious. There was simply no dodging the constitutional fact that devolved power could be recouped.

The solution suggested in the 1990 Convention document was that the Act establishing the Scottish Parliament would state that the powers therein would not be altered without the consent of the Scottish Parliament. This would in practice have meant little as it is a Westminster rule that no government can bind its successor. Regardless of what was in the Act, a subsequent government could take a different view.

Phase Two of the Convention produced a different solution: that there should be a formal Declaration in Westminster that the Act founding the Scottish Parliament would not be repealed or altered in any way to jeopardise the devolved Parliament without the consent of the Scottish people.

Same issue, same problem. No matter how solemn the intent, no matter how formal the declaration, this could not be a deal which bound future Westminster governments.

To be fair, both Convention documents acknowledged this problem and stressed that the true entrenchment of the Scottish Parliament would come from demonstrable public will, that no political party would dare to remove a democratic institution for as long as it had evident popular support.

As it turned out, that has been the answer if not the formal solution to this question. The plan for a Scottish Parliament was endorsed in a popular referendum and the scheme for a sonorous Declaration at Westminster was quietly forgotten as a consequence.

The issue which caused the biggest challenge to the Convention in its early phase was one which can never be far from the thoughts of an elected politician: the voting system.

The Liberal Democrats had long advocated proportional representation for elections. By this, they meant that parties would obtain seats broadly in proportion to their share of the popular vote. More votes overall, more seats.

Under the established system of first-past-the-post, the outright winner in an individual constituency took all the spoils. A political party could have considerable support, it was argued, with a string of good second or third places across the country, yet end up with very few seats to reflect that. The Liberal Democrats were in just such a position, especially in Britain-wide terms, which undoubtedly strengthened their adherence to the principle of voting reform.

Further, the Social and Liberal Democrats, as they were formally known then, dreamed of mould-breaking. They hoped that, if they could persuade Labour in Scotland to adopt PR, they might extend the principle to Westminster and potentially rescue their party from the political sidelines.

They made no secret of their intentions. In his statement of 4 April 1989, Malcolm Bruce employed apocalyptic language in insisting upon voting reform. He said: 'To replace the Government of Scotland by a Conservative dictatorship based on only 42 per cent of the UK votes and 24 per cent of the Scottish vote with Labour domination on the basis of 42 per cent of the Scottish vote will be resisted all the way by Social and Liberal Democrats.'

Put more simply, no PR, no deal. At the time there were significant numbers in the Labour ranks who were prepared in those circumstances to say: no deal. They could not comprehend why their party required to treat with rivals who, particularly in the days of the SDP/Liberal Alliance, had sought to supplant Labour as the alternative to the Conservatives.

They saw the Liberal Democrats struggling electorally in the aftermath of the 1987 general election and – just like the deputy Prime Minister John Prescott a decade later – they questioned what good they were to Labour.

Malcolm Bruce recalled that mood when I interviewed him in January 1999. He said: 'Some of the Labour MPs and party activists seemed to be asking themselves, "Why are we dealing with the bloody Liberals?"'

Labour, he recalls, was initially very reluctant to endorse PR – and with good partisan reason. With a substantial vote concentrated in a range of mainly Central Belt constituencies, Labour did extremely well out of first-past-the-post in Scotland, managing to gain the bulk of the seats without a majority of the popular vote. Labour had a lot to lose from PR.

There were other concerns too. Murray Elder was the Labour Party's Secretary in Scotland and later a special adviser to John Smith and then Donald Dewar. Instinctively cautious, he is adept at spotting the consequential flaws in a policy which may seem superficially attractive. It is a characteristic which occasionally infuriates his more enthusiastic Labour colleagues but it was a valuable asset to an opposition party which, inevitably, lacked civil service advice but required to subject the Convention scheme to searching scrutiny.

In a paper submitted to Labour's home policy committee on 8 January 1990, Elder set out the options regarding PR. He acknowledged that it was a prerequisite for the Liberal Democrats and noted drily that there was a 'certain amount of pressure from within the party to adopt some form of electoral reform'.

But, said Elder, the Scottish scheme could not be considered in isolation. 'It would have implications because for one part of the Labour Party to be arguing for a proportional system would be bound to affect the argument in the rest of Great Britain,' he noted. Further, he argued that PR for the Scottish Parliament would be 'likely to mean that for Scotland at least local government would, after reform, also be elected on a proportional basis'.

This was, of course, precisely what the Liberal Democrats wanted: PR in Scotland followed by PR for local government and Westminster. From a Labour perspective, however, the situation was rather different. Labour stood to lose electorally from PR in a Scottish Parliament and regarded the potential knock-on consequences for councils and Westminster with anxiety or at least disquiet.

Why then did Labour plump for PR in Scotland? The answer lies in the motivation which took them into the Convention in the first place. They remembered all too painfully that devolution had flopped in the 1970s. Scots had voted for devolution, just, in the 1979 referendum. Many, however, had voted against or abstained.

Scotland had not been sufficiently enthused. There was a particular problem in mustering a cross-party consensus and in sustaining support for devolution away from the populous Central Belt of Scotland. People in the North-east of Scotland, in the Highlands, in the outer isles, in the rural South-west all questioned whether rule from Edinburgh would be any less remote or any more to their taste than rule from London.

Devolution had ultimately led to the chain of events which brought down the Callaghan Government. General party and popular opinion, however, meant that Labour must again pursue devolution. Put simply, this time they had to get it right and that meant assembling a broader base of support.

For that, Labour needed the Liberal Democrats, who were the only other major political player in the Convention. They could not have applied the label 'broadly based' to any deal which excluded them. PR was a crucial element in that search for a wider apparent consensus.

It was felt that PR voting would lessen the concerns of rural Scotland that the new Parliament would be dominated by the Central Belt Labour Party. It was a fearful conundrum for Labour. Fearful that their Scottish support might ultimately slip to the SNP, they believed they needed to promise devolution to shore up their Scottish vote. But, to shore up devolution, they came to believe, in effect, that they must constrain the potency of that Scottish Labour vote.

Labour accepted that a broadly based deal required a broadly based electoral system. They endorsed the notion that fostering the unity of Scotland, rather than simply the large minority who habitually voted Labour, meant electoral reform.

In addition, says Bruce, once in the Convention, Labour would have found it hard to get out, recognising that they would be blamed for breaking the consensus which they had stated as a prime objective. Labour knew this too, which is why the party took such care in preparing the ground for the establishment of the Convention in the first place.

Labour saw a further advantage to PR, although this was commonly left unstated. Labour itself was a standing example of a party able to dominate Scottish politics without a popular majority – that is, without the support of more than 50 per cent of the electorate.

The private worry was that the SNP might at some future date be able to achieve a similar trick in the Scottish Parliament and so advance the cause of independence. Convention members understood that proportional voting would prevent that. True, it would stop

Labour from dominating Scotland with a minority vote. It would, however, also stop the Nationalists from controlling the devolved Parliament with a minority vote and possibly claiming a mandate to take Scotland out of the Union.

That issue surfaced again briefly during the 1997 general election campaign. At a Labour news conference in Glasgow, I invited the party's Scottish General Secretary, Jack McConnell, to confirm that the precise electoral system chosen for the Scottish Parliament had been designed to prevent the Nationalists from taking power with a minority vote. With admirable brevity, he replied: 'Correct.'

According to Malcolm Bruce, Labour endorsed PR for Scotland from a combination of internal politics and external pressure. The internal element was the perception that Labour's devolution scheme would be the stronger as a consequence and that there might be a further clamp on SNP aspirations. The external pressure was the standing threat by the LibDems to quit the Convention if they did not get their way. Bruce told me: 'There was a combination of . . . not exactly blackmail, let's call it hard bargaining . . . plus evidence that PR would be helpful.'

So PR was on the table. The 1990 Convention document, however, failed to specify the number of members of the Scottish Parliament, it failed to specify the precise electoral system and it failed to detail exactly how a further stated aim, that of gender balance, would be achieved.

Gender balance became a substantial talking point. Women activists in particular argued that, if the aim was an inclusive Parliament, if the aim was a Parliament which involved the regions of Scotland away from Central Belt, if the aim was a Parliament which crossed party lines, then fair and equal treatment of women could scarcely be neglected.

A plan was advanced which became known as 50/50 representation. Under this scheme, the Parliament would be of a sufficient size to admit one male and one female member for each constituency. This was vigorously advocated by women's groups although some were frank enough to concede that it had democratic and presentational flaws.

It was argued, for example, that a candidate – male or female – might be elected on grounds of gender balance when, perhaps, another candidate had more support. Equally, some claimed that it was placing an additional strain on an electoral system whose principal purpose was to determine the governance of Scotland. Others feared, although they tended not to stress this in public, that the voters of Scotland were not ready for positive gender discrimination.

While this debate was at its height, I covered the issue substantially and recall in particular one interview with Labour MP Maria Fyfe. We were standing, slightly chilled, outside BBC Scotland headquarters in Glasgow. I was quizzing her persistently on the perceived problems with 50/50. Finally, in polite exasperation, she replied: 'Look, this really matters. Have you got any better ideas?' The interview did not last much longer.

The 1990 Convention document endorsed the principle of equal representation for women. But, in common with its stance on the voting system more generally, it failed to specify the system to bring this about. Indeed a further clause contained a let-out in that it argued for a scheme which 'ensures or at least takes effective positive action to bring about, equal representation of men and women'.

With the passing of the years, it was again the qualifying clause which came to the fore rather than the main argument. The precise demand for 50/50 representation was overtaken by an electoral agreement pledging individual Convention parties to aim for gender balance within their candidate selection procedures.

Some argued this was where the issue should have been settled all along, that it was presumptuous to expect legislation to solve a problem which could be said to reside with party selection machinery. Others insisted it was vital to determine gender balance by statute from the outset.

In any event, the 1995 Convention document, *Scotland's Parliament, Scotland's Right*, confirmed the shift of ground. While adhering to the principle of equal representation, it laid the task of achieving this upon the electoral agreement reached between Labour and the Liberal Democrats.

This agreement was signed in Inverness on 23 November 1995 by Rhona Brankin and George Robertson for the Labour Party and Marilyne McLaren and Jim Wallace for the Liberal Democrats. It committed these two parties to endeavour to achieve gender balance by selecting equal numbers of male and female candidates and by distributing them fairly in winnable seats.

The agreement had two obvious flaws which the Convention

acknowledged. The signatories had no power to order the other parties to follow suit and they had equally no power to ensure that the vote on the night would produce gender balance, however evenly the candidates were distributed.

For their part, the Nationalists insisted that they already offered an equal chance to male and female candidates, that gender balance was largely a problem created by Labour's selection system with its historic preponderance of males from the ranks of trades unions and councils. The Tories dismissed any notion of positive discrimination, arguing that their women candidates already had every avenue open to them.

The electoral agreement fell short of the original aims of the women activists who had argued for 50/50 but, taking into account all the range of pressures upon the Convention, I believe it is perhaps the most that could have been obtained in practice at the time.

In the event, the Scottish elections of 6 May 1999 produced a gender-balanced Labour group with twenty-eight males and twenty-eight females. The Nationalist vote returned twenty men and fifteen women. Among the Tories, there were fifteen men and three women while the Liberal Democrat group comprised fifteen men and two women. In addition, three men were returned under other colours. In total, there were forty-eight women and eighty-one men returned to the Parliament, one of the highest levels of female participation in any elected chamber anywhere. But still well short of that original objective of equal representation.

Notes
1. Wright, Canon K. (1997) *The People Say Yes*, Glendaruel: Argyll Publishing.
2. Interview with Malcolm Bruce, 26 January 1999.

4 The Final Convention Scheme

The original Convention statement, agreed at the inaugural meeting on 30 March 1989, had contained three broad aims: to agree a scheme, to mobilise popular support for it and finally 'to assert the right of the Scottish people to secure the implementation of that scheme'. In short, to talk, to tell and to do.

The wording of the third objective made it sound as if the Convention would brook no obstacle. The reality, of course, was that parties wedded to democratic politics and the process of legislation had to abide by the Westminster rules. That meant there was little practical point in 'asserting the right' of the Scottish people to self-government unless those seeking reform had a working majority in the Commons.

To be fair, those participating in the Convention never had any doubt about the political realities. It was accepted that practical implementation was a matter for individual parties, although the Convention as a collective body claimed the right to monitor and encourage such implementation.

There was a small obstacle in the path of that implementation: the 1992 general election and the return of a Conservative Government under John Major, implacably opposed to devolution. John Major, indeed, showed a particularly keen interest in the constitutional debate, both from personal fascination and from a perception that his party stood to gain from the issue.

His stand against Scottish legislative self-government became ever more passionate as he evoked images of the United Kingdom, torn apart. Speaking on the BBC on 30 December 1994, he described devolution as 'one of the most dangerous propositions ever put before the British nation'. Addressing a Conservative fund-raising dinner in Glasgow on 24 February 1995, he urged Scots 'from the bottom of my heart' to resist Home Rule.

Labour, naturally, was utterly downcast at the outcome of the 1992 election. The impact on the broader Home Rule campaign was similarly severe. As Labour leader, Neil Kinnock might not have had the most fervent commitment to self-government. He had, indeed, been a passionate opponent of devolution to Wales in the 1970s. But he had pledged early legislation for devolution if elected and that prospect had vanished with his defeat.

Jim Wallace took over as leader of the Scottish Liberal Democrats after the 1992 election. He recalls Convention talks shortly after that election. 'We were all at sea,' he told me.[1] 'The Scottish Tories had returned as the government and with more MPs, the one scenario we didn't prepare for.' They had indeed, gaining Aberdeen South to give them a total of eleven seats.

Wallace recalls that it was 'hard going' with the Labour Party at this time, dealing with first Donald Dewar and then Tom Clarke who took over as Shadow Scottish Secretary for a period. The Convention was becalmed. The Liberal Democrats were internally divided on the issue, with many believing that their party had suffered at the ballot box from the perception that they were in Labour's pocket.

Labour faced internal tension too. A group of left-wing Home Rule supporters helped form a new campaign organisation, Scotland United, which aimed to build broader links than the Convention had achieved, bringing the Nationalists on board.

Scotland United held a well-attended launch rally in Glasgow's George Square a few days after the April election. Involving artists, musicians and others outside politics, the new campaign group organised a series of events throughout Scotland. It sustained pressure over its key demand: for a multi-option referendum which would ostensibly allow the Scottish people to choose between independence, devolution or the prevailing status quo.

The Labour leadership was dismissive. Donald Dewar issued a statement on 29 June 1992, commenting on formal talks between Scotland United and the Scottish National Party. 'Labour', he said, 'is not in favour of collaboration of this sort.' The SNP, he added, had made it 'brutally clear that their top political priority was the destruction of the Labour Party'.

There were other sporadic outbreaks of protest. A group called Common Cause was formed in order to muster support for change from outside the party structure. Home Rule activists began a vigil outside the Scottish Office in Edinburgh which persisted, day and night, throughout the years of the Major Government, through the next election and up to the implementation of devolution legislation by the present UK administration.

A March for Scottish Democracy brought thousands to the streets of Edinburgh on 12 December 1992 while the summit of European leaders was being held in the Scottish capital.

Protest, self-evidently, has played its part in the devolution story. The issue of reform would not arise at all if objections to the status quo had not surfaced. There was even occasional talk at this time of civil disobedience to advance the Home Rule cause.

However, two points might usefully be made. Firstly, Scotland was not remotely in a fervour of popular discontent at this time despite the impressive turnout produced by, for example, the March for Scottish Democracy. Devolution was and is a second-order issue, important for many, central for some, but not life-threatening.

Secondly, in terms of workaday politics, devolution was in the doldrums as an issue at this point. That is not in itself to downplay the impact of protest. Simply it is to stress that the Home Rule issue had mostly proceeded through practical politics rather than through demonstration or rhetoric. For practical purposes, the issue was going nowhere. A Scottish Parliament was not demonstrably closer, at least not in terms of actual implementation.

I discussed this and many other issues with George Robertson,[2] who took over from Tom Clarke as Shadow Secretary of State for Scotland in the autumn of 1993. Robertson assumed the Scottish portfolio for Labour after years in which he had made his name on defence and foreign policy issues. He had been named Parliamentarian of the Year for his relentless exposure of Tory division while the Commons was considering the Maastricht Treaty to enhance the integration of the European Union.

Robertson whimsically described my suggestion that we might discuss his period handling Scottish issues as 'an invitation to relive the nightmare'. Certainly, his spell at the core of Scottish politics coincided with hard bargaining to complete the devolution package and, of course, the furious row over Labour's announcement that devolution would be subjected to an additional hurdle in the shape of a referendum. Yet, considered in more elementary terms, Labour might also reasonably conclude that his stewardship finalised the devolution deal and helped bring about the change of government which paved the way to implementation. However, after the 1997 general election victory, Robertson was moved from the Scottish remit to be Defence Secretary.

The Scottish Secretary or shadow must command a detailed brief with a range comparable to several Whitehall departments, must organise and motivate a team, must lead a political party, must deal with the complexities of Scottish politics and must cope with the demands of a thriving and challenging Scottish media scene. It is one of the toughest jobs in politics.

Robertson told me that, when he took over as Shadow Scottish Secretary, the Convention was 'struggling to find its feet'. There was a logjam over the detail of the scheme and no clear vision as to how to break that logjam.

According to Robertson, he formed a good working and personal relationship with his Liberal Democrat counterpart, Jim Wallace. He told me: 'We trusted each other and got on well with each other. Both of us had a common interest in delivering devolution for Scotland.' Wallace agrees with that analysis.

Both also credit Jack McConnell, the General Secretary of the Labour Party, and Andy Myles, the Chief Executive of the Liberal Democrats, with forming a valuable working relationship which served the Convention well when detailed negotiations had to take place offstage to forestall persistent rows in the Executive.

The 1990 Convention report had been followed by further detailed work on such issues as the electoral system, gender balance and the daily working of the Parliament. Various recommendations on these and other issues were approved on 27 February 1992, just before the general election.

There were, however, key outstanding topics, clear gaps in the system. Robertson says that it was necessary 'to look at the Convention scheme that had been put to the people at the 1992 election and refine it. It was not nearly detailed enough.'

As I have already examined, the assigned revenues system of finance was abandoned in favour of a version of the Treasury block grant. Gender balance was addressed. The powers of the Parliament were specified in greater detail and, as I have explained, scaled down in some cases.

However, perhaps the most glaring gap remained the electoral system and the size of the Parliament itself. On the electoral system, the Liberal Democrats favoured a method known as the single transferable vote in multi-member constituencies. Broadly, this system creates constituencies which are much bigger than the usual single seat and have several members. Voters rank their preferences in order 1, 2, 3 on the ballot paper. After the top name has emerged, voters' first preferences are redistributed until all the members have been chosen. Commonly, this produces a proportional result, with parties gaining a share of the seats which matches their share of the popular vote.

But Labour objected. The system was too complex. It was too big a change. It would break the clear link between the elector and a single constituency MP. Labour favoured a variant of the list system whereby voters select a single party and MPs are drawn from a list previously submitted by that party. The more votes, the more names chosen from the list.

Under the system eventually adopted, the Scottish Parliament still has clear constituency members, with seventy-three elected first-past-the-post for individual seats. That is the same number as for Westminster plus one to allow Orkney and Shetland each to have a constituency member of the Scottish Parliament. In addition, it was finally agreed that there would be fifty-six top-up members from party lists, distributed equally across eight regions of Scotland which are equivalent to the previous European constituencies.

On numbers, the Liberal Democrats had broadly wanted 145 members: twice the number of Scottish MPs at Westminster, plus dividing the single of seat of Orkney and Shetland into two distinct constituencies.

The Scottish TUC and others were arguing for a Parliament of 200, principally to help achieve the objectives of gender, regional and ethnic balance. It was argued that the Parliament needed to be big enough to meet its democratic requirements.

George Robertson recalls that there were other 'weird ideas' floating about: all, he believes, placing too much strain on the democratic framework, expecting the structure of the Parliament to accommodate too many tasks beyond the basic requirement of representing the people of Scotland.

George Robertson was arguing for a Parliament of 112. Jim Wallace wanted 145. Essentially, they agreed to split the difference and pick a Parliament of 129. Both, however, stress it was far less crude than that. They settled upon the arithmetical combination of seventy-three first-past-the-post plus fifty-six as a top-up.

Liberal Democrat insiders insist that 129 was their baseline because, below that number, the 'proportionality' of the Parliament would be severely affected. In other words, you needed at least seven 'top-up' members in each of Scotland's eight electoral regions to allow an arithmetical chance of matching seats to votes.

Both Robertson and Wallace took considerable flak from their own parties for reaching a personal agreement in advance of formal consultation. Both insist the initiative was necessary to drive forward a project which was in danger of stalling. The issue resurfaced for Jim Wallace in particular with the subsequent suggestion that the Scottish Parliament might have to shrink in size to match the planned reduction in Westminster seats from Scotland.

There was more, much more, in the final document which emerged as *Scotland's Parliament, Scotland's Right*, presented formally at a special session of the Convention on 30 November 1995.

The powers were again defined broadly in terms of transferring the responsibilities of the Scottish Office with, of course, the key basic element that the political mandate would be exclusively Scottish. A Scottish legislative power, it was argued, would redress the situation whereby Scotland was the only democratic country in the world with her own system of law but no elected legislature of her own to determine or reform that law.

It was stressed that, while devolution to other parts of the United Kingdom would be entirely welcome, the case for Scottish self-government stood on its own merits. It would not be acceptable for change elsewhere to be regarded as a precondition for Scottish Home Rule.

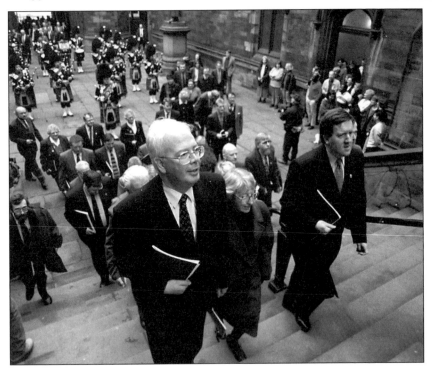

George Robertson and Jim Wallace lead the way as the Convention launches its detailed devolution scheme, 30 November 1995. (Kindly supplied by The Scotsman Publications Ltd.)

There was stress laid on the need for the Scottish Parliament to build European links and to maintain an office in Brussels.

Financing, as already discussed, was to be broadly by block grant with the retention of equalisation of resources across the UK and the Barnett formula, which determines the annual change in Scottish expenditure by relation to the annual change in the budget of comparable English spending departments.

The tone of the document – particularly on economic intervention and development – was notably more cautious than in 1990. The intention was plainly to reassure a business community which remained sceptical if not overtly hostile to devolution.

It was stressed there would be no power to vary corporation tax. The power to vary the standard rate income tax was 'unlikely to be used without a great deal of caution and prudence'. The Parliament, it was stressed, would 'want to create a vibrant partnership with industry and commerce'. There would be a 'powerful psychology of economic responsibility'. The aim was to soothe.

An internal and previously unpublished Labour memo from the time – dated 17 September 1995 – confirms this approach and gives a disarmingly frank assessment of the changes wrought in the Convention scheme from the earlier days, since the main document of 1990 and the general election of 1992. This memo was a hand-written note to George Robertson from Jack McConnell, then Labour's General Secretary in Scotland.

It is intended as a summary, a round-up of the key changes, to act as an aide-memoire to both men. Among other items, McConnell notes that the assigned revenues financing scheme has gone and that the three pence tax power has been 'put in more restrained and acceptable language' with 'other taxation specifically ruled out'.

On the Parliament's powers, he confirms the impression that Labour's new objective has been to constrain the more extravagant ambition of the earlier document. Public ownership powers are now to be almost the same as those available to the Secretary of State; the 'administration of social security' has been dropped; broadcasting has also been 'limited to SoS [Secretary of State] powers'; the notion of a role in monopolies and mergers has been replaced by 'comment on mergers affecting Scotland'; and the 'general power of competence' for the Scottish Parliament has been stopped.

In addition, the 'expectation of decentralised power to islands councils' has been dropped; spending commitments have been more cautiously phrased; schemes such as 'a women's Ministry and similar ideas [have been] left to parties'; and 'all extravagant references to transfer of sovereignty deleted'.

The memo goes on to confirm the nature of the agreement with the Liberal Democrats on the voting system – noting that the original scheme for a 50/50 scheme, for a rigidly gender-balanced Parliament (which the Liberal Democrats and many on the Labour side disliked) has gone. McConnell notes that this original statutory approach has now been replaced by a voluntary agreement, adding that 'this would have seemed impossible twelve months ago.'

Finally he sums up other changes, including the confirmation of immigration as a UK responsibility; the deletion of references to a 'Scottish Civil Service'; and the refinement of the Parliament's role in European talks, dropping, for example, the notion of a 'right' for

Scotland to lead on issues such as fisheries. McConnell notes that 'References to Europe [are] now clearly limited and in context.'

The memo concludes: 'I think that is the main list at this stage. Pretty impressive work, I think!'

It is plain from this memo – and indeed from my recollection of events at the time – that Labour's aim was to contain its devolution scheme within what the leadership would regard as workable boundaries. This was very much in keeping with the emerging strategy of the Labour Party under its new leader, Tony Blair: to keep pledges limited and achievable, to drop any promises which might be represented as extravagant. Equally, it reflected wider party concern to build a balance between Scottish Home Rule and the UK dimension.

The new overall Scottish package was endorsed by Blair, who had taken over after the death of John Smith in 1994. George Robertson argues that endorsement was highly significant, allocating a key portion of Labour's prospective UK parliamentary programme to a deal which had been negotiated solely in Scotland and with rival parties involved. More cynical observers argue that Blair's team would have been consulted throughout the negotiations. Robertson, however, insists that this was the operation of internal devolution in practice. Labour and the Liberal Democrats had a final Convention scheme. The Nationalists were advocating their programme of independence in Europe. The Conservatives were strongly playing the Union card. The battleground was clearly marked out. Then Labour revealed plans for a referendum.

Notes

1. Interview with Jim Wallace, 7 December 1998.
2. Interview with George Robertson, 26 January 1999.

5 The Referendum Row

There is no force in politics so powerful as ridicule. In the Commons, Ministers can continue to command the support or at least the sympathy of the House if they are frank about departmental or personal shortcomings. They can attack, they can wheedle, they can bluster. What they must not do is appear silly.

Spare a thought for those Liberal Democrat MPs who had to sit in close proximity to Dennis Skinner while Labour was in opposition and the two parties occupied the benches across the floor from the governing Tories. Each and every time those LibDem MPs spoke, they knew they were in danger of a sarcastic intervention from Skinner which would be picked up by the Commons microphones, prompting an already unsympathetic House to bray with destructive laughter.

It is a similar concern which prompted Jim Wallace to complain privately that the row of seats behind him in the Scottish Parliament was occupied from Day One by Dennis Canavan, Tommy Sheridan and Robin Harper.

The introduction of television cameras to the Commons produced a technique known as doughnutting. When an MP is speaking, supportive colleagues gather round in a sugary cluster, nodding sagely and mouthing 'Hear, hear' at even the most platitudinous drivel. Under the House broadcasting rules, the television camera will often cover only the speaker and his or her immediate environment. The doughnut's aim is to convince the casual viewer that the speaker has the House in thrall, that the oratory on offer is of Ciceronian standard.

Dennis Skinner is the spicy nutmeg in the Commons doughnut, with an unerring talent for spotting the precise moment when a speaker has veered into the realm of self-absorbed farce.

Labour's referendum plan, announced in opposition, suffered its worst moments in that same realm. On 31 August 1996, Labour's Scottish Executive met in Stirling. The object was to address the apparent tide of discontent with the party leadership's plan for a two-question referendum on Scottish devolution. The meeting began with disquiet over two questions. The meeting contrived to end up with support for three questions.

In a statement issued on his behalf, Tony Blair called this development 'mature and sensible'. Most political and media commentators thought it daft, an object of open derision. Bill Speirs of the Scottish TUC offered one of the more restrained opinions when he said: 'It is hard to understand how an argument between one question and two questions could have ended up with three questions.' The answer lies in the electoral arithmetic of the executive – but also in wider party uncertainty over the thrust of the Labour leadership's devolution strategy.

Folk memory plays a part here. The 1979 devolution referendum was scarcely Labour's greatest moment. True, the people of Scotland had voted by a narrow majority in favour of devolution. However, the scheme foundered on the requirement – inserted at the prompting of a dissident Labour backbencher – that devolution must obtain the support of 40 per cent of the entire potential electorate to proceed.

Abstaining or simply neglecting to vote, consequently, carried weight against devolution. The measure fell. Jim Callaghan's Government lost a vote of confidence in the Commons – with the Nationalists, angry at the fate of the devolution scheme, helping to vote him down. Labour lost the subsequent general election. Margaret Thatcher was triumphant. The Tories governed for the next eighteen years. The Labour Party of the 1990s had reasons to regard a referendum on devolution with a certain ingrained suspicion.

The party line – until it changed – was that a general election would provide the necessary mandate for devolution. Throughout the first half of 1996, in the newspapers and on television, the Shadow Scottish Secretary George Robertson stuck to that line. There was 'no question' of Labour backing a referendum. He told *The Herald* on 12 February 1996 that Labour MP Tam Dalyell was 'an isolated and lonely figure' in issuing such a demand.

This is, of course, one of the perils of politics in a multi-party set-up with an eager, watchful media. A political leader can seldom vacillate. What might be regarded as understandable uncertainty in ordinary life is viewed as unpardonable weakness in politics. The leader must sound determined. A devolution referendum is bad, it is wrong, it is a thing to be shunned by all sensible people – until, of course, it becomes the party's new policy.

The policy switch emerged from a committee chaired by the Shadow Lord Chancellor Lord Irvine of Lairg. Irvine had a useful pedigree. A Scots-born lawyer, he had been a university friend of John Smith and had recruited Tony Blair to his London legal chambers. The object of Irvine's committee was to consider the practical obstacles which might confront Labour's legislative programme in government.

Those involved at various points in consultation over the Scottish devolution scheme included George Robertson, Donald Dewar as Chief Whip, Ann Taylor as Shadow Leader of the House, Jack Straw as Shadow Home Secretary, Gordon Brown and Robin Cook.

George Robertson told me it became 'absolutely, blindingly obvious' during this committee's deliberations that Labour would have a serious problem with implementation of the Scottish devolution promise.[1]

The party was working on an assumption of a Commons majority peaking at around forty – not the 179 which was actually obtained. The Conservatives were determined to fight devolution at every stage. It could be assumed that concern over the English implications of Scottish devolution might prompt some Labour backbenchers to raise objections.

Further, the convention was that constitutional Bills had to be taken through all their stages in the main debating chamber of the Commons, rather than being consigned 'upstairs' to a committee for line-by-line consideration. Viewed from opposition, it looked as if Scottish devolution would clog up the Commons, blocking other elements of Labour's potential programme for government.

There was an additional element. The Tories appeared to be making ground with their attacks on the Tartan Tax, the proposed power for the Scottish Parliament to vary the standard rate of income tax by a maximum of three pence in the pound.

Scots, according to the Tory analysis, would pay a high price for Labour's scheme. Further – and more worrying still for the British Labour Party – the Tories argued that the Tartan Tax proved that Labour had yet to shed its image as an organisation prone to prising cash from the voters' pockets. Labour, it was claimed, was still disposed to tax and spend. Scotland might suffer first, it was argued, but England would soon follow.

It can be easy, with hindsight, to dismiss this argument, given the eventual outcome of the referendum. Again, however, Labour had a collective folk-memory that it had lost the 1992 general election partly because it had promised higher levies upon middle and upper earners.

Tony Blair and Gordon Brown, the Shadow Chancellor, wanted nothing that would associate Labour with higher taxation.

In addition, Michael Forsyth, the Conservative Scottish Secretary, had specifically demanded that Labour should subject its tax-varying plan to a referendum.[2] Admittedly, he had demanded that a two-question referendum – on the principle of devolution and tax – should be implemented only after the passage of devolution legislation.

Labour had a different approach: to subject its Home Rule plans to a referendum in advance of legislation. However, the party could attempt to argue that, in proposing two separate questions on principle and tax, it was taking up a challenge from the Tories, that it was confronting the issue. Political parties are seldom happier than when they can crow that they are taking their opponents at their word.

Put most simply, Forsyth's Tartan Tax campaign had got up Labour's nose. The referendum promise, it was argued, would at least give Labour MPs and potential candidates something to say when confronted with persistent questioning over tax. The issue of tax, they would be able to claim, was deferred until after the general election. It would never arise at all unless the voters explicitly agreed that the power should be given to the new Parliament. Even then, it was stressed, the power to tax might very well not be exercised. The calculation was that this distancing approach would neutralise the Tartan Tax campaign.

Robertson says that the referendum scheme, including the tax question, was essentially his initiative, that it emerged in detail from the Irvine committee – and in particular from the Scots on that committee.

Other insiders are far more inclined to stress Tony Blair's role. They argue that Blair took a hard look at Scottish devolution – and feared that it might stand in the way of issues which were of more immediate concern to the voters, especially in England. By this analysis, the referendum in general – and not just the tax question – was a tactic designed to quell political attacks in opposition and, subsequently, to minimise the issue's disruptive potential in government.

Donald Dewar uttered an ironic little laugh when I asked him about the genesis of the referendum plan.[3] He declined to comment in detail, adding: 'All I would say is that I think Tony had a big influence. He was very anxious that there should be a referendum to give legitimacy to what was happening.'

Blair was not, directly, a member of the Irvine committee which tackled this question. It is difficult, however, to discount his role as an offstage prompter whose voice was scarcely likely to be ignored. Blair likes to keep control of his party.

That is not to argue, as some have done, that George Robertson and ultimately the Scottish party were simply ordered to put up with a referendum, that the Scottish Labour leadership were utterly opposed to the switch. Rather it might be said that there was a convenient concordat. Blair's analysis, Robertson's analysis, the Irvine committee's analysis, all pointed to the need to address the mighty legislative challenge presented by devolution.

It is also not to argue, as some have done, that the referendum was designed to jettison devolution or, more precisely, to jettison the Scottish Parliament's tax-varying powers which were to be the subject of a specific second question.

There were undoubtedly Shadow Cabinet members and backbench MPs who would have shed few tears had devolution vanished from Labour's agenda or slid down the legislative timetable. They did not view the issue as a priority. Indeed, they feared the electoral consequences of Labour's identification with what they regarded as

an esoteric topic by contrast with the day-to-day concerns of the
voters the party needed for victory.

The referendum may partly be seen as a tactical answer to those
concerns, an attempt to contain the practical problems associated
with devolution. That does not mean that it was an overt attempt to
abandon devolution.

Robertson says the key point was that Labour's UK leadership
had accepted the entirety of the devolution scheme drafted by the
Convention. While that is true, other Convention participants insist
that the UK Labour leadership had monitored and influenced the
emerging devolution scheme throughout its progress. Its final shape,
consequently, scarcely came as a surprise.

Robertson, however, has a certain justification in arguing that this
was 'real devolution' within Labour, that the Scottish party and leadership had effectively been mandated to reach a settlement within the
Convention which would have enormous practical and political
implications for the party throughout Britain.

The key implication for the referendum, he argues, was that it
was agreed that the test of popular opinion would be held upon
the Convention scheme, formulated by the party in Scotland. With
the referendum principle and broad terms endorsed internally, the
problem was how to make the announcement, how to execute the
U-turn.

At this stage, the summer of 1996, Labour was making the final
preparations for its outline programme for government, the process
known as the Road to the Manifesto. The Scottish referendum
scheme could not be left out. Blair in particular was adamant that
the party could not promise a detailed policy prospectus including a
firm promise of a Scottish Parliament – only to confess subsequently
that the ground had shifted, that devolution was conditional on
Scottish popular support. The entire endeavour would have been
fatally undermined when it eventually emerged. Labour's overall
credibility – Blair's carefully protected reputation for political straight
talking – would have been placed in question.

It was decided to publish the referendum scheme immediately –
although Robertson concedes he 'gulped a bit at the timing' and
would have preferred more preparation, had that been at all possible.
Blair, however, was insistent.

In the event, the preparation was even shorter than anticipated.

The story leaked. On Tuesday, 25 June, the party's Scottish General Secretary, Jack McConnell, was hastily summoned to an evening meeting in London. He had got wind of the changing perspective on devolution in very sketchy outline. This meeting confirmed the intention – but, even as that confirmation came, Blair's press secretary Alastair Campbell was indicating that he had responded to questions from *The Independent* and had outlined the broad thrust of the referendum plan.

Some credit *The Independent* with journalistic endeavour in digging out the story. Others, particularly within Scottish Labour, suspect that Blair's office wanted the story to emerge in a way which indicated that London was in charge, that the anxiety of the wider party over the Scottish Question had been addressed. To be blunt, as one insider suggested to me, that 'the Scots had been put in their place.'

Whatever, it caused Robertson enormous problems both within and beyond his party. It infuriated the Liberal Democrats, who believed that the cooperational spirit of the Convention had been shattered – although, to be fair, the Convention itself had never specified whether or not a referendum would be needed. Jim Wallace, the Scottish Party leader, told me he was alerted to the prospect of a referendum by Paddy Ashdown on that Tuesday night when the story was beginning to leak.[4]

Wallace tried to speak to George Robertson in the Members Lobby at the Commons – but the Shadow Scottish Secretary was surrounded by others, preventing a confidential conversation. Robertson apparently tried to reach Wallace at his London flat later that evening – but failed to make contact. At the time, Wallace felt decidedly let down. He was furious that he was not briefed directly by his Convention partner.

The referendum, of course, also outraged substantial sections of Scottish Labour opinion.

Jim Wallace recalls that he was interviewed by me about the emerging controversy on Wednesday, 26 June for BBC Radio Scotland's 'Good Morning Scotland' programme, which I was co-presenting at the time. Heading straight to the Commons after this early morning exchange, he bumped into John McAllion of Labour's front bench, who had travelled down from Scotland on the sleeper.

Wallace says: 'I walked into the House of Commons with John and asked him what he thought about the referendum. He asked me "what referendum"? And he was the Labour constitutional affairs spokesman!'

McAllion resigned over the issue and helped to lead the internal Labour campaign against the referendum plan – and especially the second question on tax. At the same time, the former Labour Minister Lord Ewing resigned in protest as the joint chair of the Convention.

George Robertson was on the defensive. He led a tense news conference in Glasgow's Royal Concert Hall on Thursday, 27 June, alongside Jack McConnell and the party's senior Shadow Cabinet Scots, Donald Dewar, Gordon Brown and Robin Cook. This high-powered presentation was designed to demonstrate Labour's serious intent. The party line was that the referendum would make devolution 'stable and durable'.

There was one exchange from this news conference which perhaps encapsulates the atmosphere of suspicion and mistrust which surrounded the announcement. George Robertson said he had floated the referendum plan with Tony Blair when the party leader stayed at Robertson's home in Dunblane, the day after the massacre in the primary school in March.

As I recall, one correspondent, Andy Nicoll – then of *The Courier*

Labour musters its Scottish big names to defend the decision to subject Scottish devolution to a referendum, 27 June 1996. (Kindly supplied by The Scotsman *Publications Ltd.)*

in Dundee, later with *The Sun* – questioned Robertson closely on this statement, querying whether it was credible that two political leaders would sit in a town in mourning and discuss the future arrangements for Scotland's constitution. Other correspondents took up this line but Robertson apparently found Nicoll's persistence particularly objectionable and later viewed him extremely frostily as a consequence.

George Robertson told me he did indeed raise the topic of a referendum with Blair on this occasion, noting that in the presence of such an ineluctable tragedy as Dunblane, it is understandable that people will talk of something, anything other than the grim events themselves.

Far more significant than any awkward exchanges with the media, however, was the potential rift which the referendum plan created within Scottish Labour. Initially, the leadership seemed to prevail. Blair addressed the Scottish Executive in Edinburgh on Friday, 28 June, persuading them to back the change of direction by twenty votes to four, although the precise significance and relevance of this vote was later challenged.

After a truce for the Scottish school holidays, the battle recommenced in August. The focus of the complaints narrowed. If there had to be a referendum, it was argued, it should be a straight Yes or No without a back-up question on tax. A campaign for a single-question referendum was launched in the old Royal High School on Edinburgh's Calton Hill – then still the intended home for the Parliament.

The campaign was backed by MPs, the trades union Unison, women's groups and the Home Rule pressure group Scottish Labour Action. Kilmarnock MP Willie McKelvey argued that a Parliament without tax-varying powers would be a 'toothless tiger, a powerless talking shop and consequently a gigantic step down the road to independence'. In other words, the tax power was intrinsic and not optional.

In a pamphlet, four high-profile Labour movement activists, Margaret Curran, Bill Speirs, Ian Smart and Bob Thomson, warned that the referendum risked 'betraying' the people of Scotland. They viewed the second question on tax in particular as a 'wrecking device' and warned against 'the men in the dark' in Gordon Brown's office who, allegedly, wanted to dump the tax power.

It is important to understand the motivation underlying such rhetoric. That motivation still carried resonance long after the particular arguments over the referendum had been quelled. Those Labour activists who spoke out most forcibly against the referendum did so because they feared that Labour's overall attitude to devolution was suspect.

They believed that the London leadership's commitment to devolution was skin-deep, or, perhaps more accurately, that an issue they regarded as central was viewed as relatively marginal, even as dispensable, by the party in the South. In return, as I have outlined, key figures in the party in London felt that Scottish Labour seemed obsessed with constitutional change while the voters were interested in health, education and jobs.

For many Scottish Labour activists, the second question on tax was particularly objectionable because it was seen as an attempt by their own party to hobble the Parliament before it began, to restrain its powers, to curtail the measure of devolution which had been agreed in Scotland by the Convention.

They saw the referendum as mistaken, as a misplaced tactic. But more, they saw it as a curtain-raiser to potential future attempts to contain Scottish devolution, as a signal of Westminster's inherent suspicion about Home Rule. From the perspective of the critics, this was an issue of long-term principle, not simply transient pragmatism.

Labour leaders, consequently, had to fight on two fronts. They had to argue that the referendum was the best way of securing practical advance for devolution – but they also had to address, yet again, the lingering suspicion of backsliding.

George Robertson told me the concern was quite misplaced on both counts. Firstly, he 'never had any doubt at all the people would back the scheme we were putting forward' when it came to a referendum. Far from dumping the tax plan, the referendum scheme helped secure it as it 'completely neutralised' the Tory complaints over this issue during the general election.

Secondly, he argued that the referendum scheme reflected deepening support for devolution rather than persistent suspicion. By Robertson's analysis, the London leadership had completely absorbed the case for reform and had, consequently, looked seriously at how to achieve that agreed objective. The referendum was the consequence of that scrutiny.

Further, Donald Dewar told me he 'got very irritated with some of my colleagues who took the view that this [the referendum] was some sort of conspiracy to get rid of devolution – especially on the second question'.

Unmoved, Labour's most fervent Home Rule advocates continued to argue that the referendum was misplaced in practice – and ill-motivated in principle. While it lasted, this was a row quite ferocious in its intensity. It did not, however, last very long – at least in terms of open combat. This was, after all, the autumn of 1996. The general election was due in the spring or early summer of 1997 at the very latest.

Nobody in Labour ranks wanted this atmosphere of irritation and mistrust to interrupt the efforts to oust the Tories and to win the general election. Minds were concentrated.

A deal had to be reached to end the internal row – which brings us back to that meeting of the Scottish Labour Executive in the old Central Region headquarters in Stirling on 31 August 1996. Going into the meeting, views had hardened. The extent of opposition to the second question on tax powers meant that the entire referendum scheme might fail to win support. If the leadership insisted on the second question – as they did – then the arithmetic seemed to be stacking up against them.

Robertson knew he could count on eighteen votes. The critics had also mustered eighteen votes. There were three waverers, including Mohammed Sarwar, then a Glasgow councillor, later to become the MP for Glasgow Govan.

Sarwar played a key role. After a range of options had been examined without success, Sarwar proposed that Westminster should go ahead with its two-question referendum but with the proviso that there would be a further referendum, organised by the Scottish Parliament, before any tax change could be implemented. Scotland, in other words, would have a second chance to say Yes or No on the Tartan Tax.

Remember the fear was that Scots would dump the tax power – and perhaps even devolution itself – in the initial two-question referendum. Remember that those who backed devolution most avidly also believed that the scheme would be flawed, perhaps fatally flawed, without the power to vary revenue.

The logic behind the Sarwar plan was that Scots would be more inclined to vote Yes/Yes in the Westminster referendum if they had the further safeguard of a subsequent Scottish tax referendum to fall back on.

Such deals can often look attractive to participants desperately seeking a way out of an impasse, a way to square the seemingly irreconcilable. Inside the talks, Robertson saw it that way. He bought the deal and won the vote by 21 to 18. Outside the talks, it seemed absurd. Standing in the car park outside the Stirling meeting, Ian Smart of Scottish Labour Action was briefed by mobile phone. I watched his incredulity grow as he garnered the details from a sympathetic participant.

Down the years, Labour has frequently landed in such quandaries. Activists become absorbed in squaring the various interest groups within the party, rather than devising a coherent policy. They placate the powerful union, they get the big local authority on side, they quieten the maverick MP with a constituency worry. Then, exhausted, they present their patchwork plan to the public – and shrink back, astonished and hurt, when it is greeted with disdain by people who were not party to the negotiations.

Tony Blair's entire leadership approach has been to counter this phenomenon, to urge the party to focus upon the external impact of the policies themselves, rather than upon competing internal pressures.

Such a remedy, frankly, was not immediately available to George Robertson in the referendum row. He had to patch together what he could from a suspicious and divided Executive. As a consequence, at the subsequent news conference, George Robertson struggled to defend the deal. It was entirely right, he argued, that the Scottish people should be asked about their own future. But, as I recall enquiring, did they have to be asked twice – until presumably they got the answer right?

The twin-referendum scheme was ludicrous and was disowned by Robertson within the week. At yet another tense news conference – this was a peak period for tense news conferences – the Shadow Scottish Secretary declared that the second referendum carried 'no support' and was consequently dumped.

A little too late to escape damage to his political reputation, George Robertson turned the row into an issue of leadership. Nobody in the weary Labour Party could muster the energy to question his right to abandon a scheme which had after all been endorsed by the Scottish Executive and described by Tony Blair as 'mature and sensible' just a few days previously.

Inevitably, Robertson suffered. This skilled Parliamentarian – who had hounded the Tories over the Maastricht Treaty – had apparently tripped up over the intricacies of Scottish constitutional politics.

More accurately, he had the ill luck to be occupying one of the toughest jobs in politics, leader of the Scottish Labour Party, during one of its sharpest internal conflicts.

In the short term, Robertson comforted himself with the analysis of a constituent in a bowling club in Hamilton who informed the Shadow Scottish Secretary that it was 'bloody marvellous' to find a politician willing to admit he had got something wrong.

In the longer term, of course, there was an alternative comfort. Robertson told me: 'I said at the time I was prepared to be judged by the outcome.' That outcome saw the referendum carried clearly on both counts. The people of Scotland supported both the principle of devolution and tax powers and this endorsement proved its worth to Labour in speeding the devolution legislation through Parliament.

Looking back, it can be argued that George Robertson refined and finalised the devolution package in the Convention. He suffered the anguish of the referendum controversy in pursuit, as he would see it, of a longer-term gain for the cause of reform. Finally, from a Labour perspective, he contributed substantially to the party's victory at the general election which paved the way to the implementation of devolution.

Many within Scottish Labour look back on that period with dull pain – including, of course, George Robertson himself. Perhaps, however, within the more substantial and long-running drama of devolution, a sympathetic audience might be prepared to tolerate a few scenes of farce.

Notes

1. Interview with George Robertson, 26 January 1999.
2. Interview with Michael Forsyth, then Scottish Secretary, on BBC 'Reporting Scotland', 2 May 1996.
3. Interview with Donald Dewar, 16 January 1999.
4. Interview with Jim Wallace, 7 December 1998.

6 Preparing for the White Paper

George Robertson endured the frequent agony of opposition with Scottish Labour – but he was spared the challenge of dealing with devolution in government. A merciful or, more accurately, a politically calculating Prime Minister moved him from the Scottish remit to the Ministry of Defence. Donald Dewar became Scottish Secretary.

Robertson told me he felt 'a combination of relief and disappointment' at being moved from the Scottish brief. He added: 'Part of me said "I would like to see this project through" but another part of me saw it as the most brutal, bruising job in the whole of British politics.'

From a detached Whitehall perspective, the Ministry of Defence might be seen as promotion by contrast with Scotland. Starting from a neutral standpoint, Robertson would almost certainly have chosen defence, given his own background in foreign affairs. The standpoint, however, was not neutral. Robertson was inevitably concerned that his move might be interpreted as a negative reaction to the difficult days of the referendum row.

During the election campaign, I recall Robertson looking a little bemused and anxious over media rumours that he would not be given the Scottish job. Again, this was not because he desperately coveted the title Scottish Secretary ahead of all else. Rather it was the impression of temporary failure which a move might represent.

Tony Blair sought to dispel this impression when he explained the switch to Robertson. He vigorously praised his efforts in Scotland, stressing in particular the Tory wipe-out which had eluded the party in past years. But he went on to argue that the momentum of devolution must be maintained – which was better achieved by a change at the top.

Implicit in this assessment, of course, was a recognition that Robertson had been politically bruised by the referendum announcement and that he might not, as a consequence, be the best person to deliver a result in the referendum itself.

Privately, most senior Labour figures – and, even more privately, civil servants – endorse Blair's decision. They say the combination of referendum plus detailed negotiations on the legislation argued for Dewar: his political stature, his unquestioned command of the brief and his evident popularity across party lines and within Westminster and Whitehall. It is claimed, for example, that Dewar was better placed, after the row over the referendum announcement, to rebuild the cross-party allegiances which would be needed for the ballot itself.

Equally, however, there are senior Labour insiders who believe that Robertson's substantial contribution has not been given the credit it deserves. Those who take this view argue that the Convention package presented to the people in 1992 fell far short of requirements; that it was Robertson who sorted out issues like the precise electoral system while clarifying and moderating the Parliament's powers in areas like industrial intervention.

Robertson himself, however, quickly shrugged off any disappointment from the switch and grew to revel in the challenge of providing political guidance to the military, attracting the privately muttered nickname 'General George' among the more irreverent elements of Scottish Labour. He is able to look back at his spell as Shadow Scottish Secretary with a certain black humour, noting that the crisis management bunker he has been able to command in his defence role might have been useful while he was in charge of the Scottish Labour Party.

Astute readers will by now have noticed that in this assessment of various Cabinet positions, I have apparently skipped one thing: the intervening general election.

This was deliberate. It is my calculation that it will not be news to most people reading this book that Labour won the 1997 United Kingdom general election by a landslide. It is my further calculation that few will be interested in my retelling in great detail a story which they followed, more or less avidly, during the campaign itself. However, it would be perverse in the extreme to neglect the election entirely.

Put most simply, devolution to Scotland would not have happened without that general election result – or some comparable combination which returned parties open to reform and which ousted the Conservatives who had remained opposed to Scottish Home Rule.

The 1997 general election, consequently, was a critically important staging post on the route to a Scottish Parliament which I am attempting to retrace. My endeavour, however, is to focus more upon the unseen or the unnoticed, the challenges which confronted parties in framing their attitudes to Home Rule, the personal or political developments which were influential in the journey along the route.

The general election campaign, particularly in Scotland, was a curiosity in that respect. Labour appeared to want to focus upon anything but the devolution project. The Tories wanted to talk of nothing else.

Each time John Major came to Scotland, he attempted to revive the spirit of the Union which he was convinced had helped him to victory at the general election in 1992. An alternative interpretation of 1992, of course, is that Labour had not changed sufficiently, that the voters still feared Labour taxation plans and that Middle England could not stomach Neil Kinnock as Prime Minister.

Major believed that there was a dormant electoral giant, ready to crush devolution. For him, voicing opposition to devolution was not hype or temporary strategy. It was not an option to be discarded when the wind changed. He genuinely believed – and believes – that devolution is unworkable in practice and wrong in principle, fatally damaging to the Union which he regards with an almost ecclesiastical fervour.

This view was projected and endorsed in the Scottish Conservative campaign by Michael Forsyth. As Scottish Secretary, he had proved more pragmatic than his history of free-market fundamentalism led many to expect. On the question of legislative devolution, however, he was unmoved. Devolution would not work and had to be opposed.

This was the bedrock of the Scottish Tory campaign and, indeed, featured frequently in their message to England as well, following the 1992 model of attempting to 'alert' the people of the United Kingdom to the claimed danger in their midst. Certainly, the people of Scotland could be in no doubt as to the Tories' views on devolution. The people of Scotland responded by inflicting electoral obliteration upon the Conservatives. They were left without a single MP from Scotland.

Self-evidently, the 1997 collapse in Scotland could not be attributed entirely to the Tories' attitude to the Scottish Question. They lost heavily throughout England and they lost overall power. It might reasonably be argued, however, that the Scottish Home Rule issue marked the culmination of a variable forty-year decline by the party from its high point in the 1950s.

The Tories had come to be seen, fairly or unfairly, as a party whose roots lay outside Scotland, who were not identified with Scottish interests. At a time when political identification with Scottish concerns had become more important than ever, that was calamitous.

Labour's strategy in Scotland as well as England was to dwell upon populist concerns like jobs, education and health. Devolution was not entirely ignored – but it was quite deliberately treated in a different way. It was stressed that a subsequent referendum would settle the question of a Scottish Parliament rather than the immediately available general election.

The referendum consequently was used as a strategic device to help Labour surmount awkward questions from political rivals or the media: on the principle of reform or on the Tartan Tax. Labour sought by this strategy to avoid a head-to-head on devolution with the Tories or indeed with the Nationalists. Devolution was a challenge deferred.

Labour's Scottish news conferences began to follow a comforting ritual. Each day the party would pick a topic: education or health or employment or whatever. Each day the media would pick a topic: devolution.

I recall indeed being chided at the close of one such news conference by Jim Murphy, then a Labour backroom staffer, subsequently the MP for Eastwood. Why were the media obsessed with devolution?

Perhaps, I replied, because Labour had placed it at the core of their message in Scotland for more than twenty years. Perhaps because it was a substantial dividing line between the largest UK parties in an age when politics had seemingly moved into an aggregated centre.

Labour's tactic was to provide succour to those who wanted devolution; only a Labour government, it was argued, could meet their wishes. At the same time, Labour offered comfort to those who disliked devolution or harboured doubts; the election would not be the last word, there was still the referendum. Meanwhile they opted to fight the election on safer ground: the Tories' record and recent behaviour in office, and Labour's narrowly defined pledges in key areas of voter concern like class sizes, waiting lists and youth unemployment.

It is difficult to say whether this strategy played a significant part in Labour's victory. Quite probably, the contest was over long before the formal, final campaign as the voters determined to express their discontent with the Tories and decided that the new model Labour Party offered a thoroughly acceptable vehicle to express that discontent.

Labour strategists argue that it was important to prevent Forsyth's Tartan Tax campaign from destabilising Labour support. That was the reason it was so crucial to preserve the promise of a separate question on tax in the referendum. It was designed to take the bite from the Tory campaign. Arguably, however, that had already happened – to the full extent that it was going to happen – in the period following the announcement of the referendum. By the time of the election campaign, it was a question of reinforcing this message, of providing reassurance.

Labour's cautious attitude to its core strategy of devolution reflected an anxiety at the heart of the party's campaign. Readers will be familiar with the cliché that oppositions do not generally win elections – that governments lose them. More generally, this implies that the political hazards generally dog the incumbent party.

It can be said that the Tories in the run-up to the contest were making a pretty fair fist of losing the election, one way or another. But, equally, by the time of the 1997 general election, Labour seemed like the incumbents. The presumption was that Tony Blair was heading for Downing Street, that John Major was finished. Blair himself had repeatedly to remind his party that victory was not assured.

Hence, partly, the decision to place devolution at one remove by stressing the referendum hurdle. Labour calculated that – while the voters might welcome devolution – they did not want to hear about it endlessly. This reflects Labour's subsequent anxiety that the Parliament in itself will not content the Scots, that they will want substantial improvements in practical areas like industry and education.

Such tense circumstances inevitably produce occasionally bizarre behaviour. As an aside, I recall the Labour rally in Edinburgh's Usher Hall: not for the barnstorming speech by Tony Blair, when he thrust aside his notes and a faulty microphone to bawl out his key priorities to ecstatic supporters, impressive though that was. Rather I recall the Clochemerle politics which preceded the rally when Blair and his acolytes were once again pursued by a person dressed as a chicken designed, as I recall, to claim that Labour had 'chickened out' of a head-to-head television debate with the Tories.

The chicken, which followed Blair everywhere, was beginning to get to Labour, and especially the party's earnest individuals in suits. On this occasion, one senior party official had to be restrained after he declared his intention to stuff the chicken, personally. I watched, hugely amused, as alarmed party apparatchiks solemnly briefed colleagues through their high-tech personal intercom system: 'Don't touch the chicken!' The chicken duly survived – as, of course, did Labour's election prospects.

While Labour and the Tories absorbed electoral lessons, there were separate devolutionary messages from the election for both the Liberal Democrats and the SNP. The Liberal Democrats contrived to win ten seats by diligent targeting – despite a fractionally decreased share of the vote at just under 13 per cent. The Tories by contrast were wiped out in Scotland while obtaining more than 17 per cent of the vote.

LibDem strategists say they worked the system: a first-past-the-post voting system which they have consistently condemned. The 1997 general election confirmed for them, however, that under a reformed voting system they would have to punch their weight everywhere. They concluded they could not in future allow no-go areas to develop while pushing campaign effort entirely into a few key seats. Under the Additional Member System, they would need at least a discernible body of support across Scotland.

For the SNP, the general election result was relatively disappointing.

Alex Salmond had bet on at least seven MPs being returned in Nationalist colours. The outcome was six seats and a share of the vote at just under 22 per cent, which was only marginally better than the performance in 1992.

The result did confirm, if confirmation were needed, that the path to potential progress for the SNP was likely to lie through a devolved Parliament rather than through Westminster. They might have shunned the Convention, they might have repeatedly belittled Labour's plans in the past. But devolution signalled the way ahead for the Nationalists.

Strictly speaking, the Nationalists have long argued that a mandate for independence could come about through success for their party in elections either to Westminster or to a devolved Scottish Parliament.

The 1997 general election again highlighted the extreme difficulties of the Westminster route. The Nationalists fought a tough campaign, picking up three Tory seats over and above their 1992 performance. Yet they were still squeezed by a reinvigorated Labour Party battling for Westminster control with the Tories.

The voters can count. They know that the SNP, fighting Scotland's seventy-two seats, can never command a House of Commons with 659 seats. At a UK general election, the overriding question is always going to be: who will enter Downing Street?

With that key question to the fore, even the Liberal Democrats, fighting seats throughout Britain, find it hard to win a place in voters' minds. For the Scottish Nationalists, a squeeze is almost intrinsic to a UK electoral contest.

Labour, then, entered government for the first time since the thwarting of devolution contributed to their downfall in 1979. That memory hung over much of the early work. The ground had been carefully prepared to prevent a repetition.

The civil service machine moved swiftly to meet the declared determination of the incoming government that there should be legislation for a Scottish Parliament within the first session of the new Parliament. This pledge, first delivered by Neil Kinnock, was occasionally misinterpreted by the unwitting or the politically mischievous as meaning that a Scottish Parliament would actually be up and running within a year.

By contrast, senior politicians and civil servants knew that the promise of drafting and enacting preparatory legislation would itself present a considerable challenge, even with a huge government majority in the Commons. Some observers regarded the referendum as an unnecessary waste of time. Senior civil servants drafting the Home Rule legislation privately welcomed it as a breathing space.

Firstly, there would have to be the paving Bill to allow the referendum to take place. Then a White Paper setting out the Government's plans for Scotland in detail. Then the referendum itself seeking public assent to the contents of the White Paper. Then the legislation for devolution. Then finally the devolved Scottish Parliament.

The breathing space was extended by the decision – taken at an early stage by Donald Dewar – that the White Paper would not be published during the passage of the Bill setting up the referendum. Some MPs complained that they were being asked to authorise a referendum without knowing the full detail of the subject – without, in other words, seeing the White Paper. The Government insisted that they were simply being asked to pave the way to the referendum which would, of course, be based upon the contents of the White Paper.

Ministers stressed that the Referendum Bill was simply about mechanics, that the White Paper would be available well before the referendum itself and that the people would have ample opportunity to study its contents before making their choice. Ministers similarly dismissed demands that the referendum should be held after the devolution legislation had been passed.

There was occasional muttering to the effect that people were being asked to sign a blank cheque. There was dark talk of pigs in pokes. It was argued that the referendum should be based upon the final devolution scheme which emerged from Parliament, not the initial government outline.

Ministers brushed this aside for two reasons. One – and most obviously – they needed the referendum to speed the legislation through Parliament. Two – and this was left unstated – they did not envisage that the final product, after Parliament's honourable and noble tinkering, would be all that much different from the original scheme drafted by the Government.

It is a standing aim of governments to occupy inquisitive minds, particularly in the Commons. Government whips or business managers like the safety of a big majority – but equally they fret that MPs can become awkward and troublesome unless they are kept permanently busy. There is little difficulty in that regard when the Commons majority is small. Nothing occupies the minds of MPs more than the thought that their party – or more accurately their own seats – may be vulnerable.

In the absence of that sanction, governments have to find other things to fill the abhorrent political vacuum. To some extent, the referendum played that role in the emerging devolution debate. Put bluntly, the preparations for the referendum gave impatient politicians something to be getting on with – and forestalled them from nagging the Scottish Office overmuch for the detail of the White Paper and subsequent devolution Bill.

As it turned out, the breathing space was relatively short; the White Paper was published on 24 July, just as the Referendum Bill was completing its parliamentary passage.

Meanwhile, behind the scenes, of course, that question of detail was exercising minds considerably.

The first formal talks took place on the Saturday after the election at Dover House, the Scottish Office's grandiose outpost in Whitehall. Backing on to Horseguards Parade, Dover House is much envied by other government departments. The new Secretary of State had little time to absorb his new London base, to lounge in his own palatial office or explore the warren of secretarial rooms, to admire the paintings or the bust of Sir Walter Scott, to linger over the stout rope beside the staircase which reputedly assisted the lame Lord Byron to reach his discreet liaisons within this former private house.

On this particular Saturday, Sir Russell Hillhouse, the Permanent Secretary, Muir Russell, then head of the department which had overall responsibility for devolution, and Robert Gordon, the head of the Constitution Group, presented Donald Dewar with the notes which had been prepared for the incoming Secretary of State.

By this device, the civil service greets a new government with an outline of priorities and potential action based upon published political plans and, frequently, upon informal conversations before the election.

On this occasion, matters were pressing. Collectively, the Scottish Office had to be ready for a meeting the following Tuesday of the high-level Constitutional Reform Policy (CRP) committee to be chaired by the Prime Minister. This committee was to chart progress

on the Government's overall constitutional reform programme, of
which devolution was a key part.

For that first meeting, Tony Blair would expect a detailed briefing on Scottish Office proposals for implementing pledges delivered
in opposition and to be able to sign off the Referendum Bill for
introduction at the end of the following week. Further, that first
week saw the establishment of DSWR: the Devolution to Scotland,
Wales and the English Regions committee. With the Lord
Chancellor, Lord Irvine, in the chair, this body was to be the battleground for the decisive ministerial debates surrounding devolution.

Little time, then, for small talk at that Saturday meeting – or the
following day or on the Bank Holiday Monday in Edinburgh as
Dewar, his civil servants and the special advisers, Murray Elder and
Wendy Alexander, went through the details of the Scottish Office
proposals.

Murray Elder had a long pedigree in struggling with the detail of
devolution. Labour's former General Secretary in Scotland, he was a
longstanding friend and associate of Dewar and Gordon Brown. He
had also headed John Smith's office in opposition. Importantly, he
had been closely involved in the initial Labour Party decision to enter
the Convention and in the subsequent negotiations. He blended
knowledge of what the Scottish party expected with insight into
what Westminster and Whitehall would tolerate.

Wendy Alexander had followed a spell as Scottish Labour
researcher in Glasgow with a period as a management consultant.
Bright, dedicated and extremely hard-working, she was to play an
increasingly important role in implementing devolution and other
policy pledges before her adoption as a candidate for the Scottish
Parliament and her elevation to Donald Dewar's election campaign
team. Indeed, the evident influence of the special advisers during this
period prompted jealousies among the party and even in ministerial
circles.

Some felt Dewar's inner coterie had too much power, that he
consequently did not pay enough attention to party or Westminster
opinion.

An alternative interpretation, of course, is that the scale of the
practical task confronting the Scottish Office merited a somewhat
technocratic approach, that there was perhaps relatively little room
or time for observing the niceties of political or party life. Either

way, this flickering party suspicion that the devolution plan was in too few hands added to the challenges confronting the drafting team.

They had to convince relatively unenthusiastic Cabinet colleagues, they had to persuade the public in a referendum, they then had to get the devolution legislation through both Houses of Parliament – and all within the stated timescale of the first parliamentary session.

Despite the extent of that challenge, they had several key advantages. Firstly, they had learned important lessons from the frustrated attempt to devolve power to Scotland in the 1970s. Indeed, a civil service file on how to avoid the pitfalls of the 1970s had been prepared for the 1992 general election. It was swiftly dusted down and studied.

By contrast with the 1970s, it was agreed that the Scottish Office would take the lead in Scottish devolution. To outside observers, this may seem unremarkable: the Scottish Office running Scottish devolution. But the 1970s scheme had been administratively controlled from the Cabinet Office in Whitehall. This switch allowed the Scottish team supervising the reforms to set the agenda, to react speedily to developments in the interests of keeping the scheme on track.

The Cabinet Office took charge of the overall programme of constitutional change – which was significantly more ambitious and was pursued with greater vigour than the 1970s model.

Also by contrast with the 1970s, it was agreed that devolution would proceed by specifying those powers to be retained in Westminster: matters such as defence, foreign affairs and the broad economy. Everything else by definition was devolved to Edinburgh.

This was in truth a difficult enough exercise but it meant at least in theory that the endeavour was more narrowly defined than two decades previously, when Whitehall had attempted to prescribe every dot and comma of the planned Scottish Assembly's powers. It also sent a psychologically potent signal through Whitehall.

Further, the Government's plans had already been spelled out in substantial detail in the revised Convention document. Privately, more than one civil servant and even Labour politician had cause to be grateful for the intervening years since the 1992 election which had allowed the Convention scheme to be redrafted and specified.

There was at least one more source of information. Michael Forsyth, as Conservative Scottish Secretary, had sought to strengthen the role of the Scottish Grand Committee as an alternative to legislative devolution. He took the committee – comprising all Westminster MPs from Scottish constituencies – on tour around the country. He gave the committee the power to question Ministers from other departments up to and including the Prime Minister, who appeared before the Grand at a session in Dumfries. Ministerial statements, normally made in the Commons, were delivered to the Grand. Non-controversial legislation was considered in outline by the committee.

In itself, the initiative was successful. The Grand on tour proved a draw, with spectators turning up and demonstrators taking the chance to ventilate local or national concerns. The more noisy and raucous the demonstration, the bigger the smile on Michael Forsyth's face as he was able to proclaim public interest in his scheme.

In addition, civil servants were instructed to prepare details on the alternative costs and challenges of establishing a devolved, legislative body along the lines recommended by the Convention.

Forsyth intended this as ammunition in his campaign to vaunt the Grand and to undermine elected devolution, Labour-style, by highlighting its alleged expense and complexity. However, it meant that those officials asked later, by Forsyth's opponents, to implement the scheme had some familiarity with the issues and challenges to be faced. In other words, the information gathered during the course of this Tory-ordered exercise was to end up being added to the database prepared for devolution itself. It is perhaps one of the neater ironies of politics.

More generally, the civil service had known that the challenge of devolution was coming. Civil servants may be formally detached from politics. They adapt to whatever pattern of political control is thrown up by the electorate. That does not mean, however, that they are politically innocent.

When an election is looming – and, more precisely, when it is called – the civil service machine prepares for the prospect of government under a range of political options. As well as serving the incumbent administration, senior civil servants will have meetings with Opposition leaders in order to be prepared for a potential change of political direction.

This has the strictly limited purpose of gleaning direct information about their plans. It is explicitly not to offer policy advice to the

Opposition but rather to take stock of any implications of alternative policies for the machinery of government.

The objective in short is to ensure that there is no administrative or political hiatus. The Prime Minister is defeated, long live the new Prime Minister. Given Labour's seemingly dominant lead in the opinion polls in the run-up to the 1997 general election, the civil servants would scarcely have been human if they had not prepared with a certain diligence for the prospect of a change at the top.

As part of this pre-election process, the Scottish Office Permanent Secretary Sir Russell Hillhouse and his subsequent successor Muir Russell had met George Robertson, then the Shadow Scottish Secretary. The policy was formed then that, should it be required, Scottish devolution would be administratively driven from Scotland although self-evidently Whitehall would have a big say.

That allowed preparations to be made. Once the election was called, the Cabinet Office set up a new Constitution Secretariat to work through the overall jigsaw of potential reforms to the governance of the United Kingdom. This secretariat was headed by Kenneth Mackenzie, who was on secondment from the Scottish Office.

Within the Scottish Office itself, the framework for devolution was discreetly put in place. This was, after all, ahead of the election. The Conservatives had not left office. The civil service had to work on the basis that either Labour or the Tories or indeed some other combination might be returned. However, the scale of the challenge potentially presented by a Scottish Parliament meant that, within the rules, preparation was essential.

The key appointment was that of Robert Gordon. He had known that he was likely to be given a role in preparing devolution, should that prove necessary. Once the election was called, however, that outline role was formalised. He was identified as the potential head of the Constitution Group, which was to formulate and steer all elements of the devolution package, reporting to Muir Russell.

Quietly spoken and with a wry sense of humour, Robert Gordon was an excellent appointment. He combined personal skills with an attention to detail and an alertness to the political and diplomatic minutiae involved in sustaining one of the widest-ranging reforms in constitutional history.

The Scottish Office used the period of the lengthy election

campaign to identify other key personnel who would – and the conditional tense always had to be stressed – be given the task of activating reform. Civil servants were quietly diverted from their day jobs to begin the process of preparing for a possible constitutional initiative. It had previously been made clear by Labour politicians that they would wish to move extremely quickly on devolution, to exploit the opportunity which a general election victory would give. The civil service prepared.

After the election, these skeletal preparations were swiftly completed. Although devolution would affect all parts of the Scottish Office – and many would play an important role – it was decided that the Constitution Group would focus the corporate effort. Rather than disseminate the task of devolution across existing departments, the Scottish Office opted for a hand-picked squad. They were the civil service equivalent of the A Team: a description they would, no doubt, gently disdain.

Characteristically, these individuals were bright, determined and outward-looking. The Constitution Group – the A Team – looked on devolution as the biggest professional challenge they had confronted.

Professional, note. Officials cannot afford to let any political views they may hold intervene in their daily duties. Senior civil servants relish solving problems, fixing things. Devolution, by that calculation, was simply a bigger and tougher problem to be fixed.

Four squads were set up immediately after the election. There was the team preparing for the referendum under Paul Grice; the legal side under Iain Jamieson, responsible for the immense task of getting the Scotland Bill right; the powers and functions team under David Crawley, charged with negotiating the best possible settlement with Whitehall; and the outfit responsible for overall policy and the key task of drafting the White Paper under Isabelle Low.

David Crawley moved in spring 1998 to head the Schools Group and was replaced by Ian Walford. Isabelle Low moved from the Group after the publication of the White Paper to take charge of developing the Government's land reform proposals. She was replaced by John Ewing.

This strategy by the Scottish Office of operating a core group was highly significant – although naturally most public attention has spotlighted the political debates surrounding devolution. The tightly knit Constitution Group – with help from colleagues elsewhere in the

Department – provided a critically important element of persistence and constancy which blended with political direction to produce a result.

Later, civil servants – with understandable if uncharacteristic pride – were to assist on the day the Scotland Bill was published in briefing the media on a document which showed a read-through from the Convention to the White Paper and subsequent legislation. It showed, in other words, that the strategy had delivered, that the devolution scheme had been preserved in outline and detail through the trials of Whitehall and Westminster.

There was a personal element underlying this administrative task. The key civil servants tended to regard Donald Dewar with very considerable respect, admiration and affection. That is not by any means to suggest that they would not have delivered for someone they disliked or distrusted. Personal relationships, however, undoubtedly helped the sense of a team enterprise.

Dewar also required to exert his personal skills in DSWR, the Cabinet committee working on devolution, including scrutiny of the White Paper which was presented to voters in the referendum. Colleagues recall that he frequently returned from DSWR meetings white-faced and drawn – and that was when he had been successful.

Every item had to be pursued exhaustively. For Dewar, of course, this was particularly exasperating as he often had to deal at length with topics which he had discussed endlessly in past years within the Shadow Cabinet, the Scottish Labour Party and the Convention.

There were structural tensions. The Welsh Office harboured suspicions that Scotland was getting a far better deal – or that it might be seen by the voters as a far better deal. Cabinet colleagues like the Home Secretary Jack Straw, a member of DSWR, nurtured doubts about the nature of the project, reflecting wider concerns in the party that devolution was not a top popular priority.

Straw and others were not inclined, from instinct, to give too much weight to Scottish Labour's negotiations in the cross-party Convention while in opposition. More than one Minister voiced the opinion that they would not regard themselves as necessarily bound by deals struck between Scottish Labour and the Scottish Liberal Democrats. It was Labour's Commons majority which would deliver devolution, they argued, not the Liberal Democrats. Conseqently, Labour's Cabinet must make up its own mind.

Specifically, there was a serious attempt to unpick the deal with the Liberal Democrats on the voting system for the Scottish Parliament. Those who disliked the principle of proportional representation warned that Labour might be seen as setting a Westminster precedent by deploying PR in Scotland.

Further, it was pointed out that PR would almost certainly result in a Scottish coalition, that Labour would not be able to control the planned Scottish Parliament. A note of frustration occasionally entered the complaints. If there had to be a Scottish Parliament, it was argued, why not make it a Parliament with a reasonable chance of Labour control? Why give power away?

Dewar, consequently, was not confronted simply with nit-picking. Over the PR argument and other issues, he had to return to first principles, to elementary devolutionary debate.

Remember too that, while Dewar may have lived and breathed Scottish Home Rule for decades, it was relatively unfamiliar ground to others, even in the upper reaches of the party or Whitehall. They had to be convinced and convinced again on topics which Scottish politicians tended to regard as established.

There was an additional, personal source of potential tension for the Scottish Secretary. Donald Dewar's wife Alison had, much earlier, left him for another lawyer, Derry Irvine. Derry Irvine was now Lord Irvine, the Lord Chancellor and the Cabinet Minister in charge of DSWR, the committee on devolution.

Inevitably, the two were scarcely the best of friends, although insiders insist that talk of unbending hostility is entirely misplaced. Indeed, one source even suggested that a legacy of emotional guilt may have played a part in helping the two men to forge a working relationship.

Certainly, Dewar insists that Lord Irvine performed his duties diligently and with enthusiasm. According to Dewar, Lord Irvine subjected the Scottish devolution project to the closest possible scrutiny, questioning each element, each assumption carefully. But the Scottish Secretary says this scrutiny was well merited – and highly productive in that it generated a package which could survive detailed examination by both Houses of Parliament.

Within Whitehall, there lingered inherent scepticism as to whether the project could be made to work, as to whether the anomalies involved in partial devolution were sustainable. Could they tackle the Scottish Question without creating consequential problems for the governance of England or the regions of England?

There was some disquiet at the entire principle but, given the Government's majority and evident determination, most Whitehall concern spotlighted practical details.

Dewar told me there were 'enormously hard arguments' with the Treasury, who took the chance to drive a series of hard bargains on the financial arrangements governing devolution and Scotland more generally.[1] For example, the Treasury insisted that the Scottish administration should be made to face the consequential effects on welfare spending of any policy decisions it might take in areas like housing. I intend to look later, in a separate chapter, at the financial challenge which will confront the Scottish Parliament, partly as a consequence of these hard bargains.

In addition, much of the argument centred around turf wars. What impact would the powers of the Scottish Parliament have upon Whitehall? What about areas of overlap? There were wonderfully arcane discussions about the minutiae of, for example, the interplay of Scots law and companies law and how the decisions of the Scottish Parliament might impact on reserved fields.

There was a substantial fight surrounding the question of legislative competence: not just Scotland's new right to make laws but also Westminster's continuing rights. Those who might be called the devo-sceptics within the government and the party wanted to stress Westminster's continuing power to legislate for Scotland. It was argued that nothing could be done which circumscribed the sovereign Parliament of the United Kingdom.

The Scottish Office recognised that was strictly true. Even with legislative competence devolved to Scotland, Westminster could still technically exert its overarching right to pass laws in domestic matters covering the whole of the UK. Again technically, Westminster was giving a power to Scotland – but still retaining that power for itself.

Equally, the Scottish Office spotted a PR nightmare in the making. They could not allow the idea to gain ground that Westminster might in some way be able to outgun the Scottish Parliament over legislation.

Frankly, much of this was posturing. Given the Government's general disposition towards devolution, nobody seriously expected or expects that both Parliaments would simultaneously attempt to legislate on, for example, Scottish education. This would not become a legislative bidding war along the lines of 'my Bill is bigger or more important than yours.'

Rather it was about presentation. Those anxious to stress Westminster's role at the heart of all UK political life wanted specific references to Westminster's continuing right to legislate. In the event, the Scottish Office managed to contain such demands, playing down the element of Westminster's technical power over devolved matters.

Strictly speaking, the power exists: a modern equivalent of Enoch Powell's dictum that 'power devolved is power retained.' For political and PR reasons, however, this is seldom mentioned and is unlikely to provoke practical problems.

More generally, the Department of Trade and Industry demanded and got agreed rules governing the attraction of inward investment – although, strictly speaking, that issue had already been raised by the DTI. The Scottish Office was obliged to concede that Scotland could not operate entirely independently – although it fought off a suggestion that the DTI itself should be able to vet Scotland's efforts in this field, to act in effect as prosecutor, judge and jury.

Perhaps the biggest dispute of this nature concerned relationships with Europe. Politically, it had become important for Scottish Labour to be able to argue that the Scottish Parliament would have a role in European Union negotiations. This was because the rival SNP had made 'Scotland in Europe' their battle-cry. They contrasted Scotland's position with that of other countries of similar size like Ireland and Denmark who were full members of the EU with a voice in negotiations.

Again, I intend to look at this issue in detail in a separate chapter. For now, it will be sufficient to note that the starting point for Whitehall, or much of it at least, was deep scepticism on this topic. Departments like Agriculture, with a key locus in European talks, doubted whether collaborative arrangements could be made to work. Some frankly questioned the motivation behind the endeavour.

Dewar persisted, however, around the outline objective that Westminster and the devolved areas like Scotland would hold talks to reach a common United Kingdom position which would be presented in EU negotiations. Once that deal was reached, there could be no question of the Scottish Parliament pursuing its own line. Ministers from the Scottish administration might be invited to join the UK delegation in presenting this common case in Europe.

Various Whitehall departments pointed out that the two Parliaments – Westminster and Edinburgh – might end up governed by different parties. How, they queried, could a common position be forged then?

In addition, there was an extremely tricky constitutional question. The United Kingdom Cabinet is bound by the doctrine of collective responsibility. Once a position has been reached, every member of that Cabinet must advocate and defend that position, regardless of personal standpoint. The only option is to resign from the Cabinet.

However, there can be no question of enforcing collective responsibility across two administrations. The UK Cabinet cannot bind the Scottish Executive – and the Scottish Executive cannot bind the UK Cabinet. The UK government may propose a particular approach but, if Scottish Ministers do not like that approach, they can say so with relative impunity. Indeed, it may be politically imperative for them to denounce a position which has, for whatever reason, become unpopular in Scotland.

After extensive negotiations, it was concluded that the settlement machinery between the Scottish Executive and the UK Cabinet would, inevitably, be less firmly based than within a single government and parliament. This would apply in relation to European negotiations and other issues.

It was concluded that such inter-administration arrangements would proceed by way of regular departmental contact, by formal ministerial meetings through joint committees and by a series of negotiated concordats setting out the basic principles which would govern relationships between the two bodies.

As with all politics, these arrangements will largely hinge on goodwill, on personal relationships between individuals. It is freely conceded that they cannot be universally enforced. The Scottish Office is optimistic, privately calculating that, with regard to European talks, these arrangements will work 90 per cent of the time. Lingering Whitehall scepticism has been swamped by the political imperative to implement change.

That really is the wider story of the devolution negotiations. The practical obstacles were many, the scepticism was ingrained but, by contrast with the 1970s, there was a definite political will backed up by a clear parliamentary majority.

Most significantly, Tony Blair pushed for change. With the Prime Minister firmly backing devolution, there was no serious prospect that the objections raised by individual departments or by individual Ministers would block progress. Indeed, unlike in the 1970s, those raising objections knew that they could not forestall devolution itself – and tailored the nature of their approach accordingly.

Critically, then, Blair backed Dewar on key aspects of reform like the proposed voting system.

However, Tony Blair was determined to contain devolution within certain limits. One Minister told me privately that Blair was 'inherently suspicious' of devolution, that he feared its potential to run out of control. The same Minister conceded that Blair had to be given considerable credit for pushing ahead with reform, despite those suspicions.

Donald Dewar put it differently when I discussed this topic with him.[2] He told me that substantial work was done on the parameters of devolution soon after the election. Dewar said: 'I had a number of very important meetings with the Prime Minister in which we reached agreement on a number of things. There were things where the Prime Minister said: "That's not negotiable."'

Dewar declined to be specific about these non-negotiable elements. But I understand they included Blair's insistence on a clear and repeated declaration that Westminster would remain sovereign even after the establishment of a devolved Scottish Parliament.

Equally, I understand the Prime Minister wanted a precise and workable system of concordats: rules to govern relations between Whitehall on the one hand and the new bodies in Scotland, Wales and Northern Ireland on the other. I have argued elsewhere that devolution has largely arisen from very different pressures in these territories themselves. Blair's understandable aim was to subject this emerging structure to a sustainable reformed UK system of governance.

For Dewar, the stress on Westminster sovereignty was an inevitable concession – and, in truth, not even that. Scottish Labour leaders had repeatedly pointed out that devolution was not independence, that they were not breaking up the UK. Westminster sovereignty was an implicit consequence of that, acceptable provided the wording in the White Paper was not so insistent that it negated the impression that devolution would bring substantial change. That had to be negotiated in the DSWR committee and elsewhere.

Again, the principle of concordats between Scotland and Whitehall was sensible within a devolutionary framework. If this new system was to work at all, it would require basic rules. The most ardent Home Rulers might not like it, but Westminster and Whitehall would still have a considerable remit in Scotland even after devolution. Dewar's concern, of course, was not over the principle of concordats but over the detail, particularly with regard to trade promotion, the attraction of inward investment and relations with Europe.

However, I understand there was at least one further constraint, ultimately insisted upon by the Prime Minister, which subsequently posed problems for the Scottish Office and for the Scottish Labour Party.

Tony Blair favoured a cut in the number of MPs from Scotland at Westminster – despite Scottish Labour's previous insistence that this was neither merited nor planned. Additionally, Blair was adamant – to preserve the continuing outward consistency of the UK – that constituency boundaries for the Scottish Parliament should remain the same as for Westminster. This has a clear, practical consequence which threatens to change the nature of the new Parliament.

After consideration, the Government indeed decided to cut the number of MPs from Scotland sent to Westminster – or, more accurately, to abolish the artificial insistence that Scotland must have a minimum number of representatives in the House of Commons.

This was conceded in an effort to quieten complaints that Scotland is over-represented in the Commons and that English parliamentary business might in future be determined by that Scottish over-representation. Again, this was despite repeated insistence in opposition that there was no necessary connection between devolution and the numbers from Scotland at Westminster.

I shall look later in a separate chapter at the impact of devolution on England. For now, it will be enough to note the potential impact of this numbers switch for the Scottish Parliament.

The prospect is that, for the general election after next, the number of MPs sent by Scotland to Westminster will be reduced from seventy-two to around sixty or fewer. That is because Scotland's Westminster representation will be determined on a straight population comparison with England, dropping the additional members previously thought necessary to cope with the demands of processing distinct Scottish legislation through Westminster.

But Tony Blair continued to insist that the boundaries for seats in the Scottish Parliament should be the same as for Westminster. That meant the Scottish Parliament would shrink in size.

Firstly, there would be a straight cut in the number of constituency seats in the Scottish Parliament in line with the reduction in seats at Westminster. In other words, if a seat vanished from Westminster, its matching seat in the Edinburgh Parliament would go as well.

Secondly, the number of top-up seats in the Scottish Parliament would also be cut. It was argued this further cut was needed to maintain the balance between constituency and list seats, to prevent the top-up section from growing out of proportion to those seats elected by the customary constituency method.

Under this scenario, the Parliament might end up with around 104 members or so instead of the initial 129 – too few, say critics, to provide a sizeable government and opposition, to fill committees and to maintain gender balance.

From a Westminster perspective, however, Tony Blair was determined to maintain what he regarded as a clear link between the two Parliaments. With the exception of Orkney and Shetland, the constituency map for Westminster and Holyrood would be precisely the same.

I understand that this question of numbers formed part of what might be called the developing 'concordat' between the Prime Minister and the Scottish Secretary to establish the basic ground rules for devolution. Even when the issue grew in controversy later, Blair dismissed claims that the Scottish Parliament would be hobbled. Indeed, he would occasionally play down the issue in a quasi-jocular fashion, querying whether people were seriously demanding more politicians.

Dewar would not confirm to me whether the numbers issue featured in his 'ground rules' talks with the PM. He simply referred in general terms to the deal reached with the Prime Minister on a range of issues and added: 'Some of these things turned up later and people wondered why I was being so obstinate but if you reach agreements . . . you hold to them.'

The Scottish Secretary stressed that Blair was 'amazingly helpful' at the outset, during the drafting of the White Paper and through the subsequent passage of the legislation. Certainly, Blair's clear support helped drive the reform agenda forward – and helped neutralise such objections as arose. There is no suggestion he was anything other than positive over the practical task of implementing the devolution pledge. However, there was often a sense that Whitehall and Downing Street were keen to contain the scope of devolution.

That feeling of containment was evident in the controversy over numbers – which persisted during consideration of the Bill in both Houses of Parliament. Equally, it was present in the suggestion that members of the Scottish Parliament should be paid less than their counterparts at Westminster. The London perspective, perhaps understandably, was that the Edinburgh legislature must be visibly subordinate.

One source told me the challenge facing Donald Dewar in steering devolution past sceptical colleagues was a 'titanic, Tyson-like struggle'. Extending that rather apocalyptic metaphor, it might be said that Dewar had the tremendous advantage of having Blair, mostly, in his corner throughout the fight.

But Blair's insistence over the numbers issue did cause a problem for the Scottish Office. Further, that is still not finally resolved in that the reduction in Westminster numbers has yet to work through and the consequent challenge to the size of the Edinburgh Parliament has yet to emerge.

Ministers were repeatedly pressed by opposition MPs in the Commons to drop the demand in the White Paper that the Scottish Parliament must shrink in line with Scotland's representation at Westminster.

The Devolution Minister Henry McLeish was placed in a particularly difficult position. More than once, he assured the Commons during the passage of the devolution legislation that the question of the link between Westminster and Holyrood constituencies would be reviewed. More than once, MPs were left with the impression that he sympathised with the case for retaining a Scottish Parliament of 129 members, whatever happened at Westminster.

McLeish of course was not party to talks between Dewar and Blair. But he was plainly aware that the Prime Minister was adamantly opposed to breaking the link between Westminster and Holyrood boundaries. He was left in a rather unhappy position at the despatch box, formally advancing the arguments for a cut in Holyrood numbers while holding out the prospect of a rethink. Given the Prime Minister's position, the chances of a rethink were in practice minimal if not non-existent.

Jim Wallace, the leader of the Scottish Liberal Democrats, pursued this issue with vigour. For example, in the Commons on 5 May 1998 he moved an amendment to the effect that the Scottish Parliament would retain its size and shape, regardless of changes at Westminster.[3]

He argued that, otherwise, members of the new Parliament in Edinburgh would be operating nervously within the prospect that their seats might disappear. According to Wallace, 'that would lead to tension and rivalries and might distract Members of the Scottish Parliament from the work in hand. It would not be healthy for the Parliament.'

Tam Dalyell, the devo-sceptic Labour MP for Linlithgow, was more graphic still. He visualised the members of the new Edinburgh Parliament 'fighting like Kilkenny cats, squabbling like ferrets in a sack and having the sword of Damocles over them from the very beginning'.

Without resorting to animal or classical imagery, other MPs voiced a range of concerns about the Government's approach. Alasdair Morgan of the SNP demanded: 'Why on earth should we start to change the boundaries of a devolved Scottish Parliament simply because there is an argument for changing the Westminster con-stituencies?' For the Conservatives, Bernard Jenkin argued that the whole issue should be tackled before the new Parliament was elected, not after. The White Paper, he suggested, was 'a mess'.

In response, Henry McLeish offered the argument that different boundaries for Westminster and Holyrood would produce confusion in voters' minds. He conceded, however, that once a Parliament of 129 members was in place, there was 'an expectation that they might want to continue'. This was, McLeish added, part of the 'realpolitik' of the new Parliament. The Minister said the Government was still considering the matter.

It was, of course, absolutely true that the Government was con-sidering the issue. It could do no less in the face of Commons amendments and wider pressure for a rethink.

However, there was another form of 'realpolitik' to bear in mind. From the outset, in advance of the Commons debates, Tony Blair had stressed, externally and internally, his determination that the devolved Parliament would be part of a clear UK construct and that its size would, consequently, be governed by Westminster parameters. Blair tends to get his way.

This may seem an arcane argument – although there are practical consequences regarding the ability of the Parliament to scrutinise the Executive effectively or, indeed, to make up the numbers of that Executive. For the more ardent Home Rulers, however, there is an underlying issue. Is the Scottish Parliament a political entity in its own right – with a membership shaped by Scotland's requirements? Or is it a subset of Westminster?

Privately, even some key figures on the Labour side believe that the cut will not take place, that the temporary anguish of defending the reduction was undergone for nothing. By this analysis, it is argued that the Scottish Parliament, once established, will have a strong collective motivation to resist any such reduction – and that Westminster will have better things to do than to insist on pulling a subsidiary legislative body apart.

The statutory position, however, is that the Edinburgh Parliament will start with 129 members – but has an inbuilt tendency to shrink. This may be a conflict deferred.

Notes

1. Interview with Donald Dewar, 16 January 1999.
2. Interview with Donald Dewar, 16 January 1999.
3. *Hansard*, 12 May 1998, col. 220 on.

7 The White Paper

For such a momentous statement, it was a slightly halting start. Donald Dewar had risen to Labour cheers to explain the Government's White Paper on Scottish devolution to the House of Commons. The Secretary of State, however, was not initially at his fluent best.

As he stumbled over a couple of words and phrases, there was sporadic barracking from the Conservative benches. An unforgiving chamber, the Commons thrives on confrontation. Ministers can expect little mercy from their political opponents or indeed, sometimes, from their own side. It may appear infantile to observers and occasionally to participants but there is a medieval logic lurking beneath it all. Government proposals are subjected to ordeal rather than examination – the political equivalent of the ducking-stool. If an argument can survive the Commons, it should thrive in the wider world.

On this occasion, 24 July 1997, Donald Dewar appeared curiously ill at ease as he expounded the Government's plans. As the jeering increased, the Scottish Minister of State Henry McLeish – sitting at Dewar's side on the government front bench – leaned forward and snapped at the Tories: 'You're pathetic, pathetic.'

It was, however, Donald Dewar himself who rescued the occasion.

Donald Dewar tells the Commons that its power is to be, partly, devolved to Scotland as he outlines the White Paper, 24 July 1997. (Kindly supplied by PA News Ltd.)

Glancing up from his notes spread across the ministerial despatch box, he quietly informed the House: 'I am a little nervous about my place in history.' This was classic Dewar, self-effacing, underplayed. It was also self-evidently true. More than any other Labour politician, Dewar is deeply conscious of Scotland's constitutional past. After decades of effort, he seemed authentically discomfited by the sense that he was playing a role in mapping out Scotland's constitutional future.

From that moment, however, he appeared to grow in confidence. He talked of actions which 'we', meaning the people of Scotland, would take. Michael Ancram for the Conservatives queried this phrase, presumably reminding Dewar that he was speaking in the United Kingdom House of Commons on behalf of the United Kingdom Government. Ancram, of course, was formerly an MP for a Scottish constituency who subsequently sought and won a seat in England.

Dewar retorted: 'I am sorry. I made the cardinal error of assuming that I was a Scot for the moment. The Right Honourable Gentleman may have experienced some psychological amputation that removed him from Scotland but I have not.' Dewar was back on form, politely acerbic. As so often, especially with Dewar, the unscripted barb carried more force than the wordy prepared speech.

Later that same day, Dewar led a posse of politicians to City Airport in London's Docklands to catch a flight to Edinburgh for a reception in the castle. The event became known, with more than a hint of Scottish self-parody, as 'The Flight to Freedom'.

Dewar sat at the front alongside George Robertson and Baroness Smith, widow of the late Labour leader. Labour's Jim Murphy chatted with John Swinney of the SNP. Liberal Democrats mingled with Nationalist and Labour MPs.

At Edinburgh Castle itself, there was again a sense of modest Scottish pride. The setting could scarcely have been more splendid:

Donald Dewar with Baroness Smith, widow of the late Labour leader John Smith, at Edinburgh Castle, 24 July 1997. (Kindly supplied by The Scotsman Publications Ltd.)

The great, the good, the enthusiastic and sundry hangers-on celebrate the White Paper at a reception in Edinburgh Castle, 24 July 1997. (Kindly supplied by The Scotsman Publications Ltd.)

the great hall of the ancient castle, next to the chamber housing the Scottish Crown Jewels and the Stone of Destiny.

But Caledonian ostentation was out. Not a kilt in sight among the guests. Only a few discreet tartan ties. Dewar's speech a model of its kind as he told the audience – who well understood his capacity for self-mockery – that he had been 'enormously encouraged . . . almost enthused' by the events of the day.

I was covering the event 'live' for BBC Scotland – via a camera mounted in the gallery overlooking the hall. Later, I took the chance to mingle socially and I freely confess that I asked several of those present to sign my copy of the White Paper. In its own unassuming way, this event seemed genuinely historic, if that over-used description can be forgiven.

As a political journalist, I lay great stress upon remaining professionally detached. With that in mind, I hope I have contrived to cover every aspect of the Scottish constitutional debate in that fashion. I have tried to report and analyse the claimed upsides and downsides of devolution, the arguments for and against independence.

My creed with regard to political parties seeking power and elected office is a simple one. It is to give them all absolute hell, on every occasion. Subject every argument to analysis. Take nothing for granted. Question every assumption. That way the conscientious reporter can be reasonably sure of remaining detached.

This does not mean that one cannot be pleasant and friendly with politicians. Many I regard as friends. It does mean, however, that journalism and politics are different trades – and that the public interest is eroded when those trades overlap or are confused. Politicians are seeking to present their case in search of public support. Journalists should be seeking to present all sides of an issue. Sometimes these two aims will appear to coincide. Often they will clash.

This approach of mine is deliberately dogmatic, a personal defence mechanism against any temptation to let objectivity slide. I offer no verdict on other journalists who may pursue a different approach. This is simply my own way of operating.

On the occasion of the White Paper reception in Edinburgh Castle, however, the self-styled seeker after truth became a hunter after autographs. I was neither for nor against the White Paper or its contents. I fully intended to subject the Government and its opponents to searching scrutiny. That particular night, however, I felt a curious need for a souvenir.

Ever alert to journalistic objectivity, I made sure that my autographs were cross-party. For example, Brian Monteith, the Tory who was to lead the No campaign in the referendum, was at the reception and signed my document in characteristically enigmatic fashion. On the front page, he prefaced the devolution text by writing: 'This tax time bomb is ticking already. . . .' Flipping over to the back page, he offered a simple conclusion as he wrote: 'BANG!' Monteith argued at that point that Scotland would reject the tax proposals – and that the entire scheme might be undermined as a consequence.

Perhaps understandably, it is the Cabinet scribbles on my document which stand out on later inspection and, thankfully, help to confirm my self-image of nurtured neutrality. Donald Dewar's inscription read: 'For Brian Taylor (whom I often curse but only professionally).' George Robertson addressed his autograph 'To Brian who promised to give me a hard time – and delivered!'

The White Paper initially evoked a dual response. Its publication was an historic event. There was an undeniable air of excitement which affected even those politicians who had opposed or voiced reservations about devolution. That atmosphere inevitably extended to the media world.

On the other hand, this was a government publication from a political party. Its subject had been at the very core of partisan controversy in Scotland for decades. There was to be a referendum, inviting the people of Scotland to cast their votes for or against the proposed Parliament, for or against the accompanying tax powers. It was critically important that this document was subjected to detailed scrutiny.

The White Paper itself opens with an introduction by the Prime Minister and a foreword by Donald Dewar. The tone is set right from the start with the Scottish Secretary's declaration that 'Scotland will remain firmly part of the United Kingdom.'

The document then summarises the new approach: a law-making Parliament, a Scottish Executive headed by a First Minister 'which will operate in a way similar to the UK Government and will be held to account by the Scottish Parliament'. That Parliament will cover the broad range of Scottish domestic affairs: health, education, the law, home affairs, local government including social work and housing, economic development, transport, the environment, agriculture, fisheries and forestry, sport and the arts.

Then Scotland's reformed place in the wider constitutional set-up.

Broadly, the White Paper envisages that legislation to set up the new Parliament will proceed by specifying those powers which are reserved to Westminster, including foreign policy, defence and national security, macro-economics such as the currency and the broad tax system, employment law, market arrangements governing UK trade, social security, most aspects of transport safety and regulation and, importantly, the constitution of the United Kingdom.

Under the White Paper, the Queen is to remain Head of State for the UK in its entirety. In case anyone has not got the message by now, it is further stressed that 'the UK Parliament is and will remain sovereign.' The tone is perhaps a response in kind to Jack Straw's reported concern that earlier drafts of the White Paper seemed rather 'too Braveheartish' – in other words, relying too much on quasi-nationalist sentiment.

The balancing act continues, however. The very next section emphasises that the Scottish Parliament will be 'involved as closely as possible' in UK decision-making on Europe – while foreign policy overall remains reserved to Westminster. It is envisaged that Scottish parliamentary Ministers can join UK delegations at EU Council of Ministers talks and 'in appropriate cases' could speak for the UK. Westminster is sovereign but there is to be a clear role for Edinburgh in an aspect of foreign policy.

Finally, in this summary section, the nitty-gritty. The Parliament will consist of 129 members: seventy-three directly elected on a constituency basis plus fifty-six additional members from top-up regional lists. Each Parliament will normally sit for a fixed four-year term, unlike Westminster's variable feast where election dates are generally determined by the governing party. The referendum to decide whether any of this happens is to be held on 11 September 1997.

Funding will broadly follow 'the existing arrangements for financing the Scottish Office', which means a block allocation of money from the Treasury, varied annually according to a formula based upon a population comparison with England. Subject to the referendum, there will be a power to increase or decrease the standard UK rate of income tax by a maximum of three pence in either direction with liability to be determined by residence in Scotland. The Scottish Parliament will also control local authority spending and taxation.

In subsequent sections, the White Paper proceeds to outline constitutional history and to note the potential powers of the new Parliament – which range from liquor licensing to the protection of animals as well as the main domestic issues. It then specifies in detail the powers remaining at Westminster, which are to include – in addition to the chief categories – such matters as broadcasting, abortion law, genetics, drugs, firearms regulation, immigration, equality legislation, gambling, nuclear safety, the safety of medicines and the licensing of theatres and cinemas. Broadly, anything which is not reserved to Westminster is by definition devolved.

It notes that 'the boundary between reserved and devolved matters' can be adjusted in future: in other words, that devolution might be extended or curtailed. It comforts those remaining at Westminster with the thought that 'Scotland's members of Parliament will continue to play a full and constructive part in the proceedings of the House of Commons.'

It specifies the mechanism for ensuring that Scottish devolution works within the UK, including a liaison role for the Scottish Secretary in the Westminster Cabinet and the creation of a new post of Scottish law officer in Whitehall to advise the UK Government. Scotland's established law officer posts of Lord Advocate and Solicitor General are to transfer to the ambit of the Scottish Executive.

The White Paper proposes removing the statutory requirement for Scotland to have a minimum of seventy-one MPs at Westminster. In effect, this presupposes a cut in numbers from the seventy-two members despatched by Scotland to Westminster at the general election in 1997. The new Parliament is to be given the power to supervise local government and quangos in Scotland.

To avoid conflict with Westminster, it is envisaged that the Presiding Officer of the Scottish Parliament will have the power to check whether planned Scottish legislation goes beyond the powers of the legislature. In the last analysis – if the UK Government and the Scottish Executive fall out – the dispute can be referred to the Judicial Committee of the Privy Council consisting of at least five Law Lords.

In foreign policy, it is stressed that the UK must continue to 'speak with one voice'. Specifically with regard to Europe, the White Paper envisages a role for Ministers and officials of the Scottish Executive in European Council talks – while again stressing that they must 'support and advance the single UK negotiating line' which they will have had a hand in formulating. The UK lead Minister will take overall charge of the negotiations: in effect, deciding when or if a Scottish contribution is merited. The Scottish Executive and Parliament will be obliged to implement relevant European legislation and directives.

In the finance chapter, it is envisaged that the existing 'block and formula' system for funding Scotland will continue. As outlined above, this means a block grant from the Treasury voted by the House of Commons and varied annually according to a formula which allocates Scotland a fixed proportion of the increase (or decrease) in budgets of comparable English spending departments like Health and Education.

It is stressed that it is up to the Scottish Parliament to reallocate priorities as it sees fit. For example, although it will automatically get a share of any increase in spending on English education, it need not spend that money on education in Scotland. It can devote the cash to housing or health or whatever it chooses.

In a key section – which we will examine in detail in a separate chapter on finance – it is noted that the formula 'will be updated from time to time' to take account of population and other changes. This has now happened. The Barnett formula (devised by Joel Barnett, Labour's Chief Secretary to the Treasury, in the late 1970s) is finally beginning, although perhaps only marginally, to achieve its objective of narrowing the gap in spending between Scotland and England.

Another key sentence notes: 'Any more substantial revision [of spending] would need to be preceded by an in-depth study of relative spending requirements and would be the subject of full consultation between the Scottish Executive and the UK Government.' As we shall examine later, this clause – while ruling out any immediate scrutiny of Scottish spending – would allow the Treasury in future to mount such an examination, perhaps from a perspective which regarded Scotland as over-funded.

The chapter then goes on to specify the Scottish Parliament's power to vary the standard rate of income tax. At this point, it was envisaged that one penny on income tax in Scotland would raise £150 million a year. Subsequent changes, most notably the 1999

Budget, have increased that figure to £230 million. The White Paper's promise, then, to maintain the real value of the tax power through index-linking has been effectively overtaken, although the principle remains that UK budgetary decisions should not undermine the tax powers of the Scottish Parliament.

The chapter specifies that savings and dividend income should be exempt from the tax-varying power – and that there should be no power for the Scottish Parliament to alter VAT, corporation tax, National Insurance or the upper and lower rates of income tax.

The test of liability for the proposed new tax is to be Scottish residence. The cost of setting up the new system is estimated to be £10 million for the Government and £50 million for employers – with annual running costs, if the tax power is used, of around £8 million for the Government and £6 to £15 million for employers.

It is stressed that the Scottish Parliament must bear the consequences of its tax decisions – higher spending if it increases tax, lower spending if it cuts tax – and so is obliged to return money to the UK Treasury. It is further stressed that the Scottish Parliament will have full control of local authority finances in Scotland – prompting critics to forecast that parsimony by the Parliament will simply force up council taxes and local business rates. Labour subsequently attempted to offer assurances on this.

Equally – in a little-noticed section – it is made plain that the Scottish Parliament must take the knock-on financial impact from any spending decisions it makes. It is stressed that UK taxpayers as a whole must be 'insulated' from the impact of decisions which increase costs in Scotland. For example, if council taxes and local authority rents soar, that will push up benefits and rent rebates claimed by Scottish tenants, increasing a social security budget which is due to be met by Westminster. The White Paper stresses that such costs would have to be borne in mind in calculating the annual block grant to Scotland.

The White Paper spells out the electoral arrangements: the PR voting system, the eligibility of UK citizens including peers and the clergy to stand for the Parliament along with Republic of Ireland citizens and EU citizens resident in the UK. It urges women, members of ethnic minorities and disabled people to consider putting themselves forward for the Parliament.

It stresses, as we have already discussed, that there should be common UK and Scottish constituency boundaries and that, consequently, any cut in representation at Westminster from Scotland would cut the size of the Scottish Parliament.

The document outlines the arrangements for the Parliament itself – including the proviso that the Senior Salaries Review Body will recommend pay levels for members of the new legislature in the first instance. It will be up to the new Parliament to fix its own allowances. The First Minister, not surprisingly, will 'normally be the leader of the party able to command the majority support of the Scottish Parliament' – and will be appointed by the Queen. Law officers will be appointed by Royal Warrant and need not be Members of the Scottish Parliament (MSPs). Standing orders are to be left to the new body to decide.

Finally, the White Paper specifies plans for a new parliamentary building at an estimated cost, then, of between £10 million and £40 million. The site at that point had not been identified, although it is noted that the long-anticipated choice, the old Royal High School on Edinburgh's Calton Hill, has 'serious disadvantages' of limited space and poor public accessibility. Donald Dewar, of course, subsequently opted for a new building at the foot of the Royal Mile opposite Holyrood Palace. The White Paper concludes by commending its contents to the people who will decide in a referendum.

I am uncomfortably aware that this detail will inevitably have been tedious for those who are familiar with the White Paper and its contents. The old hands will by now be yelling: 'We know all this, get on with it!' My apologies to them.

I thought it right, however, that this account of the process of Scottish devolution should include at least one section which spelled out the scheme in a broadly unvarnished form. Otherwise, there was a risk of replicating the more irritating arts reviews which endlessly parade the critic's psychological insight without even the faintest account of the subject under discussion. The reader may be relieved to know I do not propose to trawl through the devolution Bill or Act in similar detail.

The White Paper, naturally, was picked apart by every political party and interest group in Scotland. Nobody perhaps paid closer attention to it than the leaders of the Scottish National Party. They had to decide whether to offer their support to the detailed scheme for devolution in the September referendum.

This quandary may seem curious – particularly to observers of the Scottish political scene from outside who may be inclined to elide or confuse devolution and independence. Such observers frequently focus upon the SNP as the driving force for constitutional change and presume that their support for any form of Scottish Parliament is unquestioned.

As I have argued elsewhere, the Scottish National Party is rather a product of a general desire for self-government in Scotland. It argues for one particular form of self-government: constitutional independence for Scotland and the severing of the Treaty of Union with England. It has amended that platform but only to transform previous hostility to the Common Market into warm support for independent Scottish membership of the European Union.

The Nationalists, consequently, are not devolvers. They want a separate Scottish state. There is a section of their membership which continues to regard devolution as a Unionist trick to placate the Scots and to mute demands for full-scale independence.

Given that background, the leadership of the SNP had to tread relatively carefully. They repeatedly refused to offer their endorsement to the devolution scheme in advance of publication of the White Paper. Indeed, they were sharply attacked by Labour for their 'silence' on this question.

However, it would be misleading to suggest that Alex Salmond and the wider SNP leadership were studiedly neutral on this question. They did not idly scan their copies of the White Paper and conclude: 'Well, that looks worth a go.' Rather it is my firm impression from covering their deliberations at the time that they were itching to back the devolution scheme. From their perspective, it was a clear advance upon the status quo. Alex Salmond was already on record as saying that devolution was his second preference after independence.

They had expressed one key concern. Would there be a 'glass ceiling', as they put it, to Scotland's ambitions? This phrase is generally used to reflect the various forces which militate against the rise of women or ethnic minorities in the workforce. The SNP feared a statutory limit to reform of Scottish governance. They feared in short that there would be legal obstacles, specified in the White Paper, which would hinder Scotland from moving to independence.

They said that their fears on this topic had been heightened by remarks made, in opposition, by Labour politicians including George

Robertson and others which suggested that there might be specific limits. Such remarks, of course, must be seen in the context of Labour's desire at the time and subsequently to stress that devolution should not be seen as a precursor for independence, that they were not one and the same.

In any event, Alex Salmond told me that those fears were largely eased in private discussions with Donald Dewar at the Scottish Office.[1] Salmond says he was given 'an absolute guarantee' that there would be no formal obstacle to Scottish independence – beyond, of course, the small matter of winning popular support for such a move.

Dewar's wider objective was to secure Nationalist support for the White Paper in the referendum. In retrospect, it can be seen that Scotland backed the principle of devolution by three to one. In advance of the ballot, however, Dewar could not be so certain. Would 1979 repeat itself? Would Scotland turn aside at the last moment from the path of change? Would the Scottish response be an apathetic shrug of the shoulders? Dewar needed at the very least to neutralise any SNP hostility to his package.

In speeches and interviews over this period, Dewar regularly deployed a formula on this question: that he personally opposed independence and believed it damaging but that Scotland's constitutional future lay in the hands of the people of Scotland. Salmond says this formula was agreed in talks between the two leaders. This statement of popular sovereignty was what the SNP wanted. Nationalists say it effectively accepted that independence would be determined by a Scottish mandate rather than a UK one.

It could be argued that Dewar was saying no more than that he is a democrat. He was also saying no more than previous Conservative leaders, including Margaret Thatcher and John Major, have said. Scotland can have independence if the people of Scotland want it; Labour, Tory and Liberal Democrat politicians do not generally think that they will.

There is a further point. It should be noted that the White Paper is not silent on future constitutional arrangements. It specifies that the Constitution and the Crown are among the matters reserved to Westminster.

This implies – and Scottish Office civil servants have privately confirmed this to me – that a referendum on Scottish independence could only be called by the Westminster Parliament. The Scottish

Parliament has no power over the Constitution and, consequently, could not pass the legislation necessary to call a constitutional referendum. If it attempted to introduce such legislation, it would potentially face a challenge from Westminster that it was acting beyond the limits of its powers, that it had ventured *ultra vires* in the splendid Latin phrase.

Is this not the 'glass ceiling' which the SNP had feared? Salmond says no. Strictly speaking, it is the Labour Government's intention in the White Paper that a binding referendum can only be called by Westminster. However, Salmond cites the further power for the Scottish Parliament to discuss anything it pleases in domestic or international politics.

Given that power, he argues, the Scottish Parliament can consult on anything it pleases. It might choose to hold a plebiscite to determine popular opinion on independence. To those who say it would be acting illegally – and incurring costs for which it had no authority – Salmond cites the example of the referendum on the control of water services called by Strathclyde Regional Council, Labour's former power base in the West of Scotland which vanished under Conservative local government reform.

That 'referendum' on 22 March 1994 had no formal legal base – yet its substantial vote against the privatisation of water supplies in Scotland is generally credited with helping to persuade the Tories to abandon any notion of taking water out of the public sector north of the Border.

Salmond accepts that, as with most other instances of countries gaining independence from the UK, the legislation to establish Scottish independence would have to be processed through the Westminster Parliament. However, he told me: 'The decision is not one for Westminster. The decision is one for the Scottish people.'

Salmond told me the SNP's previously preferred route to independence was an SNP popular mandate in an election, then negotiations with Westminster to establish the nature of the independence settlement, then finally a referendum on that settlement among the Scottish people. That might be called the High Road to independence.

However, he pointed out that Labour had pursued an alternative approach with regard to devolution. Despite criticism, mainly from Conservative opponents, they had held a referendum before legislating for a Scottish Parliament. The referendum had been on the contents of the White Paper, not the minute detail of the Scotland Bill.

That, according to Salmond, provides a 'fine precedent' for the SNP holding a referendum on independence before proceeding to negotiations with Westminster. A 'simple majority' of those voting in Scotland would be sufficient to ensure that those negotiations got under way.

This would be the Low Road: an SNP minority administration securing sufficient support in the devolved Parliament, perhaps after a gap of several years, to hold a test of public opinion on independence.

Salmond, of course, formally clings to the prospect that the SNP might at some point win such a clear majority of seats in Holyrood elections that Westminster would move to open talks immediately. In such circumstances, the referendum would still follow the outcome of those talks. However, he has repeatedly indicated that he does not presently think such an outcome likely, particularly given the PR voting system for the Scottish Parliament which was deliberately designed to prevent a party from gaining a majority of seats on a minority of the popular vote. The first Scottish election in 1999 tended to confirm that analysis, with the SNP gaining thirty-five of the 129 seats on offer.

In reality, then, Salmond envisages the SNP stepping along the Low Road of gradualism rather than the High Road of a clean break. There is also a strategic reason for stressing the Low Road option. It is the SNP's calculation that voters will be less frightened by the prospect of 'becoming independent' by a gradual process, than they are by the notion of a sharp fracture in the Union.

The final act in each scenario would be the passing of an Act at Westminster establishing an independent Scotland. I questioned whether the SNP leader could ever envisage Scotland lodging a Unilateral Declaration of Independence. Salmond thought it was unlikely such a step would be needed but told me: 'If the Westminster Parliament decided for reasons best known to itself not to process the Act then that is what would happen, the Scottish Parliament would declare UDI.'

A referendum on independence is seen in practice by the SNP as following upon their election to shared power in a Scottish Parliament. They do not accept that Westminster would have a constitutional block upon such a development. Tactically, of course, the

Nationalist leaders have deliberately tried to play down the notion that there may be such a block.

They were, as I have argued, predisposed to endorse the White Paper. They were inclined as a consequence to lay more stress on the formula that Scotland would determine her own future than on a strict interpretation of the White Paper that only Westminster can call a referendum. In other circumstances, it might have been very tempting for SNP leaders to pounce on the White Paper's provision that the Constitution is reserved to Westminster. There might have been talk of an unfair clamp upon the aspirations of the Scottish people At this point in history, however, the Nationalist leaders were intrinsically disinclined to acknowledge that there might be any constitutional problem with calling an independence referendum after devolution. Such a notion did not fit their broader strategic view that devolution could evolve into independence without too much difficulty.

Nationalist leaders, then, were seeking a formula which retained independence as an option – while placing it, effectively, at one remove. Their argument is that a vote for the SNP is not in itself a vote for immediate independence. There would be a further referendum – just as Labour stressed there would be a further electoral test of devolution after its general election victory in 1997. The objective, again, is to lessen any 'fear factor' adhering to the prospect of independence.

Equally, however, Labour has been justified in arguing that a vote for the SNP can be seen as the first step in a process which is designed, by the Nationalists, to lead to independence. In precisely the same fashion, the Tories had a reasonable case when they warned voters that, if they did not want devolution, they should not take the risk by voting Labour, by voting for the party offering change. The voters, of course, are free to heed or ignore such warnings.

There is a further question which is whether, having won an election, the SNP could subsequently win an independence referendum. Nationalists argue that, once over the hurdle of supplying the SNP with majority support, the people of Scotland would move relatively readily to full independence. Others cite the example of Quebec, where the Parti Québécois can command electoral support but has failed to win referendum backing for breaking from the Canadian federation.

That, however, is a different issue from the debate over the mechanics of establishing a referendum on independence in the first place. The legitimacy of such a referendum is, self-evidently, important but in practice I believe the argument rests more upon politics than constitutional nicety. I think it unlikely that there would be legalistic objections to an independence referendum if Scotland had demonstrably voted for the SNP in a devolved Parliament or for a political combination which facilitates such a ballot.

To be fair, Donald Dewar never sought during the passage of the devolution legislation or the run-up to the Scottish parliamentary elections to rely upon any constitutional hurdles.

Wise parties know that people do not take kindly to suggestions that their democratic options are limited in any way. As I have pointed out, the power to call a binding referendum is – strictly speaking – reserved to Westminster in the White Paper and the devolution legislation. Dewar, however, has always stressed that he relies upon the 'sense' of the Scottish people to reject the option of independence: in other words, to forestall the SNP from putting the question to the test.

By contrast, of course, the Nationalists rely upon their expectation that the people of Scotland will turn to full-scale independence. In any event, in determining their reaction to the White Paper, they chose to focus more upon the prospect of independence than upon the strict letter of the law, which was that the question of a referendum was reserved to Westminster.

The SNP leadership was, as I have said, at least predisposed to argue for the White Paper in a referendum while reserving the right to seek to increase the powers available to a Scottish Parliament when the detailed legislation came before the House. Only a specific and clearly worded prohibition in the White Paper upon an independence referendum would have deterred them. There was no such explicit prohibition and they chose to play down the fact that the White Paper reserved the Constitution to Westminster. They chose to ignore a decidedly inconvenient obstacle in the path of their aspirations.

That predisposition to endorse was sustained through support for the notion from the SNP executive. Finally, in the City Halls, Perth, on 2 August 1997, the SNP's National Council – the governing body between party conferences – agreed by a large majority to campaign vigorously for a double Yes vote in the September referendum.

Gordon Wilson, the former leader of the party, was among those who counselled against this approach. In a powerful speech, he warned delegates that devolution was a 'blind alley', that the party would suffer electorally from attaching itself to the unsatisfactory policy of a rival party. Wilson drew upon his experience of leading the party through the 1979 devolution referendum to urge delegates to reject a repeat performance.

His passion, however, failed to sway delegates, who preferred the argument that devolution was better than the status quo – and that the voters of Scotland would find SNP opposition to the Labour scheme incomprehensible.

Gordon Wilson told me later that he maintained his personal stance in the referendum itself.[2] On question one, covering the principle of devolution, he altered his ballot paper to vote for the option of independence. On question two, regarding tax powers, he voted No – believing that the devolved tax power is a 'trap' to load a financial demand on the people of Scotland and cut cash support from Westminster.

In August 1997, however, devolution supporters could live without the backing of Gordon Wilson provided they could guarantee that the SNP as a whole would be on board for the referendum which was due the following month.

Notes

1. Interview with Alex Salmond, 4 December 1998.
2. Interview with Gordon Wilson, 28 November 1998.

8 The Referendum and the Scotland Bill

The referendum to determine Scotland's constitutional future was held on 11 September 1997. Those with a sense of history noted – either with enthusiasm, irony or a shiver – that it was the 700th anniversary of William Wallace's victory over the English at the Battle of Stirling Bridge.

However, it was contemporary death rather than ancient conflict which overshadowed much of the campaign leading up to the vote. First, Paisley South Labour MP Gordon McMaster committed suicide. In a note, he complained about the treatment he had allegedly received from certain party colleagues including the neighbouring MP Tommy Graham. This reopened a long-running controversy about the infighting and power politics of Labour rule in Paisley and throughout the West of Scotland.

Then, on 31 August, Diana, Princess of Wales, was killed in a car crash in Paris. With less than a fortnight to the vote, the Government had to decide whether to postpone the referendum and how to handle the campaign if they went ahead.

I telephoned Donald Dewar on the Sunday morning after Diana's death. He was understandably downcast: shocked, as were others, at the events surrounding the death of the Princess but, additionally, at a loss as to how to proceed with regard to the referendum. I sounded

him out regarding the options but it was plain that the development
was too abrupt, too stunning to permit an instant decision.

Later, after conversations with the Prime Minister and others,
Dewar concluded that the referendum would go ahead – but that
the campaign would, obviously, be put on hold.

The argument in favour of proceeding was that preparations were
considerably advanced for the Scotland-wide ballot and count on
11 September. The issues, it was argued, were clearly understood.
The people were ready to decide. Delay would be utterly disruptive.
In addition, the Welsh devolution referendum was due the week
after Scotland voted. Labour's strategic hope was that a positive vote
in Scotland would help convince Wales, which had voted decisively
against devolution in 1979 and was still deeply divided over the
question. If Scotland postponed, Wales would have to postpone also
to maintain that potential knock-on impact. The entire timetable
would unravel – and possibly elements of the devolution package
with it.

There was, however, a further concern beyond the question of
timing. Devolution was partly predicated upon identity, upon an
argument that people could be comfortably Scottish and British. A
new politics for a dual identity. Would the death of Diana, a royal
icon, tend to make people stress their British identity and neglect
their Scottish adherence? Would it, to be blunt, affect the vote in the
referendum?

For reasons of diplomacy and taste, this concern was seldom stated
explicitly in the days after the Paris tragedy. It lingered, however, in
the minds of those who fretted over the possible Scottish result. In
the event, it would appear that the people of Scotland were able to
separate their varying responses to the death of Diana from the
political choice confronted in the referendum.

Campaigning resumed after the funeral. The now truncated contest seemed somehow less acrimonious. It was as if Diana's death – or
perhaps rather the emotional outpouring which followed – obliged
the politicians to focus upon authentic issues.

The campaign had opened formally on 19 August with a cross-
party launch under the banner of Scotland Forward, the group
formed to act as an umbrella organisation pressing for a double Yes
vote in the referendum. In practice, however, campaigning was well
under way before that.

Scotland Forward had been inaugurated on 15 May, the same day that Donald Dewar launched the government Bill needed to legitimise the Scottish referendum. Its chairman, businessman Nigel Smith, said at the Edinburgh launch: 'We need to provide a single, unifying force in Scotland during this campaign.'

Again, this reflected a memory of 1979, when the Yes forces in the referendum had been divided on party lines and, arguably, less effective as a consequence. Nigel Smith and other key individuals, like Esther Roberton who had worked with the Convention and Bill Speirs of the Scottish TUC, concluded that it was important to provide a framework outside party politics which, nevertheless, party politicians could join.

Scotland Forward certainly achieved that and provided a coherence to the Yes campaign. It could be assumed that Labour and the Liberal Democrats would work together, given their cooperation in the Convention. What was more troublesome was involving the SNP. In that sense, Scotland Forward was a vehicle for assisting the Nationalists to campaign for devolution without feeling that they were joining a Labour Party organisation.

There were difficulties with Scotland Forward, however. Even

Henry McLeish, the Devolution Minister, advances the Scotland Forward campaign in the run-up to the September 1997 referendum. (Kindly supplied by *The Scotsman* Publications Ltd.)

before the general election, there had been a degree of jockeying for influence among those likely to be involved in the formation of such a cross-party organisation. Key Labour officials were said to be concerned that the emerging plans lacked sharp focus.

That concern surfaced again during the referendum campaign itself. On 21 August, Lord Steel of the Liberal Democrats – who had jointly chaired the Convention – told 'Good Morning Scotland' that Scotland Forward was run by 'well-meaning but politically inexperienced people'.

In other words, Scotland Forward was regarded as rather amateur by professional politicians. Officials from all three parties – Labour, the Liberal Democrats and the SNP – recognised that it was tactically essential to present the united front which Nigel Smith had described. They tended, however, to be privately rather dismissive of the organisation. The work on the ground, it was stressed, would be done by the political parties concentrating on the communities where they were each strongest.

Partly, this was a cultural clash between the politically aligned and those who evinced a non-partisan interest in Scottish self-government. This cultural clash was a regular feature of the Convention, where high-minded sentiment frequently conflicted with low politicking. Partly, though, it reflected an anxiety that the various parties' distinctive positions should not be entirely submerged.

This was an instinctive response. Each of the parties knew that disunity must be avoided in the Yes camp. Equally, each wanted their distinctive standpoints understood. Labour wanted it known that devolution or, more precisely, the White Paper which was the issue in the referendum, was an initiative from their party. The Liberal Democrats believed they had a longer pedigree over Home Rule – and wanted to get that across. The Nationalists were concerned to sustain the longer-term case for independence and to explain their support for a Yes vote in terms of a staging post on the road to that ultimate goal.

To be fair, Scotland Forward never suggested that it could supplant the political parties. It was always understood that party effort would continue. Scotland Forward simply hoped to provide a vehicle which could stress the common ground between the parties and, of course, to involve other non-partisan groups. Using that as a yardstick, Scotland Forward succeeded.

Their campaign launch, however, on 19 August was an awkward affair. It was completely dominated by persistent media questioning over Tommy Graham MP and allegations concerning party membership and his treatment of neighbouring MPs, including the late Gordon McMaster.

Later that same day, Graham's solicitor confirmed that his client had been suspended by the Labour Party pending an investigation. The following day, the 20th, Labour confirmed tight new rules for the selection of candidates for the Scottish Parliament. At the time of the media launch of the Yes campaign, however, none of that had happened.

The launch was held in the old Royal High School in Edinburgh – the building which had been destined to house the 1970s Scottish Assembly and which had stayed in gently decaying readiness ever since. Present were Donald Dewar, Alex Salmond, and Menzies Campbell for the Liberal Democrats – standing in for Jim Wallace, who was less than pleased to find that the launch had been scheduled for a day which he insists he had warned in advance did not suit his diary. In attendance, also, a posse of supporters connected with Scotland Forward.

Following my 'give them all hell' policy, I pursued questioning regarding the potential impact of the Graham affair on their campaign. As I recall, I was not the first to raise this issue – and certainly not the only journalist to seek an answer. However, irritated by what I perceived as evasion and condescension from the platform, I was perhaps the most persistent.

Former Labour councillor Paolo Vestri, who was chairing the event for Scotland Forward, responded to this persistence by calling me a 'prima donna'. Campbell Christie of the Scottish TUC said the general line of questioning was 'balderdash, media hype'. To his credit, Donald Dewar declined to take this approach and insisted on attempting to answer the questions, urging us, however, to bear in mind the 'big historical picture' of Scottish self-government.

I freely concede that the mist descends over my eyes a little when I perceive that a politician, any politician, is trying to dodge a question or trying to patronise the media or trying to question our motives. The underlying assumption on this occasion appeared to be that the wicked media had sullied what was meant to be an historic launch with nit-picking questions.

By contrast, I would argue that the organisers of a launch must be prepared to have their case tested. Labour in particular should have better anticipated questions on this issue and should have been ready with answers.

The Tories subsequently attempted to make use of the Graham affair, using his image on a poster attacking devolution. Certainly, Labour and the other partners in the Yes campaign were concerned at the possible impact. It is impossible to gauge but, in practice, it appears to have been minimal. In the longer term, Tommy Graham was cleared of any claims that his behaviour might have contributed to Gordon McMaster's death. He was, however, eventually expelled from the Labour Party on other charges relating to his conduct of party business. The MP continued to protest his complete innocence.

If the Yes campaign had a troubled launch, the No camp appeared to be facing still greater problems. In the 1970s, the No campaign had been well organised and notably well funded. This time around, things were different.

The Scottish Conservative Party had made plain that, following its general election defeat, it had neither the funds nor the inclination to organise a full-scale No campaign of its own. In June 1997, Tory peer Lord Fraser assumed the role of coordinating, partly, the preparation of such a campaign. His 'honest broker' job was apparently to reassure potential supporters that funds would not be diverted to the Conservative Party.

The No campaign which emerged was largely drawn together by Brian Monteith, a splendidly maverick free-market, libertarian Tory and former acolyte of Michael Forsyth, who maintains a connection with the harsher realities of Scottish life through his passionate support for Hibernian FC. Monteith provokes admiration and suspicion in varying measure within Conservative ranks. He is, however, a likeable individual, a hard worker and a media-friendly public relations professional: the right type, in short, to organise a campaign.

That campaign, however, faced difficulties from the start. Unlike 1979 – with a Labour Government in trouble – devolution 1990s-style was an initiative from a new Labour administration elected with a massive majority.

Businesses, large and small, may not always have the most acute antennae when it comes to politics. Indeed, business leaders can occasionally be remarkably naïve about the rude political realities.

Generally, however, they can count. They swiftly calculated that Labour was likely to be the UK power for quite some time, with a governing influence over the business sector. Not, all in all, the best time to poke one's head over the parapet to oppose a key plank of that Government's legislative programme. Better all round to let this devolution thing take its course. Perhaps the Scottish Parliament wouldn't be as bad as it seemed. That Donald Dewar seems a reasonable bloke.

So the business sector, broadly, steered clear of the formal No campaign. The forecast multiple big names in support of a No vote simply did not emerge.

Lord Weir of Cathcart, head of the Glasgow engineering firm, spoke out against devolution as he had done in the 1970s. But perhaps the most significant business intervention came from Sir Bruce Pattullo, the Bank of Scotland Governor. Speaking on 21 August, he attacked the proposed tax power for the Scottish Parliament while stressing that he was making absolutely no comment on the first question in the referendum, the principle of devolution.

He complained that the referendum question on tax did not specifically confine itself to income tax. More importantly, however, he spoke out against the prospect that Scotland might end up with a different income tax regime from that applying in England. The impact of this, he said, would be 'slow and corrosive' on the business sector.

Perhaps because he was one of very few business voices formally raised against aspects of the devolution plan, Sir Bruce's remarks appeared to have a substantial impact. They certainly seemed to get to the Labour Party. On a visit to Scotland two days later, the deputy Prime Minister John Prescott advised the Governor to 'play around with your money but just leave us to get on with our politics'.

This was one of those remarks which might have been better left unsaid. The whole point of a referendum, after all, was to extend decision-making beyond the narrow political field into wider public life. If the Governor of the Bank of Scotland had a genuine concern over the financial impact of a particular proposal, he was entitled to say so and indeed almost duty-bound to say so. The people of Scotland could weigh the impact of his comments in their wider contemplation of the choice before them. John Prescott would have been wiser, in this instance, to let Scotland get on with that choice.

Others in the Yes camp feared that the tax question was about to dominate the referendum as some had forecast when they spoke out against the decision to have a two-question ballot.

Certainly, tax was the very core of the No campaign.

Their strategy was to spotlight the tax power and hope, by that tactic, to undermine the whole case for devolution: to target tax as the soft underbelly of devolution. They believed they could defeat the second question and hoped thereby to wound the entire scheme, reflecting that the Liberal Democrats and several Labour MPs had previously warned that the devolution package would be flawed, perhaps fatally flawed, if the tax power vanished.

The limitation of the No camp's ambition is perhaps best expressed in the slogan which they paraded when Brian Monteith, Donald Findlay QC and others launched the campaign at Murrayfield Stadium. They were urging the Scottish people to Think Twice: an implicit acknowledgement that the people were predisposed to vote Yes and needed to be reminded of the alleged perils.

The Think Twice team tried their best. At the launch, Donald

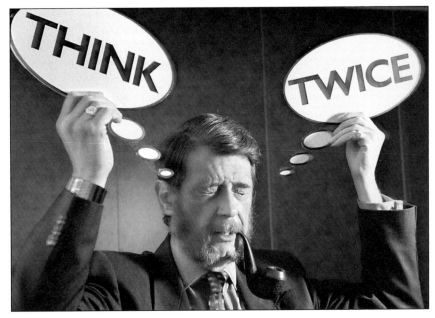

Think Twice, advises Donald Findlay, as the opponents of devolution launch their referendum campaign. (Kindly supplied by Murdo MacLeod.)

Findlay happily acceded to the photographers' request to hold two cardboard 'thought bubbles' up beside his whiskered face, while he placidly smoked his pipe. They could not have been more obliging to the media and to the wider public. The resources, however, were not there.

That presented the media with something of a problem. Should the balance of our reporting reflect the fact that the Yes camp was out-punching their opponents? Or should we attempt to present both sides of the argument and leave the public to judge? One or two in the Yes camp appeared to believe that the media – and particularly the BBC – were responsible for overselling the No campaign.

I argued then and still argue now that it was important for the public to be given the widest possible range of information with which to inform their judgement. That did not mean, as some seemed to think, inventing a No campaign where none existed. The doctrine of 'give them hell' applied to the No team too.

It did mean, however, confronting each side with arguments advanced by the other: the essence of democratic decision-making, in other words. I hope and believe that the media played a useful role in ensuring that the choice made by the people of Scotland on 11 September 1997 was an informed choice.

For Donald Findlay himself, staunch Unionism of a more questionable nature later generated trouble. Findlay had to resign as Vice-Chairman of Glasgow Rangers football club after he was recorded singing bigoted, sectarian songs at a celebration of the team's Scottish Cup victory.

But back to the referendum. The Yes camp were producing the big names. On Sunday, 7 September, just days before polling, Sean Connery addressed a cross-party rally in the old Royal High School on Calton Hill in Edinburgh. The hall was hushed as that famous voice quoted from the Declaration of Arbroath and told his normally partisan audience: 'This entire issue is above and beyond any political party.'

Connery, of course, is a Scottish Nationalist of long standing. He has supported the SNP financially and in other ways, including lending his voice to party political broadcasts. His intervention that Sunday was thought valuable by all participants in the Yes campaign. It came the same day as an opinion poll in *Scotland on Sunday* had suggested that majority support for the tax-varying power might be weakening.

Subsequently, his role in Scottish politics formed the core of a substantial row when Labour Ministers were accused of blocking a knighthood for him on the grounds that he was a Nationalist and that the honour might have boosted the SNP. Donald Dewar has repeatedly refused to comment on this issue – and declined to do so again for this book – but SNP leaders insist their suspicions have substance.

Alex Salmond's version of events – and I stress it is his version – is that Donald Dewar endorsed and welcomed Connery's participation in the autumn referendum campaign while knowing that in the summer of that year, as Scottish Secretary, he had expressed reservations about a possible knighthood for the actor. According to Salmond and others, the first suggestion within Labour ranks that Connery might be used in the campaign had come from Peter Mandelson.

Salmond told me that he and Connery had lunch with Donald Dewar in a private room at L'Amico, a restaurant in London's Horseferry Road, on 7 August 1997 to discuss the campaign and Connery's potential role. On the way there, Salmond said Connery asked him what sort of man Dewar was. This, seemingly, is Connery's customary approach; he likes to weigh the merits of an individual, to know what he is dealing with. Salmond said – in response to Connery's enquiry – that Dewar was trustworthy.

Salmond told me that he reflected on this meeting when the controversy over the knighthood emerged much later.[1] He said: 'When the knighthood issue came up, I was able to date it. Dewar had already knifed him in the Scottish Office. We sat down to lunch and Donald had already knifed him. It was a breach of trust. It was a surprise. I didn't think he would do something like that.'

Salmond says his longer-term opinion of Dewar has altered as a consequence of this event. Without commenting on the details in any way, Dewar's supporters say Salmond protests too much, that his anguish is curious from someone who seemingly disdains the baubles of political life, that there are frequent and varied discussions about honours, that no decision is cut and dried.

In any event, this controversy was for later and did not feature during the referendum. The main concern of the Yes team in the final few days of the campaign was that the tax question might not carry popular support.

Financial issues, more generally, had stayed in the foreground. Sir Malcolm Rifkind, the former Conservative Cabinet Minister, writing in *Scotland on Sunday* on 31 August, explained why he would be voting No, despite supporting devolution in the 1979 referendum.

He attacked the decision to hold the vote on the White Paper only but, more significantly, he spotlighted the financial aspects of the settlement which, he claimed, featured inherent instability. Devolution, he argued, would generate an early conflict over cash between Scotland and Westminster, with either spending cuts or tax rises as a result.

He wrote: 'I was and remain sympathetic to the argument that Scotland with its own distinctive law, administration, education and ethos could benefit from a devolved legislature.' The financial flaws of this particular scheme, however, prompted a No vote.

Opponents said his reasoning was bogus, that many Tories had opposed devolution in 1979 on the very grounds that there was no power to vary taxation and so provide the devolved legislature with a measure of financial responsibility of its own. Now they seemed to want to target those tax powers.

However, tax was still the worrying point for the Yes campaign. Donald Dewar had decidedly gloomy moments during the campaign when he thought that the tax question was lost. He bought the argument that it ran entirely counter to modern political thinking to confront the electorate directly with the potential cost of their political decisions.

Further, one source told me that Tony Blair shared this analysis. At an Edinburgh reception after the campaign was relaunched, the Prime Minister was heard to say that the tax question was in trouble. No matter how often Labour and others stressed that it was only a tax power, not an actual tax increase, which was on offer, the concern persisted in the Yes campaign.

Privately, senior politicians had to consider what happened if the tax element was rejected. Tony Blair and others insisted that the package did not stand or fall on tax. There could be a powerful, law-making Parliament without the tax power.

Labour, it was understood, was prepared to legislate for such a Parliament. During the referendum, of course, the party argued that the people of Scotland should be prepared to grant full powers to the planned new body including the power, in certain circumstances, to vary the rate of tax.

The Liberal Democrats were on record as opposing a Parliament which lacked tax powers. Speaking in Edinburgh on 21 September 1996, the party's Scottish leader Jim Wallace had said that a Parliament without such fiscal powers was 'not worthy of the name'. Implicit in that argument was a presumption that the Liberal Democrats would vote against such a scheme in the House of Commons.

They argued that a Parliament without the limited flexibility of tax powers would be utterly subservient to Westminster. The constitutional structure, it was claimed, would be unstable and might hasten the arrival of independence: a development which devolution was supposedly designed to forestall.

However, privately, Wallace recognised that it very much depended on the outcome of the referendum. If, for example, the people of Scotland voted decisively for a Parliament – and just as decisively against tax powers – it would have appeared perverse for the Liberal Democrats to attempt to frustrate the evident choice of the electorate.

In the event, of course, the concerns of the Yes camp proved groundless, although one observer told me that backstage at the main count in Edinburgh on the very night of the referendum Donald Dewar was still sounding anxious. In Dewar's case, such pessimism is probably an ingrained defence mechanism.

On the night of 11 September, I was in BBC Scotland's headquarters at Queen Margaret Drive in Glasgow. We were coordinating a results programme from the capacious Television Studio A with Kirsty Wark in the chair while I tried to offer reasoned analysis and our team of top-class number-crunchers fed through the data at lightning speed for Peter Snow to turn into graphic representations in his infectiously eager fashion.

From the first results, it appeared clear that there was going to be a substantial Yes majority on the first question – and that the tax question would also get through. That impression was confirmed each time we crossed to the main counting centre in Edinburgh to hear Neil McIntosh, the former Chief Executive of Strathclyde Region, announce another result from around the country.

Perhaps the image of the night was that of Alex Salmond and Jim Wallace emerging together from the Edinburgh counting centre and punching the air in delight at the outcome.

The final result, however, was slow in coming. As I recall, the Highland result was delayed. In Studio A we stayed on air, talking until dawn about ever more abstruse topics while waiting for that final declaration. Once, years previously, Neil Kinnock had justified his relative neglect of devolution in a Scottish conference speech by asserting that he hadn't talked about weather conditions in the Himalayas either. That night, as the discussion dragged on, I think we would have been only too glad to subject the Himalayan climate to searching scrutiny.

Finally, we had to give up and hand over to our colleagues from BBC breakfast news. The Highland result, of course, came shortly afterwards.

The final picture showed that Scotland had voted decisively for a devolved Parliament with tax-varying powers. There was a 60.4 per cent turnout, lower than general election levels but substantial none the less.

Edinburgh's Parliament Square, 12 September 1997 – and the Prime Minister helps celebrate the double Yes vote in the referendum. Donald Dewar threw caution to the wind and called the result 'most satisfactory'. (Kindly supplied by The Scotsman Publications Ltd.)

Some 1 775 045 or 74.3 per cent voted Yes to a Parliament while 614 400 or 25.7 per cent were against. That left Scotland three to one in favour of devolution. On the tax question, 1 512 889 or 63.5 per cent voted Yes with 870 263 or 36.5 per cent against. Scotland had voted by nearly two to one in favour of tax powers. Every area of Scotland voted for the Parliament on question one. Only two areas, Orkney and Dumfries and Galloway, voted narrowly against the tax power.

That clearly empowered the Government to introduce its Bill, the Scotland Bill, to legislate for a Scottish Parliament. The Bill, of course, was already in elementary form as work paralleled the efforts to produce the White Paper. The Scottish Office drafting team worked flat out to get the Bill ready before the end of the year. It was produced on 18 December 1997 and given outline approval in the form of a Second Reading by the Commons on 13 January 1998 after a two-day debate.

The Scotland Bill contained 40 000 words of precise, legislative prose. It apparently took 60 000 person hours of ministerial effort to produce, or one word every hour and a half. It had 116 clauses when it was published. There were eight schedules setting out the consequences of devolution in minute detail.

Yet when Donald Dewar stood up in a Glasgow hotel to introduce the Bill to the media, he turned his attention in particular to Clause 1, Part One. It read simply: 'There shall be a Scottish Parliament.' Dewar repeated the phrase with a smile: 'There shall be a Scottish Parliament – I like that!'

That clause and that wording survive into the final Scotland Act as, indeed, does much of the Bill. After such careful preparation, the Government was not inclined to let the House of Commons or the House of Lords take its legislation apart. The Bill and the Act very substantially follow the detailed pattern of the White Paper.

I do not intend to repeat that detail now but for the record it may be helpful simply to list those powers which are reserved to Westminster in the Bill. Everything else by definition is devolved.

The Bill, then, provides that Westminster retains power over: the Constitution including the Crown, foreign affairs including relations with Europe, the civil service, defence, macro-economics including almost all tax and budgetary matters, social security, child support, abortion, embryo research, broadcasting, pensions laws, the regulation of financial services, the currency, drugs control, data protection, firearms, immigration, national security and counter-terrorism, betting and gaming laws, extradition, competition law, import and export controls, consumer protection including weights and measures, telecommunications regulations, electricity, most oil and gas regulations, nuclear energy, most road, rail, air and marine transport laws, the regulation of many professions, health and safety, judicial pay, ordnance survey, time – and, finally, 'the regulation of activities in outer space'.

Mostly, Scots seemed prepared to accept this bar placed upon their country's capacity to launch a shuttle or a Mars space probe. Much of the debate in the Commons and the Lords, however, centred upon efforts to amend other aspects of this reserved list and thereby to extend the powers available to the Scottish Parliament.

The decisive result in the referendum had changed the political climate. The Tories declared that they would abide by the will of the people. They set about their endeavour to transform themselves from the chief opponents of devolution into its self-styled true defenders, the party who could entrench a devolved Scotland within the Union.

The fear of a guerrilla campaign against the devolution Bill from the Opposition or from the Labour backbenches simply evaporated. The Government felt able to accede to Tory demands that all stages of the Bill would be considered by the Commons as a whole. That is customary with constitutional Bills but there had been talk of breaching the convention and sending the Bill 'upstairs' to a smaller committee of MPs.

Again, that prospect vanished with the referendum result. The Tories promised that they would not offer unwarranted obstruction to the Bill if it was considered on the floor of the House. The referendum, in short, had produced the goods. It had fulfilled its objective of easing the devolution legislation through Parliament and preventing the creation of a Westminster logjam.

When Donald Dewar began parliamentary proceedings on the Bill in the Commons on 12 January, he offered the opinion that the subsequent debate on the detail of the legislation was likely to be 'routine'. In a sketch the next day, Ben Brogan of *The Herald* said that the supposedly historic Second Reading of the Scotland Bill was 'about as exciting as watching paint dry'. Exactly, Brogan explained, as the Government intended.

The Tories battled gamely. From the front bench, Michael Ancram said the Bill was 'so badly drafted, it's for us as Conservatives, the one party that started out against devolution, to try for the sake of the United Kingdom to make these proposals work.' The Labour majority – or those MPs who bothered to attend – hooted with laughter.

In the subsequent weeks and months, MPs and peers worked through the detail of the legislation. Despite the substantive efforts by opposition politicians to alter the legislation, the proceedings were as Donald Dewar described: routine.

The Liberal Democrats tried, among other issues, to strengthen the provisions on gender balance in the Parliament. The Nationalists wanted further powers devolved in the fields of broadcasting, finance and relations with Europe. Specifically, they wanted a statutory right for Scottish parliamentary Ministers to attend meetings of the European Council of Ministers.

Ministers knocked that back, as they did the sustained attempt to devolve the issue of abortion to Scotland. This produced an intriguing coalition of interests between liberal thinkers who believed it was illogical and inconsistent to deny the Scottish Parliament discretion in this field – and opponents of abortion, including the Roman Catholic church, who harboured hopes that Scotland might be prepared to sanction a stricter regime. On balance, Ministers argued this was best left as a UK issue.

There were changes, however. Perhaps the most significant concerned the tenure of judges. The original plan had been to allow the appointment and, more importantly, the dismissal of judges to be in the hands of the Scottish Parliament. This produced complaints from the legal profession that there would be unwarranted political interference in the judiciary as a consequence. The final arrangement, as amended, provides for a tribunal of inquiry to investigate any complaints against individual judges.

The Prime Minister will retain the power to recommend to the Queen the appointment of the senior judges, the Lord President of the Court of Session and the Lord Justice Clerk, with the proviso that there must first be a nomination for such individuals from the First Minister of the Scottish Parliament.

The First Minister holds the power to recommend the appointment of other judges and sheriffs. Judges can be dismissed by the sovereign after a vote by the Scottish Parliament – but only if they have been found to be unfit for office by a tribunal. Political whim alone will not suffice.

Among other changes, the rules were clarified on whether the Scottish Parliament might be straying inadvertently beyond its powers into areas reserved to Westminster. This 'overlap' problem was addressed by a new test: whether the principal purpose of the measure in question was aimed at Scotland.

The rules were also tightened on members' interests to provide that this issue might become statutory rather than simply in the standing orders of the Parliament. More generally, financial scrutiny procedure for the new Parliament was tightened for the Act. The definition of those liable to pay should the Parliament exercise its tax-varying powers was clarified.

In addition, the Scottish Parliament was given an amended protection against legal challenge – although, strictly, the powers of the new Parliament can be questioned in any court in Scotland, however humble.

Indeed, it is possible that the courts may have to continue the discussions as to the relative powers of the Edinburgh and London Parliaments, especially if an aggrieved individual launches a complaint. In a lecture, Lord Gill of the Scottish Law Commission speculated that the Government's 'legislative intent' might end up being 'interpreted and filled in by the courts'.[2] However, he added reassuringly: 'These are all matters with which a flexible and adaptable judiciary is capable of dealing.'

As the Bill proceeded through Parliament, Ministers proclaimed themselves gravely concerned at the possibility that the unelected House of Lords might frustrate the evident will of the Commons and the Scottish people over devolution. There were dire warnings of the consequences should such an eventuality occur. Democracy, it would appear, was in jeopardy.

In truth, I believe there was an element of affectation about such warnings, not unconnected with another government initiative: reforming the House of Lords. Ministers were seeking to stir up a froth of indignation at the Lords. In response, peers, including the Tory leadership in the Upper House, repeatedly offered assurances that they would not delay the legislation beyond their duty to scrutinise it thoroughly.

The Scotland Bill duly carried through all stages in both Houses of Parliament and received royal assent on 19 November 1998.

Notes

1. Interview with Alex Salmond, 4 December 1998.
2. Lecture by Lord Gill, delivered to a seminar organised by Strathclyde University's Centre for Professional Legal Studies, 27 February 1998.

9 The Scottish Labour Party and Donald Dewar: a Profile

I have long felt a particular affinity for Scottish literature. From the sympathetic glories of Sir Walter Scott to the brutal drollery of Irvine Welsh, I think our best writers can offer an insight into the Scottish character in all its varied forms. As well as these highways of literature, I like to wander down some of the byways. There is a splendid trilogy of novels by Guy McCrone, entitled *Wax Fruit*, which captures the past flavour of mercantile Glasgow. The Glasgow merchant family at the heart of the work is depicted on a trip to Vienna, absorbing the obligatory European culture in their upwardly mobile way. One member of the party, however, seems less than enthralled. 'Henry was sitting, glum and unhappy-seeming, as many Scots do when they are excited,' we are informed.

This is true character insight – indeed foresight. Change the name and it could be Donald Dewar. Labour's Scottish leader, Scotland's First Minister, is a charming individual who has inspired warm affection across a wide range of Scottish society. But he has also built a reputation for his determination to remain underwhelmed.

Nothing must be permitted to stir an extravagant response. We all know the caricature, the Scot accustomed to setbacks who will bask in the sunshine, discern a tiny cloud in the distance and observe: 'Aye, looks like rain.'

Dewar's party colleagues have long been accustomed to operate according to the law of inverse responses. If Donald is glum, they say, things are generally OK. If he is bestowing smiles on one and all, start worrying. Dewar, of course, is considerably more complex than this whimsical rule of thumb would indicate.

His wit can be satirical and, occasionally, even a little hurtful while he can appear oblivious to the reaction he sometimes provokes. I once sat behind him at a wedding ceremony during which – there is no other word for it – he heckled under his breath, apparently disinclined to make concessions to solemnity.

Equally, though, I have watched him evince the most genuine concern for colleagues – or indeed for strangers encountered in the course of political canvassing. Dewar does not press the flesh with a fixed, televisual grin. Indeed, he cordially loathes photo-calls, particularly when they force him into an uncomfortable environment. On one occasion, I caught him staring with undisguised horror at a dumper truck which an eager PR officer suggested he might care to steer.

Dewar's manner – his occasional abruptness in both social and political life – is, I feel certain, at least partly a defence mechanism, forestalling high expectations for fear, presumably, of subsequent disappointment.

Yet at the same time he can be charming company both at public events and in the society of close friends. He is highly intelligent, extremely witty and with a range of observation and understanding far beyond the narrow party focus occupied by so many in politics. Dewar is a character, forged by his easily tolerable foibles. He is a quite remarkable blend: a professed pessimist, perhaps, without remotely being a misanthropist. An admirer of humanity, alert to its faults.

Most in the Labour Party are Dewar fans. A few privately call him 'Big Donald', a deliberate parody of a casual, back-slapping approach which, of course, sits ill with the restrained recipient. Some, however, feel that he is out of touch with the party's roots: with the trades union and council bedrock. They find his more arcane pronouncements irritating.

Dewar is not remotely the model of a modern political leader. For one thing, he defies the categorisation which seems to be obligatory in these simplistic, pigeon-holed times. Try thinking of him as New Labour or as Old Labour – and discover how futile the endeavour is.

Learning a little about Donald Dewar is, however, a dangerous thing. The caricature says he is utterly uncomfortable on holiday. Certainly, one wicked Scottish newspaper diarist once offered a prize for the first authenticated sighting of Dewar incontestably on vacation and demonstrably enjoying himself. As far as I am aware, the reward went unclaimed. D. Dewar is not the wow of the beachside karaoke set.

Equally, I and other journalists accompanied him on a trip to Barcelona where he held talks with Jordi Pujol, the political leader of Catalonia. We gathered in the ancient courtyard of Pujol's HQ, sipping *cava* – the Catalan answer to champagne – under the gently waving orange trees. D. Dewar looked and sounded decidedly content, a man reborn, a man who had concluded there is more to life than checking the minutes of the Constitutional Convention.

This is a man who looks ascetic but has a healthy appetite, an art-loving solicitor who, none the less, has a keen and genuine interest in football. Some have even claimed to see him as a species of brooding romantic, a Kelvinside Heathcliff, although I know the very notion would provoke a guffaw from the man himself.

A keen sense of the absurd and a reluctance to appear overblown perhaps prevent him from being a stunning party conference orator. He always appears to draw back from the fatuous phrase which, nevertheless, seems necessary to stir the political blood of the contemporary, less discriminating audience.

By contrast, he is an excellent debater, alert to sharp cross-party exchanges, and a brilliant after-dinner speaker, with comic timing which would not disgrace Les Dawson. In a mock mournful voice, he will describe, for example, previously sharing a Commons office with the youthful Tony Blair who was, apparently, wont to burst in and yell excitedly: 'Morning, DD,' to the anguish of his less effervescent colleague.

Born on 21 August 1937, Donald Dewar first demonstrated his wit and discursive skills in the student debating chamber at Glasgow University: the academic home of John Smith, Menzies Campbell and Charles Kennedy, among many others. He had previously attended Glasgow Academy. Dewar was MP for the notoriously marginal Westminster seat of South Aberdeen from 1966 to 1970.

He returned to the Commons via the Glasgow Anniesland by-election of 1978. He became Scottish Secretary after the 1997 general election and now, of course, has opted to continue his career through the Scottish Parliament. On Thursday, 13 May 1999, he was elected First Minister.

Dewar can appear unworldly, either inadvertently or by deliberate contrivance. He once asked Michael Connarty – a fellow MP with a distinctly neat hairstyle – how he achieved his remarkable coiffure. Connarty said he used mousse. 'But', said Dewar, 'isn't mousse something you eat?'

He is a modern-day Manichean, a combination of contradictions. Perhaps fitting in a party which has historically swithered over its attitude to Scottish self-government. For Labour – even the Scottish party which Dewar leads – is not an instinctive party of devolution. By that, I mean that it is not a first principle for the party. Labour has largely followed public opinion on this question, rather than leading it.

The history of the party in Scotland may be traced back to 1888 and Keir Hardie's foundation of a Scottish Labour Party, although the modern British Labour movement may properly be sourced to a London meeting on 27 February 1900. Throughout the century, devolution has prompted tension within Labour. That sporadic conflict is entirely understandable. It arises from the differing perspectives of those devoted to advancing the cause of Labour in Scotland and those attached to the British or international agenda.

Indeed, at an earlier stage many Socialists – including several in Scotland – were inherently suspicious of Scottish self-government, which they equated with nationalism and the Right. Glasgow or Dundee workers, they would argue, had more in common with workers in Manchester and Liverpool than with the bourgeoisie in Scotland.

Others have taken an alternative tack, arguing that social reform could be advanced within Scotland by reform of governance. Occasionally, as during the long years of Conservative rule after 1979, it appeared that the Left in Scotland were partly advocating devolution in frustration at Labour's inability to make progress in British politics.

Many of the earliest advocates of Socialist parliamentary representation in Scotland were sympathetic to the Home Rule cause – either through direct principled support for self-government or mistrust of the prevailing British state establishment or the belief that socialism could more easily be advanced in a small political arena. Alongside that, however, were always others who felt this ran counter to the movement's internationalist ethos.

In practical terms, the Home Rule issue was frequently overshadowed by the efforts of the Labour movement to build and sustain a Westminster parliamentary majority. For example, the wartime coalition Scottish Secretary Tom Johnston was a Home Ruler – but the Attlee Government, which won a spectacular victory for Labour in 1945, took no steps to implement devolution, concentrating instead on applying British state solutions to the deep social and industrial problems of the time.

Throughout much of the 1950s and 1960s, Labour in Scotland concentrated on issues such as boosting the economy and spreading social provision. The party appeared either hostile to Home Rule or, more accurately, uninterested although there were thoughtful figures, including a young Donald Dewar, who advocated Scottish self-government when it was relatively unpopular inside the Labour movement.

Most trace Labour's adoption of devolution to the rise of the SNP in the 1970s, when the Nationalists gained first seven and then eleven seats in the two general elections of 1974.

Certainly, the two events are coterminous although, as I have argued elsewhere, I think it is more strictly accurate to say that Labour was responding to a non-specific mood for a recognition of Scottish identity which the SNP represented. That self-same mood, in other words, both forged the SNP and threatened the established Labour Party.

Had that mood been uniformly and ineluctably for straightforward independence, there would have been little a party like Labour could do, short of overturning its commitment to the Union. Rather, the mood which was partly expressed through SNP support was perhaps less clearly defined. It was for significant self-government, for recognition of Scotland's distinct position.

Labour leaders, then, responded – but remained rather reluctant devolvers. Indeed, the Scottish Labour executive voted against devolution in the summer of 1974 – although, anecdotally, the balance may have been tilted by a relatively poor attendance caused by a clash with TV coverage of the Scotland–Yugoslavia World Cup tie. Harold Wilson's Government persisted with devolution and Scottish Labour's seeming reluctance was overturned at a subsequent party conference.

The tension, however, persisted. In the 1970s, Labour MP Jim Sillars led a breakaway Scottish Labour Party in protest at the British party's alleged lack of genuine commitment to Home Rule. Sillars, of course, later joined the SNP.

In the Scottish and Welsh devolution referendums of 1979, prominent Labour figures like Robin Cook, Neil Kinnock, Brian Wilson and Tam Dalyell voiced strong opposition to the changes proposed by their Government. The Welsh plan was heavily defeated while the Scottish scheme was scuppered by the 40 per cent rule.

Over succeeding decades, however, support for devolution became steadily entrenched within Scottish Labour. This was partly, as I have argued, in response to the party's inability to gain success at the UK level. MPs and activists thwarted in the search for Westminster power sought to redraw the boundaries, to create a legislature which they could command.

Perhaps more than that, however, the motivation for the party membership and activists was the developing popular mood of Scotland, the apparently persistent support for a measure of self-government. Scotland was grasping the Saltire and Scottish Labour could not be seen to be brandishing the Union flag over-eagerly.

Labour, in short, followed Scotland, not the other way round. This is not, of course, an ignoble posture for a democratic party but equally not perhaps the image which contemporary Labour likes to present. Political parties – and especially a party like Labour which has maintained substantial support in Scotland – generally like to represent themselves as leading 'their people' or at least as being in synchronisation with popular sentiment.

While it is reasonable to analyse Labour's genuine motivation in this field, we should also acknowledge the capacity of the party to detect and reflect a changing popular mood. By contrast, the Conservatives stood against the changing political tide in Scotland and paid the electoral price as a consequence.

The Labour Party in England, of course, could scarcely be expected to pursue this course with the same fervour. Devolution was party policy, but it was not a policy which was much loved in

London. MPs from England mostly understood that the Scottish party required to follow the mood of Scotland – or, more commonly, they grasped the raw politics of countering the SNP.

Some, including MPs from the North-east of England, resented the notion of a Scottish Parliament. They feared that Scotland would gain bigger clout in attracting internationally mobile industrial investment. Others feared that too much attention would be paid to devolution at the cost of more mundane policies likely to be popular in England.

Most, however, tolerated devolution – if they thought about it at all. For these MPs and activists, perhaps understandably, devolution was never a policy of the same nature or calibre as the minimum wage or schools provision or NHS structures, something to be debated and promulgated. Devolution was needed to placate the Scots. It was a strategy, not a policy.

Even today, there are senior figures in Labour ranks who question that strategy, who fear the end game. As I have said, it is not instinctive in perhaps the way that support for equality of opportunity is instinctive. Devolution has to be learned and relearned, especially by Labour leaders outside Scotland who still wonder whether the party is conceding ground to an alien concept of nationalism.

In September 1995, I prepared a series of items for BBC Scotland on the detailed consequences of devolution: the big, underlying issues which were sometimes neglected in coverage of the endless cross-party bickering.

For one of these items, I interviewed Welsh Labour MP Dr Kim Howells, then the party's constitutional spokesperson in Jack Straw's team. The interview was remarkable, an outpouring of anxiety at his party's constitutional strategy in Wales and Scotland. Howells told me: 'I did not become a Labour MP in order to take part in the Balkanisation of Britain and I am profoundly anti-nationalist.'

Nationalism, he added, always contained underlying elements of a sort of fascism. In addition, he questioned the plan for tax-varying powers in Scotland. Howells' statements were disowned by Jack Straw and he was subsequently moved to another remit but he was voicing a strand of Labour thought, undoubtedly more prevalent in Wales and England than in Scotland, but authentic none the less and still apparent.

It is not that the party in England or the London-based leadership is overtly hostile to devolution. But the attitude of many MPs when they thought about devolution has been: 'If we must'. There has been a dissonance of approach within the Labour Party across the Border between Scotland and England.

Tony Blair has regularly voiced frustration at the apparent obsession of the media in Scotland with the topic of devolution, resorting privately to colourful language to caricature the Scottish press pack. That conflict is born out of the dissonance between Labour politics in Scotland and England on this question.

Members of the media suspect that Blair is not an instinctive devolver. When they quiz him on the subject, they are frankly trying to catch him out, occasionally posing ever more arcane questions to test his knowledge and standpoint.

I freely confess to indulging in the same pursuit from time to time – while acknowledging that I have a certain sympathy for Blair on this matter. For example, he attempted to justify the Scottish Parliament's tax powers in an interview with *The Scotsman* by pointing out that the lowliest parish council in England had a certain degree of discretion over finance. Would it not be ridiculous, he argued, to deny discretion to the powerful Scottish Parliament?

Blair was, in truth, contrasting one with the other, stressing that the Scottish Parliament was an influential and significant body by comparison with the humble parish council. Sections of the Scottish media, however, chose to assert that he had compared the Scottish Parliament with a parish council, that this was an unpardonable slur on Scotland's dignity. Given the sensitivities, his simile might have been more carefully chosen – but the reaction was out of all proportion to the remarks and, indeed, misrepresented them.

In response, Blair's advisers – Team Blair – have become deeply suspicious of the Scottish media. Their constant complaint – which has a certain basis in fact although it is overstated – is that the Scottish media have been obsessed with devolution by contrast with the Scottish people.

I recall observing Tony Blair as Prime Minister answering questions from the public in the Glasgow Film Theatre. As the enquiries ranged from employment law to social policy and education, a piece of paper was thrust into my hand. It was a scribbled note passed from Alastair Campbell, the Prime Minister's ever-present press secretary, and read: 'These are the real concerns of the public.' I glanced towards Campbell and he responded with a cheeky grin.

However, if there is substance to the claim that the Scottish media are obsessive about devolution – and I think there is – then Team Blair can sometimes seem dismissive not just of the Scottish media but of the Scottish political dimension and even the place of the Labour Party within that.

While endorsing devolution, sections of the London-based party appear occasionally to elide or ignore its consequences for their own party, to play down the distinctive nature of Scottish politics. They seem to feel their Scottish colleagues are simply being perverse in stressing that Scottish political dimension.

I recall the despair on the face of the Scottish Labour official who had just faced an awkward conversation with a colleague from party headquarters in London. The occasion was the Perth and Kinross by-election in May 1995 caused by the death of Tory MP Sir Nicholas Fairbairn.

This was not natural Scottish Labour territory – and indeed the contest was eventually won by Roseanna Cunningham for the SNP. But the London Labour man refused to accept such an analysis.

Such constituencies in England, apparently, were ripe for Labour takeover. In vain, the Scottish party official tried to explain the four-party structure in Scotland, the role of the SNP. This, seemingly, was defeatist. Tony was looking for victory in seats like this. As the Scottish party official said to me later: 'They just don't get it.'

This is not simply a matter of policy. I get impatient with those who characterise the party in Scotland as uniformly unreconstructed 'Old Labour' while the party in England is apparently all Blairite 'New Labour'. There is no reason to suppose that people in Scotland are any more intrinsically resistant to new political ideas than the people of England under New Labour or, for that matter, the people of Germany under the Social Democrats.

The party in Scotland may be of a somewhat different overt character to the emerging profile of the party in England but that is perhaps because its previous decline was less precipitate. Its power bases in unions and, especially, in Scottish local government remained entrenched. It does not mean that Blairite ideas will be or are rejected out of hand by the electorate.

Rather it is to do with atmosphere. Team Blair can occasionally seem exasperated with Scotland. With a massive Commons majority and a humbled Tory opposition, they have become accustomed to unalloyed success.

Scotland in the run-up to the May elections seemed to bring nothing but problems: troublesome MPs, question marks over Labour local government, the Nationalists, opinion polls. The election result – a coalition instead of total Labour power – only increased the tendency for the party in London to pigeonhole Scotland under 'trouble'.

It is to some extent an exercise in doublethink. Team Blair know that Scotland is different; that is why the Labour Government implemented devolution. They appreciate the identity issue expressed most obviously through the Nationalists but also relevant to their party in Scotland. They grasp the concept. Yet at the same time they appear to cling to the contrary opinion: that Scotland can and must be confronted with exactly the same political tactics as in England.

This phenomenon produced problems in the past for Donald Dewar. When Labour seemed to be slipping behind the SNP in the Scottish parliamentary opinion polls in 1998, Dewar was given a decidedly hard time privately by sections of the London-based party. Those around Blair simply could not accept, could not comprehend the notion of failure.

Dewar was advised to take a tough line with the media – who were regarded as troublesome – and with the SNP. MPs with a less than sure grasp of Scottish politics were heard to voice the opinion that 'Donald should sort it out,' as if the existence of a challenge had not occurred to the leader of the Scottish party. Dewar's own stewardship of Scottish Labour was called into question at this stage.

The Scottish election campaign was marked by further significant tension within the party. Mostly, this has been attributed to a difference of emphasis between London and Scotland. This, I feel, is an oversimplification. Certainly, key London officials believed that the party in Scotland was simply not up to the task presented by the 6 May poll. Disparaging remarks were uttered – evoking occasional responses from the Scottish-based squad. There were, however, other elements.

There were personality clashes within the team supposedly orchestrating the campaign. There was difficulty caused by suspicions that certain individuals were promoting their own prospects rather than the party. There were persistent claims of factions entrenching the influence of Gordon Brown or Tony Blair. Perhaps most significantly, there was lingering resentment that Donald Dewar's own team appeared to have been rather marginalised in the control of the campaign.

Mostly these personal and structural tensions – of a sort which can occur in all parties – were subjugated and controlled. They may even have had a productive side, enhancing internal competitive effort. In Labour's case, however, the internal conflict had a direct, later consequence with the resignation of Alex Rowley as General Secretary of the Scottish party exactly a fortnight after the 6 May election.

Rowley had been a successful and innovative leader of Fife Council. He had important connections in the trades union movement. Most importantly of all, however, he was a close constituency ally of the Chancellor, Gordon Brown. Despite holding one of the highest offices in the UK, despite busying himself with international financial negotiations, Brown still takes an exceptionally close interest in the minutiae of Labour's internal power structure. He likes to have friends at all levels of the party.

Brown was instrumental in helping secure Rowley's appointment as General Secretary just a little over a year before the Scottish elections. Partly as a consequence of the background to his appointment, Rowley had to endure a whispering campaign against him virtually from the start of his period in the post.

Rowley is deeply imbued with an authentic Labour ethos. He can be a thoughtful and intelligent advocate of the need for reform within the party. However, he faced complaints on two fronts: firstly, that he was Brown's man rather than Scottish Labour's and, secondly, that he simply was not up to the job. It was argued that his communication and motivation skills were limited. Those closer to him, however, insist that he is a skilled political tactician who should have been redeployed rather than undermined. On his departure, several senior union leaders protested fiercely that the party had lost a valuable asset.

During the early period, during the preparations for the election, it was very difficult to determine who was in charge of the Scottish Labour Party's campaign. Was it Donald Dewar? Or Helen Liddell, his deputy who had previously been asked by Tony Blair to shake up the Scottish operation? Or Henry McLeish who had helped coordinate the 1997 election campaign in Scotland? Or Alex Rowley, who was the General Secretary? Or Gordon Brown?

The options steadily narrowed as the campaign went on. Rowley was marginalised. McLeish was utilised but was definitely not in charge. Liddell was scarcely evident in the national campaign and was later passed over for the job of Scottish Secretary. Dewar was the party leader and First Minister in waiting – but Labour media mythology also devised another role for him, as 'Father of the Nation', a quasi-presidential figure, somehow above squalid politics.

If matters were uncertain at the very beginning of the campaign, by the end there was absolutely no doubt. Gordon Brown took direct personal command of the campaign, with help from key aides like Douglas Alexander, the bright and personable winner of the Paisley South Westminster by-election. By all accounts – including those from people who are not instinctive supporters of the Chancellor – Brown's energy, discipline, motivational skills and sheer talent were critical to the campaign.

However, another figure also entered the scene: John Rafferty, later to become Donald Dewar's Chief of Staff in the office of First Minister. Rafferty took time off from his job running the National Lottery Charities Board in Scotland to assist the Labour campaign. A quintessential fixer, his most prominent Labour role in the past had been to devise and maintain the party's strategy against the poll tax in the 1980s, steering a careful path away from the demand for Labour to organise an illegal non-payment campaign. Donald Dewar, Shadow Scottish Secretary at the time, was exceptionally grateful for his assistance.

Rafferty is a discreet, smartly dressed executive type – softly spoken, with a cultured West of Scotland accent and a speaking style which can veer enticingly between Runyonesque polite precision and subtle menace, according to the taste of the listener. I should add that, personally, I have never found Rafferty anything other than entirely affable.

Those close to Rafferty say that his defining nature is meritocratic. He has relatively little patience with the bureaucracy and structural niceties which can dog political parties. Rather he identifies core tasks involved in an operation and sets about achieving them. This is a characteristic he shares with Tony Blair, who is also preeminently a 'can do' politician who refuses to be bound by dogma or cherished party customs.

His arrival, however, posed an intrinsic challenge to Alex Rowley, who found that his stewardship of the party came under further question as Rafferty exerted more and more influence. A powerful personality will almost always break through the hierarchical structures of an organisation – and this is what happened during the Labour election campaign. Rafferty's influence extended as Rowley's declined. The General Secretary of the Scottish Labour Party was marginalised at a unique moment, the first elections to the new Scottish Parliament.

There are two alternative interpretations of Rowley's ultimate departure. One is that he was effectively dismissed by Labour's Millbank headquarters at the insistence of John Rafferty. The other is that he resigned in response to the tensions which had built up during the campaign.

In terms of straightforward fact, Rowley resigned. He was not sacked. It is equally the case, however, that his resignation followed talks in which he had been confronted with concern as to his performance. Cabinet sources insist that Rowley's departure was not simply a case of London Labour sorting out recalcitrant Scotland: the scenario which instantly attracted the attention of the observing media.

Rather it is claimed that Scottish Labour intended an organisational shake-up in any case – and that it had become clear, within both Scotland and London, that Rowley was not best suited to a managerial role in charge of the recruitment and motivation of staff. There was the prospect of redeploying him as head of a new political unit where, it was argued, his skills might have been put to good use.

Alex Rowley himself says that he was grateful for continued support from individuals like Gordon Brown and Donald Dewar – but that, fairly or unfairly, he had plainly lost the confidence of Millbank including Margaret McDonagh, the overall General Secretary in London. As a consequence, he chose to go. Significantly, he does not blame Rafferty directly.

Quite separately, there is said to have been disquiet among those who were despatched on Donald Dewar's campaign battlebus.

Departing from Edinburgh's Parliament Square at the start of the campaign, Dewar toured the length and breadth of Scotland, evangelising Labour's cause, while others managed the campaign from the Glasgow headquarters.

By one interpretation, this was a curious decision, recalling for some the decision to despatch John Prescott around the country in the 1997 general election. Others, however, insist that Dewar came to revel in his role, meeting voters and addressing genuine concerns. It was argued that this was Dewar's greatest strength, the potential leader of the nation meeting the people. Equally, Dewar was very far from being out of the spotlight. His tour itself generated publicity and, in addition, he featured at several national news conferences and on numerous election debate programmes.

Dewar, then, was able to dismiss with confidence any suggestion – in the media or elsewhere – that his place at the physical centre of the campaign had been usurped. While carrying out his tour, he was careful to monitor, influence and direct developments elsewhere. He was, indisputably, the party leader if not the campaign controller.

Apparently, others in the bus party were less contented. The squad included, at various points, Westminster MPs, Dewar's adviser Murray Elder, and Lorraine Davidson, the party's director of communication. Some members of the battlebus team, it is claimed, felt rather left out of events. They felt they were traipsing round the country when the strategic campaign decisions were being taken back in Delta House, the party's Glasgow HQ, by acolytes of the Chancellor and by relatively new arrivals like John Rafferty.

One source even suggested to me that the battlebus featured alongside its high-tech equipment a puppet or doll nicknamed 'Rafferty', which was 'no doubt kicked from one end of the bus to the other'. This, I feel sure, is one of those apocryphal election tales which are perhaps enhanced in the retelling.

It would not do to overstate matters. Tensions and jealousies are endemic to political parties and are heightened at election time. Physical absence from the centre of decision-making can exacerbate anxiety for those accustomed to being closely involved in strategy. Equally, however, Lorraine Davidson, who had been assuring everyone that the battlebus was the most splendid fun, resigned from her post shortly after the election. There had previously been rumours that she was discontented.

On his departure, Alex Rowley raised another issue: the question of Scottish Labour autonomy. He made plain his belief that the party in Scotland must be given more discretion to run its own affairs.

This issue is certain to provoke further conflict. In many respects, Labour – the party which has implemented legislative devolution – is the least devolved of any of the major parties. Key matters like staffing of the Scottish party have customarily been determined in London.

On policy, too, there are those who believe that the Scottish party must be seen as virtually a wholly owned subsidiary of the British party, with little flexibility or distinct powers of initiative.

Such an approach was firmly advocated by Matthew Taylor of the Institute for Public Policy Research, a former assistant General Secretary of the Labour Party, writing in *The Guardian* on 11 May 1999. He argued that the emergence of distinct Scottish Labour policies would jeopardise the presentation of a single British Labour 'brand'. He added: 'Devolution gave the people of Scotland and Wales the right to elect their own government, not to redesign the political platform of each party.'

Further, he said: 'To suggest that devolution to the Scottish Parliament means that Scottish Labour politicians have free rein to redesign the party's values and core policies is to deny the very definition of a political party.' A cynical observer might paraphrase that as 'you can have your own Parliament if you insist but you must not dare to do anything different with it.'

Certainly, devolution need not be seen as a form of defiance. There is little point in the new Parliament opting for different policies from Westminster simply for the sheer fun of trying a different road. Equally, devolution is utterly pointless if political parties – including Labour, the leading party in Scotland – are unable to adapt their policies to the immediate circumstances and needs of Scotland. There is simply no function in having 129 MSPs, including twenty-two Ministers, if their policies are wholly or largely predetermined by the party machines in London.

Taylor's article, of course, is only one view. I would not want to suggest that it is the established London Labour perspective. Equally, I do not believe that it is a maverick standpoint. Scratch a nib across the Westminster Cabinet list and you will be underlining the names of several individuals who also feel that the Scottish Parliament must not be allowed to diverge from British policy.

On a note of caution, I am alert to the danger of seeming to overstate this tension between the party in Scotland and England. Senior Millbank officials worked effectively alongside the Scottish party during the election campaign. It may have been tough for some but it worked. Labour mostly rebutted potentially damaging topics like the Private Finance Initiative – even when a senior union leader quit the party in the middle of the campaign over exactly this issue. Other potential problems – like the role of the unions and the Parliament's tax powers – were also contained.

Further, perhaps what is ultimately striking is not any lingering suspicion within the party in London about devolution and the Scottish dimension to politics. The remarkable – and arguably creditable – phenomenon is that, despite those concerns, the Labour Party throughout Britain has proceeded with devolution in response to an apparent demand by the Scottish people.

Labour, though, does confront a structural problem. If they are to be truly the 'Scottish' Labour Party, how much emphasis are they to place upon that element? They remain, after all, also a British party seeking a mandate to govern the United Kingdom. Their Scottish efforts are, in banking terms, a significant branch contribution to a network effort.

In opposition, Labour contrived successfully to appear both Scottish and British, to avoid the problem which beset the Tories, who found themselves labelled an English party in a part of the UK, Scotland, which was turning more towards a Scottish identity.

In government, however, the structural contradictions within Labour have been more evident. The Scottish Nationalists, of course, are entirely a Scottish party. The Scottish Liberal Democrats are autonomous, with a federal relationship to the London-based party. The Tories recreated themselves in Scottish garb. Scottish Labour, by contrast, has witnessed, for example, London party involvement in the vetting of candidates for the Scottish Parliament. For a brief period, Scottish Labour appeared to be trying to out-Nat the Nats. They tried to depict themselves as Scotland's true national party, to contest the SNP on the Scottish identity question. The snag was that this undermined the effectiveness of powerful assets like their UK leader, Tony Blair, and their network of British and European connections.

If Labour was to deck itself in tartan, to depict itself as a quintessentially Scottish party, then every visit to Scotland by Tony Blair would be a reminder that this was a charade, that the Scottish operation was, at least partly, a subset of a bigger machine. What could be an advantage – Labour's British strength – would become potentially a flaw.

Labour concluded that it must retain a Scottish dimension – but should abandon any attempt to outgun the SNP on Scottish national identification. The Nationalists could always trump Labour in that game.

By contrast, Labour leaders concluded they should pursue two paths. Firstly, they should contest the SNP on precise policies of relevance to individual people and families: hence the conflict over taxation. Secondly, they should draw Scottish lessons from their wider links: hence the attempt to translate an international issue, SNP opposition to the NATO bombing of Yugoslavia, into a question mark supposedly placed against the Nationalists' capacity to reflect Scottish opinion.

It is certain that the nature of the Scottish Labour Party will change. It will, I believe, become more autonomous over time and in the face of strong resistance. It will find itself looking more to Holyrood. This change will accelerate as time moves on and, progressively, its Scottish parliamentary leaders are individuals who have had no connection with Westminster and no experience of London politics. That is part of the dynamic of politics.

It seems likely, however, that the inherent tension – between a party dedicated to Scotland and a party seeking UK power – will remain. Labour leaders are adamant they can cope with both dimensions. This will be one of the more intriguing Scottish political stories in the years ahead.

10 The Scottish National Party and Alex Salmond: a Profile

If the very phrase 'Scottish Labour' can be said to represent inherent tension, then Scottish Nationalism has historically combined a series of dichotomies.

Is it a movement or a party? Does it believe in independence at one jump or gradually? Do its voters all believe in independence? Should it adopt a political platform tailored to the existing political structures or focus almost exclusively on overturning these political structures? Is it left, right or centre or none of these?

As party leader since 1990, Alex Salmond is the individual who has played by far the biggest role for the SNP in shaping its response to these questions. Quite frequently, the answers – when fully understood – have departed from popular assumptions about the SNP. Quite regularly, the answers – when fully grasped – have annoyed key members of the party.

Senior strategists concede that debates over these issues have been decidedly sharp at various points in the history of the SNP. They argue, however, that the SNP has broadly settled its overall approach.

The SNP is incontestably now a fully formed political party. In addition, its strategy for achieving independence is now, in reality, completely gradualist. It is a social democratic left-of-centre party with a full policy range encompassing everything from the economy to social issues to defence and foreign affairs.

By addressing these questions – however history ultimately treats them or him – Alex Salmond has claimed a place as one of the most influential Scottish Nationalists of the twentieth century. His record has made him a significant political figure in his own right, a feared adversary.

Salmond is a complex character who blends intensely private thoughts and emotions with an occasionally jovial outward appearance. Perhaps it is his own nature, perhaps it is the essence of Nationalist politics, the perpetual challenge of overturning the established constitutional structure, but Salmond seems more than most a driven politician. He can seem sometimes possessed by politics.

In company, particularly private company, Salmond can be charming, intelligent, diverting and intriguing. He is without doubt one of the closest and most thoughtful observers of the political scene, acutely aware of potential problems and opportunities for his own party and his rivals.

In public, particularly in political debate, he can occasionally seem over-assured. He dislikes failing or indeed admitting weakness in any form. That can be both advantageous and problematic, occasionally at the same time. That determination to remain on top, which is vital for a successful political career, can sometimes spill over into a self-confidence approaching arrogance.

When he made his broadcast in March 1999 criticising the NATO bombing of Yugoslavia, he could have made his intentions clear in measured, restrained vocabulary. Instead, he used the phrase 'unpardonable folly', he chose an absolutist tone in setting himself apart at that time from other political leaders in Britain and NATO.

As a long-term observer of politics – rather than participant – I am probably imbued with an inclination towards the relative approach to events, rather than the absolutist. Indeed, it occurs to me with a slight inward grin that I have even contrived to insert the word 'probably' into that statement of my position.

Political judgement is almost never an absolute question – and is almost always presented as if it were by parties seeking support from the voters and fearing that the electorate will distrust anything short of an unquestioning statement of beliefs. If there were not many sides to each question, if every decision were obvious and clear-cut, then there would be little need for ministerial judgement, little need for political debate and controversy.

It is one of the less appealing aspects of adversarial partisan politics that it seldom permits a genuine discussion of the multi-faceted elements of a political decision. A Minister under pressure cannot commonly voice uncertainty – and ask for a few suggestions. Opposition leaders must give the impression that they have a complete plan ready for implementation if only the Government would get out of the way and allow real talent to take over.

This flaw in partisan politics – and it is only a flaw, not a fatal weakness – is undoubtedly made still worse when parties are strictly whipped into line behind a leadership position or when backbenchers cravenly submit to a leadership line. There is nothing more valuable in democratic politics than the backbencher who gently voices mild concern over a government decision or poses a few questions or wonders whether alternative strategies have been suggested. Opposition criticism can be disdained. Backbench criticism, if modestly voiced, often requires answers.

This digression is intended to argue that determined commitment in politics can be both a virtue and a problem – and is undoubtedly enhanced by the contemporary nature of partisan debate. Alex Salmond has long been a committed individual.

We were at St Andrews University together in the early 1970s, in the days when that noble and magnificent institution was a ferment of New Right politics. Control of the student political body wavered between the Conservatives and the broad Left – but the notion of new thinking, the authentic sense of a movement in creation, was on the Right.

This has been much commented upon – and some may suspect that it is the product of later legend. For once, however, this is a legend which had evident and quite remarkable substance at the time. Students and lecturers were authentically discussing and propagating the free-market, libertarian thinking which was later to influence Margaret Thatcher's Government from 1979.

Michael Forsyth was a St Andrews student at that time – but there were many others, including Dr Madsen Pirie and Eamonn Butler, who went on to found the free-thinking Adam Smith Institute. Collectively, they came to represent part of a growing intellectual challenge to established Conservative thinking, indeed to the consensual establishment more generally, questioning and probing accepted doctrine.

In the midst of this was Alex Salmond, an economics and history student and already a dedicated and thoroughgoing Nationalist. My role then, as now, was that of detached observer. I was editor of the student newspaper, *Aien*, while pursuing a degree in English literature and language.

Salmond in his student days was a lean and energetic individual who wore what I was later to lampoon as a Maoist cap while he rushed about the old town pursuing the cause of Scottish Nationalism. Clearly on the Left, he could easily have been an influential figure within the university Labour Club.

Indeed, he confessed to me that he had once voted Labour at St Andrews in a contest where there was no SNP candidate. He neutralised this, however, by also registering to vote in his home town of Linlithgow – where there was an SNP candidate to gain his support. Such options were available to wandering students.

Salmond, however, is something of a paradox: an undoubted Nationalist who nevertheless displays few of the customary characteristics of cultural Nationalism. He dutifully attends the party's Bannockburn rallies – but appears more at home expounding the alleged economic benefits of independence.

In explaining this, Salmond again confirms his image as a calculating politician, where little is permitted to be haphazard. He told me that 'the SNP weren't short on passion or on commitment to Scotland. They required a bit more economic and political rigour.'[1] Salmond reckoned he could supply that – rather than a lusty voice to add to the chorus of 'Flower of Scotland'.

He explains his own attachment to Nationalism in terms of a relatively simple sense of Scottish identity. He told me: 'The underlying force for change in Scotland is the change in people's perceptions of their identity. Scotland is an infinitely more Scottish place than it was fifty years ago – not in every sense, of course, but in the key senses that matter for political change. People's identity is now Scottish first, in some cases British second, in some cases British not at all. That doesn't mean we are yet in the position where people feel no affinity to Britain but it does mean we are in a position where that affinity is very loose.'

Salmond, of course, has not been universally popular within his own party. A significant section of the SNP distrusts his strategic approach, believing that he does not lay sufficient stress on the core objective of independence. Looking further back, he is distinguished as one of the very few individuals to lead a political party which previously expelled him.

He was – briefly – thrown out of the SNP in the early 1980s as a leading light in the '79 Group which attempted, after the 1979 general election, to reshape the SNP as a party of the Left. This was judged to be factionalism, to be operating a party within a party, and Salmond was disciplined. Other key members of the '79 Group included Roseanna Cunningham, later to be MP and MSP for Perth.

This episode reflects a prevalent theme of earlier Nationalist thinking: that the SNP was in existence solely to agitate for independence and not to make a partisan political choice between Left and Right. Such matters could be left to the electorate after independence.

Indeed, I can well recall SNP conference speakers from earlier days who regarded partisan political comment as virtually a betrayal of the movement, as calculated to alienate one section of the population or another from the true quest of independence. Implicit in this argument was a presumption in some quarters that the SNP itself would not necessarily survive the process of independence, that it might fracture into component political parts after the dissolution of the Union.

It has been Alex Salmond's perpetual endeavour to close down that avenue of thinking within Nationalism, to invite the SNP – in his phrase – to 'make choices within Scotland' as well as simply choosing Scotland.

Born on Hogmanay in 1954, Alex Salmond took the Westminster seat of Banff and Buchan from the Tories in 1987 and became leader of the SNP three years later, succeeding Gordon Wilson. Salmond had earlier been an economist with the Royal Bank of Scotland, specialising in the energy field.

An accomplished politician, he has frequently got under the skin of his rivals. His attention to detail, his neat one-liners, his predilection for interrupting: all are calculated to infuriate partisan opponents. Labour and the Conservatives regard each other as the Opposition. Both are inclined to view Salmond and the SNP as the enemy.

Salmond can be affable, even funny. Far from being a remote intellectual, he is a Hearts supporter who follows racing keenly and likes a bet, pursuing an occasional career as a tipster. He is, however, far from 'clubbable': relatively aloof, a little detached perhaps from the allegiances across the party divide which sometimes form in politics. Perhaps that is influenced by the sense of political mission which so often accompanies Nationalist endeavour.

Yet Salmond has none of the bitter, humourless flavour which such politics occasionally engenders. He is a Nationalist, born and bred, but has little patience for those in his own party who sometimes feel the need to question the patriotism of others who do not share their views. He will attempt to persuade people to vote for the SNP – but does not regard resistance to this message as tantamount to treachery.

Many politicians in other parties, I know, will read that assessment with a shriek of dissent. Salmond, they will say, gives absolutely no quarter to others who do not share his views. He misses no trick in caricaturing Unionist rivals as London lackeys.

All true – but, from long experience of covering Nationalist politics, I would argue that Salmond and others who think like him have wrought a transformation in the SNP. There was a time when, for many in the party, a balanced perspective was to carry a chip on each shoulder.

Salmond, by contrast, epitomises civic, inclusive Nationalism. He urges Scotland to shape her own political destiny, abjures any culture of blaming England and stresses that Scottish citizenship would be based on residence and choice rather than ethnic origin. All, perhaps, familiar opinions now – but there have been moments in the past when it was by no means clear that this was the image which Scottish Nationalism would uniformly present to the world.

The SNP came into existence on 7 April 1934 following the merger of two predecessor parties. There had been a number of pro-independence organisations, often founded on cultural concerns, from the early years of the twentieth century.

The Scots National League was founded in 1921 on a platform of Highland land reform and Gaelic revivalism. The Scottish National Movement grew out of the Scottish literary renaissance. In 1927, John MacCormick – a key figure in Home Rule politics – formed the Glasgow University Scottish Nationalist Association. These groups came together in January 1928 to form the National Party of Scotland. A separate organisation, the Scottish Party, was founded in 1932. Eventually, these two merged in 1934.

The early years of the party were spectacularly unsuccessful on the fringe of Scottish politics. From foundation to the early 1960s, it hovered around 1 per cent in overall support, reflecting the fact, of course, that limited resources meant it presented relatively few candidates: only two, for example, in each of the general elections of 1951 and 1955.

The Nationalists won their first Westminster seat in 1945, when Dr Robert McIntyre won a wartime by-election in Motherwell, only to lose again a few months later in the face of Labour's general election triumph.

In the debate between romantic Nationalism and political pragmatism, McIntyre was very firmly on the pragmatic wing. He was known in his early days as a party hard man who laid down the law against a background of factional conflict. I recall interviewing him in his tidy home in Stirling, not long before his death. He argued that it was critically important to present the Scottish people with a practical, political answer to their unfulfilled sense of national identity. Indeed, he informed me in a quiet, unassertive way that he believed it was only the existence of the SNP as an organised political force which had prevented the wider nationalist movement from descending into sporadic violence. The wilder forces, he said, had been contained.

This argument, presented entirely without sentiment or exaggeration, somewhat startled me but of course we tend to take for granted the virtual absence of violence or indeed disruptive protest from the Home Rule movement in Scotland. It is a curious presumption when one has only to look over the water to the island of Ireland to find an example of a self-government cause which has been immersed in violence.

There have been sporadic incidents, of course, the occasional letter-bomb, and no doubt the security authorities remain vigilant. But the Scottish National Party remains a resolutely democratic and civic organisation. In a Scottish context, such a remark seems trite, almost unnecessary and unwarranted. However, nationalism elsewhere has not been so benign and it is perhaps worthwhile to examine the nature of the Scottish manifestation.

One occasionally hears it said, from both Left and Right, that Scottish Nationalism is inherently wrong, inherently misplaced. Both appear to argue that the phenomenon is disruptive and almost counter-intuitive.

From the Left, one sometimes hears it said that nationalism as a creed runs counter to international cooperation, that there is something inherently fascistic about it. From the Right, one quite frequently hears the argument that nationalism within the British Isles is destructive of the common Unionist heritage, that it further weakens Britain's role in Europe and the wider world. Both also occasionally argue that the Scottish manifestation of nationalism gives succour to disruptive sub-state movements elsewhere.

As I outlined above, I am not an absolutist. These are arguments for the Nationalist movement to address. I have to say that, on balance, I do not find that they are ultimately sustainable in their own right with regard to the SNP.

Firstly, unless there is to be a world government, there must be governmental organisations which are commonly, easily and under-standably based on national allegiance or on combinations of national allegiance. These allegiances have historically been shown to shift. They must ultimately be based on popular acceptance. Otherwise what is in play is not national self-identification but colonialism.

Those on the Right who condemn Scottish Nationalism as dis-ruptive are, ironically, often the same individuals who resent what they regard as European Union interference in the governance of the United Kingdom. They appear to feel – in the manner of Voltaire's Pangloss – that all is for the best in the best of all possible worlds, that the UK has reached a state of absolute constitutional perfection which must not be jeopardised by any questioning from within or from outside.

Those on the Left who question the elemental nature of nation-alism have, I feel, had more substance to their concern in the past. I recall conducting picture research for an item on the SNP and feeling distinctly uncomfortable as I surveyed scenes from a party confer-ence long past when a 'colour party' marched to the front of the hall with banners aloft on commands from the platform.

However, that mock-militaristic element is absent from the mainstream of the modern SNP. Further, Salmond and the broader leadership have taken pains to offer a civic and inclusive nationalism which eschews ethnic origin as an issue.

There are, it should be said, occasional anti-English sentiments raised within the confines of Scottish Nationalism. But the prepon-derant appeal remains inclusive – and the party has made deliberate efforts to recruit support among Scottish residents of varied origin. This is an issue to watch, an issue for the media to monitor, but it is not, I would argue, an incontestable ground for rejecting Scottish Nationalism.

Then there is the question of fostering nationalist movements elsewhere. For the thinkers within the SNP, this is perhaps a more significant challenge. They comfortably summon up comparison with Scandinavia where Norway and Sweden separated, or with the 'velvet divorce' which transformed a single state into the Czech Republic and Slovakia. They tend to turn their thoughts away, however, from the Balkans and ethnic, religious and political division.

This is undoubtedly a challenge for the SNP to surmount on two counts: firstly, the basic question of whether Scottish independence would foster any such divisive elements in the British Isles and, secondly, the question of whether the assertion of Scottish independence might be said to represent an added destabilising challenge to an already shaky global political order.

With regard to this question, I would say this is an issue to be debated across the various parties and among the electorate. The parties must propose and the voters must choose. I do not, however, believe that it is an issue which is clearly settled from first principles, that there is something inherently and unarguably destructive about the notion of Scottish nationalism, of Scottish independence.

It does not seem to me reasonable to argue – from first principles – that Scotland must abandon all notion of independent self-government for fear of encouraging disruptive protest elsewhere or unbalancing geopolitics. To argue that Scotland should not be independent is an entirely valid political point of view. To argue, however, that Scotland cannot and must not be independent is of a different order and is, again, reminiscent of the colonial perspective which argued that Indian or, before that, American independence was inherently wrong.

For the avoidance of any doubt, let me stress two things. Firstly, I do not attribute the above views to the mainstream opponents of the SNP. Almost without exception, senior politicians including successive UK Prime Ministers have freely conceded that Scotland could be independent – and have been content to argue their case against such an initiative. They have argued from pragmatism, not generally from spurious first principles. Occasionally, however, the other form of reasoning has been allowed to muddy the waters.

Secondly, to examine the counter-standpoint, I am not for a moment asserting that the case for Scottish independence can be asserted positively from first principles. Rather I believe that nations are political and constitutional arrangements, generally derived from geographical and historical motivation with a continuing existence dependent on internal popular acceptance and the tolerance of other states.

In short, there is no reason, inherently, why Scotland should be a nation state. Equally, there is no reason, inherently, why Scotland should not be a nation state. The same, incidentally, applies to the United Kingdom or France or Germany. Under their current boundaries, each is a political and popular construct.

The SNP's contention is that Scotland naturally forms a national governmental unit. Other parties contend that Scotland's future prospects rest more securely on shared sovereignty within the United Kingdom. These contentions represent a political choice. Neither can be said to be either inherently right or inherently wrong.

In its earliest days, the Nationalist movement in Scotland largely pursued efforts to build a consensus with supporters of various forms of Home Rule in established parties. Frustration in that field led the SNP to follow the path of seeking partisan electoral support. The modern party is generally traced to Winnie Ewing's by-election defeat of the Labour Party in Hamilton in 1967. There have been other by-election successes: Margo McDonald in Glasgow Govan in 1973; Jim Sillars, again in Govan, in 1988; Roseanna Cunningham in Perth and Kinross in 1995.

The party's period of greatest apparent promise in Westminster politics occurred in the 1970s. In the February 1974 election, the Nationalists took 21.9 per cent of the popular vote in Scotland along with seven seats. In the October contest the same year, they increased that to 30.4 per cent and eleven seats. The objective at that time was to secure a majority of the Westminster seats in Scotland – and to petition for repeal of the Act of Union.

Although no formal renunciation has been made, it is clear now that the Westminster route is unrealistic. The distribution of Nationalist support, relatively thinly spread, certainly militates against

success in a first-past-the-post system. Even with nearly a third of
the popular vote in the later election of 1974, the Nationalists gained
less than a sixth of the seats in the Commons from Scotland. Other
performances, of course, have fallen far short of even that peak.

In any case, the advent of a Scottish Parliament has changed the
rules. The Nationalists will now concentrate their endeavours on
winning success in a purely Scottish political arena. The mandate for
independence is now defined in terms of support within the
Edinburgh Parliament – a mandate which, the party concedes, was
denied in the 1999 contest.

In the previous chapter, I spotlighted the tensions within the
Labour campaign in the Scottish elections of 1999. They were,
however, alluded to relatively obliquely during the campaign itself.
By contrast, the apparent tensions in the SNP camp became the focus
of substantial media attention.

Nationalists will say, with some justification, that one reason for
that disparity in treatment is that Scotland's newspapers are generally
hostile to the SNP. Journalists working for papers which supported
Labour or the Union or both were, instinctively or under editorial
guidance, on the lookout for cracks in the Nationalist construction.

Equally, however, there were flaws in the SNP approach reminiscent of an earlier Labour Party. Party leaders did not prepare their
response exhaustively to each and every eventuality, each and every
consequence of a policy announcement. To be blunt, they occasionally
resorted to bluster to cover gaps in presentation. In a separate chapter
on finance, I intend to examine the problems which surrounded the
SNP's publication of its economic assessment. In summary, it was
detailed but not detailed enough.

There were other examples, seemingly trivial but instructive. One
particular day, the Nationalists volunteered a policy for enhancing
the teaching of modern languages in primary schools. This was their
key announcement for the day in question. At the news conference,
I inquired: 'Which languages would you propose to teach to primary
children?' Nicola Sturgeon, the education spokesperson, was unable
to specify, although she did indicate a comforting preference for
European tongues. She was rescued by Mike Russell, the Chief
Executive, who suggested, as I recall, French and Italian.

In the early stage of the campaign, there was a substantial media
focus upon Alex Salmond. It was claimed that he appeared out of

sorts. There was vague talk of problems at the core of the SNP. It should be said immediately that no evidence whatsoever was adduced to back up these claims of fundamental or structural difficulties.

I should add, however, that the party leader did not seem to me to be at his best on the day the manifesto was launched, Thursday, 8 April.

It is difficult to be precise. His opening presentation seemed low-key. He seemed unnecessarily irritated by some of the questions. Certainly, they ranged far beyond the scope of the manifesto itself but that is part of the election process. The sharp leader – and Salmond is incontestably sharp – tackles and rebuts questions, the penetrating and the vacuous, the distinct and the repetitious. That particular day, he seemed to me to be wearying of the task.

After the manifesto launch, a photocall was held at the old Royal High School in Edinburgh. I took the chance to suggest, solicitously, to Salmond that he looked and sounded a little tired. I wondered whether a previous problem with back pain had resurfaced. Never, he insisted, had he felt better.

SNP insiders say one potential problem arose with persistent media enquiries about peripheral matters, not related to politics. As so often before in other circumstances, these enquiries came to nothing but it is at least possible that they distracted Salmond to some extent from the task in hand. Others concede that the entire leadership team, relatively small in number, began the formal campaign somewhat fatigued after the extensive and lengthy preparations of the build-up period.

Equally, though, Salmond performed well at subsequent points throughout the campaign. He argued his case vigorously and with conviction in the various broadcast debates. If there were problems at the outset – and I believe there were – then Salmond and the wider party rallied to give a good account of themselves as the election contest progressed.

More generally, informed sources concede that the SNP was simply outgunned by Labour. The Nationalist campaign was bigger than ever before, it had more resources, it was highly effective. Yet it still could not match Labour – where the Scottish and London organisations combined to produce a constant flow of research material, sharp attacks on opponents and round-the-clock rebuttal. Nationalists were strong on the ground. Labour had the edge at headquarters level.

One senior SNP source told me that they later identified a basic flaw in their approach. They were unable, for lack of personnel, to separate long-range strategy from day-to-day planning. The same individuals had to conduct both tasks, placing enormous physical and time pressure upon them. Every informed analysis of Tony Blair's election success has identified this separation of powers as a key element in ensuring that the 'big picture' was not lost in the basic drive to run the campaign on a daily basis.

Internal SNP critics claim that the problem was exacerbated by the dominance of a relatively small leadership clique which was determined to maintain control of the campaign. Naturally, key leadership figures do not see it that way.

However, there is already talk within the upper reaches of the SNP of transforming the nature of campaigning in time for the next Scottish parliamentary elections. Some talk of Project 003 – referring to the date of the next Holyrood contest. By that point, it is argued, the party must have substantially refined its policy-making process and have completed the division of strategic and organisational planning.

I would argue, further, that there was a structural problem confronting the SNP. From the moment in September 1997, when the Nationalists joined Labour and the Liberal Democrats in campaigning for a double Yes vote in the referendum, they faced the potential for political dysfunction. They became again what they had been in the earlier 1979 referendum: a party of independence arguing for devolution, arguing for another party's platform, pledging to make that devolved Parliament work for the benefit of Scotland.

I should stress that I believe the strategy of offering to work with the grain of devolution was correct – and inevitable. The voting public, who often blur the distinction between devolution and independence, would have found an SNP No campaign in the referendum incomprehensible. Similarly, the voters would not take kindly to a party which implied that it was out to undermine a devolved Parliament before it had even opened.

The SNP had to contest the Parliament on offer: the devolved Parliament. They could not fight the election purely on independence. An independent Parliament does not exist. While working with devolution, they could not and did not wish to ignore their core objective of independence. The result – a mixed message of devolution and independence – was inevitable.

That does not mean that the consequences for the SNP of this inevitable strategy were necessarily positive or even neutral. The Nationalists, I believe, faced a fundamental mismatch which they have yet to resolve satisfactorily. They struggled, in the face of Labour attacks, to transform independence into a choice deferred, into an issue to be settled by a subsequent referendum.

Strictly speaking, the SNP were only seeking to match tactics deployed by Labour at the 1997 general election. Labour argued then that a vote for Tony Blair was not inherently a vote for devolution, that there would be a subsequent referendum, that the election hinged rather on issues like jobs, health and education. But in the 1999 Scottish campaign – by dint of persistent repetition – Labour contrived, at least in part, to equate a vote for the SNP in a devolved Parliament with a vote for independence.

Naturally, there were other reasons why the SNP did not win more seats. Some voters may have been deterred by the Nationalist plan to reverse for Scotland only the Chancellor's planned cut of a penny off the UK standard rate of income tax, although SNP leaders insist that was a vote-winning formula.

The Kosovo broadcast may have had an impact. One senior strategist suggested to me that, while the broadcast had been entirely right and justifiable, it had perhaps cost the party three to four seats, either in terms of key marginals or numbers from the top-up lists. Such an assessment, of course, is impossible to ratify or challenge. Others in the SNP say there was evidence that canvassers faced initial hostility immediately after the broadcast but that the impact waned and that the criticism came mostly from individuals who were determined to vote against the SNP in any case.

I am aware that I am in danger of over-emphasising the negative side of the campaign for the SNP. There were a series of successes. The party produced some effective hits against Labour: for example, on the use of private finance for public projects.

There was also a change of emphasis when Salmond took the campaign out on to the streets, declaring that it was time for SNP leaders to 'get the jaickets off and get stuck in'. This switch was prompted by internal party anger at the nature of newspaper coverage but it did seem, psychologically, to energise the wider Nationalist campaign, to convince supporters that the party was ready to fight. A negative motivation – anxiety over press coverage – was turned into a positive gain for grassroots Nationalists.

The Sean Connery rally in Edinburgh on 26 April was memorable – if not, perhaps, a seminal moment in Scottish politics, as some Nationalists appeared to think. Most newspaper coverage spotlighted Connery's condemnation of the 'control freaks' in, presumably, Labour who had overturned the collaborative spirit of the referendum. My own personal recollection is of Connery's forecast that the devolved Parliament would 'evolve with dignity' into full-scale independence.

The result of the election, too, was relatively successful for the SNP. Their 1997 voting performance would probably have translated into around twenty-eight Scottish parliamentary seats under the revised electoral system. They obtained thirty-five – a significant advance – and narrowed the gap behind Labour, especially in the second vote.

The Scottish Parliamentary elections – and the Nationalists hope a little star quality will rub off from Sean Connery, their most famous supporter, 26 April 1999. (Kindly supplied by The Scotsman Publications Ltd.)

The problem for the SNP was the contrast between relatively successful reality and earlier expectation of far more. Opinion polls in the summer of 1998 had suggested that the Nationalists were in the lead over Labour. In addition, while they took Inverness East, they failed to capture any other key constituency seats. Victories in Govan and Ochil – while they would not have fundamentally altered the arithmetic of the Parliament – would have added a presentational gloss to the SNP's performance.

These, however, are transient matters compared with the question of core strategy. Policies can be altered. The new cadre of thirty-five salaried MSPs and their back-up team will in themselves enhance the potential for the Nationalists to combat Labour. They will form a state-funded vanguard for independence. The deeper issue is the party's core objective and how it is presented.

Without stating it too bluntly, the Nationalists have substantially changed their strategy over the years. As I have previously noted, the SNP used to argue that they would win a majority of seats in a political contest in Scotland, they would then negotiate an independence settlement with London and they would subsequently submit that settlement to the Scottish people for endorsement or rejection in a referendum. Strictly speaking, that avenue remains open. If the Nationalists were to win an absolute majority of seats in the Edinburgh Parliament and if Westminster were to accept that as a legitimate mandate for independence talks, then the previously established path might be pursued.

A new realism is abroad in the upper reaches of the SNP, however. They know they are not going to win a majority of the Scottish seats at Westminster. They know, too, that the PR voting system was deliberately designed to make it difficult for them to win a majority of the Scottish parliamentary seats on their customary minority voting support, even a substantial minority.

The true objective now is to help the devolved Parliament to bed down, to demonstrate that Scottish Home Rule can be successful and to assemble at some subsequent point a coalition of interests for an independence referendum, comprising Nationalists and perhaps free-thinking Labour politicians, Liberal Democrats or even, unlikely as it might sound, Scottish Tories who believe that a party of the Right could flourish in a separate Scotland.

In the mean while, the flame of independence is to be kept

burning by a persistent campaign which parallels the party's efforts to demonstrate the relative success and popularity of devolution. Again, there is a significant body of opinion – including within the SNP's Shadow Cabinet and Scottish parliamentary group – which believes that the party's advocacy of independence has become too apologetic. These critics were furious when independence was listed in last place among ten key objectives for the May election.

However, Alex Salmond made his intentions clear long before those Scottish parliamentary elections. In a lecture in November 1998,[2] Salmond foreshadowed his determination that the Nationalists must work within the new devolved Parliament rather than following any alternative strategy such as attempting to destabilise the new body in the hope that disquiet and popular discontent might provide a motivation towards independence.

Salmond said then: 'I see this period as one that cries out for ideas – practical ideas for the future governance of Scotland in the devolved areas within the competence of the Parliament which can be implemented in the first four-year term and ideas for the nation as it begins to gain experience of government and looks to building on that experience.'

For a Nationalist party, this is of course a potentially hazardous approach. Two problems loom. The voters may never turn to independence, however positively the SNP presents itself in a devolved Scottish Parliament. The party meanwhile may end up resorting to support or tolerance of devolution.

As I have said, a substantial section of the party – including key senior individuals – distrust the gradualist approach. Whatever assurances are given to the contrary, they believe that Salmond and his aides are trying to lull the Scottish people, to lure them into independence by stealth. Salmond's critics do not believe such an approach can work. They fear that, in the mean time, it is the SNP which will suffer a transformation by stealth, steadily shedding its support for all-out independence.

The prospect is not that the Scottish National Party actively turns against independence. It is rather that key Nationalists among the thirty-five-strong group in the new Parliament and among their supporters may become inured to devolution. They may become institutionalised by the devolved settlement, rather like fervent Eurosceptics who are elected Members of the European Parliament and are then steadily entranced by the apparent power and importance of Brussels and Strasbourg.

Gradualism may become so much a part of their psyche that independence is increasingly marginalised. If they come to believe that all-out independence is hard to sell, then it may become tempting to play down that aspect in pursuit of political power or cross-party accommodations within the Scottish Parliament.

One parallel is with Catalonia, one of the semi-autonomous provinces of Spain with its capital in the beautiful and wealthy city of Barcelona. The Catalans have a clear cultural identity, their own language which they propagate enthusiastically and a history, admittedly relatively distant, of self-government distinct from Spain. During his years as leader of the Catalan Nationalists, Jordi Pujol has contrived to maintain relatively firm control of the region's government by vigorously pursuing sectoral interests for Catalonia and by exerting political pressure on Madrid.

He is a politician for whom the adjective 'wily' might have been invented. Pujol, however, has come to disdain any notion of breaking away from Spain. Indeed, he became notably irritated when I asked him about this prospect during an interview.

Pujol's power base lies in playing Catalan provincial interests against Spanish federal interests. Equally, he is able to exert a degree of influence at the European level – maintaining a Catalan presence in Brussels, for example – without over-reaching himself and usurping or appearing to usurp Madrid's role in representing the interests of the Spanish member state. In short, he knows his political place.

The parallel, of course, is not exact. Catalonia's relationship with Spain is decidedly more subordinate than that between Scotland and England. There are fewer of the overt signs of nationhood such as a separate legal system, separate church and separate sporting teams which mark out Scotland. In addition, Catalonia is only one of a series of provincial governments which cover the whole of Spain, with powers which vary according to each area's demands.

However, senior Scottish Nationalists are aware of the Catalan model.

The thinkers among the SNP leadership privately acknowledge that it is at least theoretically possible that Scottish Nationalism might go the same way, accommodating in part to the devolved settlement.

Again, I stress that I do not remotely envisage that the SNP would abandon the objective of independence. Rather the potential scenario is that the emphasis falls ever more strongly upon making devolution work, upon perhaps extending the powers of the devolved Parliament into new domestic areas such as the party suggested during the passage of the Scotland Act. Gradualism becomes semi-permanent.

In a curious way, the globalisation of politics may militate both for and against this scenario. On the one hand, it is entirely possible to envisage Nationalists – or at least ardent Home Rulers – who would not necessarily agitate permanently for the establishment of a separate Scottish armed force or separate diplomatic network. Such individuals may well be content to extend Scotland's domestic potency and leave such historic trappings of statehood to wider, international collective organisations.

Equally, however, I believe that the European Union dimension may provide pressure the other way. Since adopting a pro-European policy, the SNP has made much of the demand for a 'seat at the European top table'. It is difficult to see that lessening in the immediate future unless the UK Government handles particularly sensitively the accommodation of Scottish interests within the new collective arrangements for relations with Europe.

The familiar answer to Nationalist demands for Scotland to become a distinct member of the EU is that Scotland has access to greater influence through adherence to the UK, one of the most powerful members of the club with considerable voting and diplomatic clout. The UK's punch, it is argued, can be exercised in Scotland's interests – while small member states gaze on impotently from the sidelines.

However, if that were incontestably true and if it superseded all other interests, then Vienna would seek to have its opinions within the EU advanced by Berlin and Dublin would defer to London.

There is, undoubtedly, merit in the argument that a bigger nation can exert greater influence. There can, however, be a counter-argument: that a small member nation can occasionally extract a concession on an issue of vital interest to its own citizens in return for supporting a larger voting bloc on wider matters. Such leverage may, of course, diminish with expansion of the EU, especially if the Union's internal voting system is reformed to narrow still further the scope for individual nations to exert a veto.

For now, the demand for European representation is likely to exert considerable sway within the SNP, perhaps helping to keep it focused on the wider aim of independence. In addition, Salmond's main emphasis is upon financial powers. I asked him how he defined independence in an interdependent continent and world. It was, he said, controlling the substantial portion of state revenues which were not voluntarily pooled with the European Union. He told me: 'I would have thought the defining element of independence is controlling 97 per cent of your revenues, as within Europe. Even if it is 90 per cent, that is definable independence.'

So there are longer-term fiscal and political goals to keep the Nationalists wanting more. Equally, however, as I have outlined above, there may be pressures the other way. What if it could be demonstrated that the Scottish people had become satisfied or relatively satisfied with the degree of self-government tendered by devolution or by some further enhancement of devolved powers?

The gradualists in the SNP might come to feel that the only obstacle to power in the available, devolved Parliament was their adherence to independence, to a radical transformation of the Parliament's nature. Even subconsciously, as they become accustomed to the new Parliament, to its devolved dynamic, they may find themselves trying to play and win the game by the existing rules, rather than devoting all or most of their efforts to changing the rules.

When I interviewed Gordon Wilson,[3] the former leader of the party, he was alert to this prospect. He told me: 'There are temptations in following the Catalan model because they can settle for regional status and it has a certain logic, it has merit in itself.' Wilson, of course, was speaking as a 'so-called fundamentalist' who has tended to regard devolution as a trap to placate the Scots. He would be utterly opposed to succumbing to the temptations of the Catalan model.

From that standpoint, he told me he was not keen on an early independence referendum. He added: 'You should only hold referenda when you are going to win them. There's not the consensus yet for independence. It's coming, though.'

Wilson offered his view that the Nationalists were far safer in opposition in a devolved Parliament, that they would be less inclined to fall under the spell of devolved ministerial power.

Finally, he envisaged that the Scottish National Party might – I stress might – diverge or even split under the new Scottish political settlement, that it might be impossible to sustain the gradualists and the fundamentalists under the same political banner. Wilson's scenario is that the party might well be pulled in two directions, one motivation being to work with the grain of devolution, the other to press relentlessly for independence.

Politics is dynamic. All parties represent an assembled coalition of interests, sometimes more or less united, sometimes frankly uneasy. When an emerging divisive issue becomes more important than the motivation which initially forged the coalition, then the party realigns or splits. This happened with the Liberals over Irish Home Rule and, more recently, it has regularly loomed as a possibility for the Conservatives over Europe.

Salmond and other Nationalist leaders, of course, do not envisage any realignment in the SNP or the wider Nationalist movement – at least, not this side of independence. They believe that a core position has been established: to demonstrate the worth of limited Home Rule and so advance to independence, however that is defined in an interdependent continent and world.

As a concrete example of that supposedly united perspective, Salmond included several leading fundamentalists within his Shadow ministerial team.

Constant unity, however, is far from guaranteed. It is not intrinsic in Scottish politics that there must be one party and only one party advocating autonomous Scottish government. It is at least theoretically possible that there might be a divergence between the gradualists and the fundamental supporters of independence.

It is instructive to reflect that just as there is no single definition of devolved power, so there may be no single goal shared by those who would commonly call themselves Nationalists. Certain earlier advocates of nationalism, indeed, were occasionally pressing for reform which might now be characterised as devolution.

Rather, Scotland's constitutional options may be represented as a spectrum, ranging from full incorporation within the United Kingdom through various forms of devolution to virtual domestic autonomy to independence inside or outside the European Union.

To emphasise, I am by no means firmly forecasting a rift within the SNP. The more likely scenario remains that the gradualists and the fundamentalists will find a way of accommodating their differing positions, their different emphases within a common party structure. Just as for Labour, however, the new Scotland may bring pressures as well as potential for the SNP.

Notes

1. Interview with Alex Salmond, 4 December 1998.
2. Lecture by Alex Salmond, Strathclyde University, 26 November 1998.
3. Interview with Gordon Wilson, 28 November 1998.

11 The Scottish Conservative Party and David McLetchie: a Profile

Political parties are permanently in search of the fabled 'big idea'. This can be a policy initiative like the Tory endorsement of the sale of council houses to sitting tenants. It can be an ear-grabbing slogan like Tony Blair's determination to remain 'tough on crime and tough on the causes of crime'.

It must catch the imagination, scramble for attention. There is apparently little room for complexity or subtlety in the modern political world. Most politicians now follow the doctrine: outline what you intend to say, say it, then sum up what you've just said.

In this regard, I am reminded of the splendid parody of political campaigning which, I think, I first heard in a Liberal review, that scurrilous self-parody which was such a feature of Liberal conferences in the past.

The sketch portrayed a team of earnest Liberal campaigners, beards and sandals at the ready, rehearsing their chant in the manner of left-wing protesters at a jobs rally or outside the US Embassy. 'What do we want?', the lead chanter demanded. Came the reply: 'The single transferable vote in multi-member constituencies!' The prompter pursued: 'When do we want it?' Answer: 'In due course.' You get the point. No punch.

Not long after he was elected leader of the Scottish Conservatives,

David McLetchie was asked by *The Sun* to outline his vision for Scotland.[1] 'We stand', he replied, 'for the folk that take their turn at cleaning the stair.' Perhaps not quite the intellectual ferment of Hayek's *The Road to Serfdom*. Not quite the call to political revolution of *The Communist Manifesto*. Yet for Scotland's Conservatives, a worthy and indeed noteworthy aim.

Andy Nicoll – the paper's Scottish political correspondent and an estimable Dundonian with a droll sense of humour – drew upon his own origins to remark that McLetchie's objective appeared to owe more to the Broons, Scotland's couthiest family of comic fame, than to contemporary politics.

McLetchie was, however, acknowledging and reflecting a fairly obvious fact. For a range of reasons, the Scottish Tories appeared to lose touch with the everyday concerns of the Scottish people. Further, they came to be seen as quintessentially an English party, remote and distant.

Unfairly or not, their crusade for the Union, coupled with fervently expressed opposition to devolution, conspired to place them outside the Scottish body politic. While not actively anti-Scottish, they appeared to some extent to be something other than Scottish. Their loyalties appeared to lie elsewhere.

This was bluntly admitted on the very first page of the Tories' manifesto for the Scottish Parliament, which acknowledged that the Scottish people had come to believe that Conservative policies had 'London stamped all over them'. The manifesto reflected on the general election collapse and noted plaintively: 'On May 1st 1997 the people of Scotland told us what they thought – we got it wrong.'

This manifesto was published on 8 April 1999. The day before, a leaked copy arrived for me in a plain brown envelope delivered to the BBC's Edinburgh office. Consequently, I was able to regale BBC viewers that evening with early news of a political first: a manifesto which opened with a public apology.

At the 1997 general election in Scotland, the Tories had indeed lost every remaining Westminster seat. The obliteration which had been predicted for the 1992 contest finally worked through. From that moment, the Scottish Tories set out on a long transitional road to change, a process which mirrored the party's previous internal transformations.

According to the party's historian Gerald Warner,[2] the predecessors of the modern Scottish Conservatives were 'the only party consistently and unanimously opposed to the Union' between the Scottish and English Parliaments in 1707. Warner traces the Tories back to the Jacobites of the late seventeenth and early eighteenth centuries.

In sharp contrast, for much of the twentieth century, Conservative adherents north of the Border were known as the Scottish Unionists, founding their appeal firmly upon the preservation of the United Kingdom and adopting the nomenclature of Northern Ireland politics in the process. In addition to their customary middle- and upper-class support, the Tories were able to garner working-class Protestant votes as a consequence. In short, they pitched for the Orange vote.

Tory fortunes have long vacillated in Scotland. They quailed before the all-powerful Liberal Party in the nineteenth century. They thrived in the early 1930s, partly as a consequence of internal problems besetting the emerging Labour Party. Finally they peaked in 1955, gaining a majority of Scotland's seats, thirty-six, and more significantly an overall majority of votes cast, attracting 50.1 per cent of the popular vote in Scotland. To date, they are the only party to achieve this feat in Scotland since the arrival of universal suffrage.

From that point, the history of the party in Scotland up to the Scottish parliamentary contest was one of slow, persistent decline – punctuated by occasional brief revivals. The general election of 1997 gave them 17.5 per cent of the popular vote and left them at that time with no Westminster MPs, no members of the European Parliament and no Scottish councils under their control.

The Scottish election of May 1999 returned them to parliamentary politics. They gained eighteen seats in the new Scottish legislature, one more than the Liberal Democrats who ended up joining the governing coalition with Labour. Yet the Conservative share of the vote – midway between 15 and 16 per cent in both the constituency and list sections – was still a very poor performance, worse even than the 1997 result which was widely and rightly described as a catastrophe for the Tories. The Scottish Conservatives did not win a single constituency seat, although they came very close in Ayr.

Expectations, however, played a part in the party's relatively buoyant response to the outcome. Scotland had got used to the Tories as a marginal party. They had become accustomed – unlike their counterparts in England – to deploying a particular species of self-deprecating, black humour in describing their own prospects. When they won seats – albeit through a PR system which they had deplored – it seemed like a triumph, particularly when they came ahead of the LibDems. Consequently, they smiled and smiled; but, privately, their sharper strategists knew that the result confirmed that the Tories still face a substantial fight to regain their status in Scotland.

The decline of the Tories has been attributed to various factors: the steadily entrenched, seeming dominance of the Labour Party, the rise of a rival power base in the shape of the SNP, individual constituency targeting by the Liberal Democrats, Scottish hostility to Margaret Thatcher.

Many Tories, however, would concede that there has been an underlying cause, a core problem. Across Europe, parties of the Right like the Gaullists and the German CDU have tended to represent themselves as the patriotic parties. It is certainly a card which the Tories play strongly in England. The trouble for the Tories in Scotland is that they came to be identified with the wrong patriotism – wrong, at least, for their hopes of electoral success.

They regarded themselves as British patriots. The voters in Scotland, however, steadily came to see matters in a different light. Particularly under Margaret Thatcher, the Tories became identified in the popular mind with England – even with English nationalism – at a time when Scottish identity was apparently becoming more important to Scottish voters. The Tories were brandishing the Union flag while Scotland was tentatively, then confidently, grasping the Saltire. For a party seeking electoral support, this was a disastrous combination.

An earlier indication of this trend was perhaps the evaporation of the working-class Orange vote. A few Tories still regret the party's decision effectively to disavow any appeal to such sentiments when, in 1965, the party formally changed its name. The Scottish Unionists became the Scottish Conservative and Unionist Party. From that moment on, the Conservative element was more prominent than the Unionist – although the second strain was never entirely neglected. Indeed, it was frequently stressed.

The West of Scotland in particular remains sadly sectarian, even today. Indeed, it is one of the more depressing aspects of Scotland that even supposedly intelligent individuals in business or public life can occasionally find it funny or faintly daring to refer to the supposed icons of Scottish sectarianism, to prate of Parkhead and Ibrox in terms remote from football. Sectarianism is, of course, insular, small-minded, sapping and tedious.

In reality, however, any serious prospect of appealing to an Orange vote had vanished for the Tories by the time of their name change. The vote no longer existed, at least in a form which could be targeted and gathered. The Scottish working and middle classes steadily came to base their electoral choices on matters other than religion: on financial motivation or class loyalty or, increasingly, Scottish identity.

If Warner is right in tracing the origins of the Scottish Tories, then politics had come full circle. The party which began as the inheritors of Jacobite sentiment, implacably opposed to the Union of 1707, had arrived close to the point of obliteration partly as a consequence of their apparently unquestioning support for that Union.

I discussed this phenomenon with Sir Malcolm Rifkind,[3] who became President of the Scottish Conservatives after losing his seat and his Cabinet place in the general election of 1997. Rifkind endorsed the analysis that the Conservatives had lost out partly as a consequence of their popular identification as an English party at a time of growing Scottish identity.

That, he said, had been particularly evident in the Scottish reaction to Margaret Thatcher, Prime Minister from 1979 until 1990. Assuming an ironic grin, he told me: 'She was three things for the Scots: she was a woman, she was English and she was a Tory. They could forgive one or maybe two of these things. But they could not forgive all three.'

Rifkind, however, drew comfort from a sense of history when he pointed out that the Tories had been down before in Scotland, subsequently to thrive.

He confirmed that the Tories in government, during his tenure as Scottish Secretary and at other points, had regularly considered the question of Scottish governance, had looked indeed at various points at the issue of an elected Scottish legislature or assembly.

It had always been concluded, relatively swiftly, that the Tories could not endorse legislative devolution. For one thing, they were, mostly, against it in principle. They believed that asymmetrical devolution – providing legislative power for Scotland without comparable provision for England – threatened to jeopardise the Union.

For another, there would have been intolerable internal strain from such a policy. It might have bought passing popularity from the Scottish voters – although that is questionable – but it would have fractured the coalition of interests which comprised Scottish Tory activists, outraging the staunch Unionists and baffling the undifferentiated middle while probably stopping short of satisfying the generally unstated demands of the devolutionists, closet and self-confessed, within Tory ranks.

Seen in that light, then, the 1997 general election result and the subsequent establishment of a Scottish Parliament cleared the decks for the Tories – although it was, of course, a thoroughly painful way to achieve such an aim. Their objective has been to neutralise the Scottish Question, to convince Scots that the Tories are again at least worthy of consideration on the basis of economic and social policies, free from the taint of being a party whose roots lie outside Scotland.

The Tories have toyed with the Scottish Question repeatedly in the past. As outlined elsewhere in this book, most of the administrative devolutionary changes, including the establishment of the Scottish Office, have come under their supervision. John Major's Government attempted – in a process popularly known as Taking Stock – to reform the handling of Scottish business, including more imaginative use of the Scottish Grand Committee of MPs.

In addition, at various points in the past the Tories have issued statements of support for some form of elected devolution – most obviously through Edward Heath's Declaration of Perth at the Scottish Tory conference in 1968. In the 1979 referendum, the former Conservative Prime Minister Lord Home advised Scots to vote No – so that a better devolution Bill could be subsequently introduced. To no one's surprise, this freelance offer later came to nothing when the Tories gained power.

Such initiatives reflected political pragmatism, political fear. The Scottish Tories could see that Scotland apparently wanted some imprecise form of self-government, some governmental recognition of Scottish identity. In the circumstances, they occasionally attempted to go with that flow. Indeed, many contemporary Scottish Conservatives have form as past advocates of devolution, a legacy of their party's vacillation on the topic. Occasionally, entertaining little pamphlets from the past, scribbled by youthful enthusiasts, have turned up to bring a bashful glow to the faces of their now-mature authors.

The big change in Tory attitudes to devolution came when Margaret Thatcher became leader of the Conservatives in 1975. After a very brief period sustaining the Tories' Declaration of Perth tolerance of the policy, she came out firmly against elected devolution. In opposition, she condemned the Labour Government's 1970s attempts to devolve power to Scotland so severely and with so little quarter that key members of her Scottish front bench, including Alick Buchanan-Smith and Malcolm Rifkind, felt obliged to resign their posts.

In truth, her principled, even dogmatic stance was more in tune with the underlying attitudes of the party. Customarily polite and docile towards the leadership, the Scottish Tories had broadly opted to live with Heath's Declaration. They were, however, frankly happier with the Thatcherite approach. They were and are Unionists. They did not trust devolution – and in many respects still feel exactly the same way.

Their approach was more in keeping with the appeal issued by Michael Forsyth in a speech to West of Scotland Tories in January 1996. Speaking of devolution in terms which make it sound like a rabies scare, he urged the party: 'I implore you, for the sake of all our people, to do everything humanly within your power to alert your friends, your neighbours, your communities to the dangers of what is being planned for them.'

Forsyth duly implored, the Tories duly alerted their friends, the people duly voted overwhelmingly for devolution and the party duly turned around and endorsed the change which they had reviled for years.

What has happened is a bit like the scenario which some Tories privately envisage with regard to the party's disputes over European integration. Quietly, a few senior Tories are praying that Blair will manage to take Britain into the Single European Currency, that the issue will be settled, that it will no longer be available as the standard around which Euro-sceptics can cluster. This is not, of course, the formal leadership perspective which remains hostile to British membership of EMU (European Monetary Union) for the lifetime of this Westminster Parliament and the next.

With regard to Scotland, the position is somewhat similar. The Tories did not like devolution. They did not want it. They knew that their stance was electorally damaging but could not see a way out of the bind. Now that devolution has arrived, the correct strategy – frankly, the only strategy – is to accept change, to strive to be supportive: to make the best of it.

Following the 1997 defeat and the subsequent devolution referendum, the party rallied. There was a curious sense of relief that the issue was so clear-cut. The Tories had no Scottish MPs, Labour had a huge Westminster majority, devolution was certain to happen. There could be no question, no argument that something had to change.

The changes were overtly substantial. Firstly, a commission chaired by Lord Strathclyde produced a new structure for the party, sweeping away the old division between the formal, professional party and the voluntary Scottish Conservative and Unionist Association. The title of the Strathclyde report, 'Made in Scotland', signalled the new direction.

Then Sir Malcolm Rifkind chaired a policy commission which outlined the party's direction, subsequently reflected in the Scottish parliamentary manifesto. At the launch of the commission report in Edinburgh, Rifkind reflected that a new, more open politics now appeared possible. He spoke of a 'golden age' returning to Scotland, a throwback to the Enlightenment and Edinburgh's reign as the Athens of the North.

The age was not sufficiently golden, however, to tempt Sir Malcolm and other senior party figures like the Chairman Raymond Robertson to put their names forward for the Scottish Parliament. They preferred to retain the possibility of returning to Westminster. It was left consequently to David McLetchie to head the party's pitch for the Scottish parliamentary campaign after he defeated ex-MP Phil Gallie in a leadership contest.

McLetchie was caricatured, often by people who did not know him especially well, as the quintessential grey man. He came to the leadership, admittedly, as an Edinburgh solicitor, bearing the badge of Scottish professional respectability. Equally, however, he is a supporter of Heart of Midlothian Football Club – an allegiance which brings with it sufficient pain to fire the soul of even the steeliest legal figure.

I will freely confess that I like David McLetchie. For the avoidance of doubt, I should state that I like each of Scotland's political leaders. (For the avoidance of further doubt, I should state that my personal approbation of politicians is not universal.)

McLetchie was a student associate and longstanding friend of Sir Michael Forsyth, which led him in early newspaper portraits to be categorised as a rabid, unthinking right-wing zealot.

Firstly, Forsyth himself is considerably more thoughtful and open to ideas than some caricatures would represent. Secondly, McLetchie has not borrowed his every waking thought from his colleague. His economic thinking is free-market; he is, in short, a self-confessed Conservative. However, he has demonstrated the potential to be open to a range of ideas on the social policy front. The luxury of opposition, of course, particularly in the early days, is that one can voice such ideas freely.

McLetchie's Edinburgh origins were relatively humble, particularly in comparison with the silver spoons delivered orally to several of his party colleagues. Despite his staid profession, he can be exceptionally droll company and is an acute observer of politics.

Cicero he is not. The attempt to build up his oratorical presentation at the Scottish Conservatives spring 1999 conference in Perth backfired somewhat. He appeared a little uncomfortable with some of the rhetorical twists made available to him. In addition, he puzzled a few colleagues by delivering then, in advance of the elections, a pledge that the Tories would effectively support Labour in the event of a Scottish parliamentary confidence vote.

McLetchie's justification was that any alternative to Labour would presumably involve the Nationalists. In the event of a straight choice, the Scottish Conservative and Unionist Party would do nothing which might advance the cause of independence. Ultimately, the logic was impeccable, although it might have been wise to prepare the ground within the party first.

Since that early effort at party conference, McLetchie has shown himself to be a sharp performer in cross-party broadcast exchanges. As leader of the party in the run-up to the May elections, McLetchie signalled the new road ahead for the Scottish Tories. They were to remain 'staunchly Conservative' – but to put the interests of Scotland first.

He delivered a speech to party candidates at Hampden Park in

Glasgow,[4] the national home of Scottish football. In a conference suite, admittedly, rather than on the field of play, but an emotively chosen venue for all that.

To follow New Labour, McLetchie was offering New Unionism. He said Conservatives could no longer resist the mood swing which was evident in Scotland, the 'stronger cultural nationalism' which had become evident. The Tories' failure had been to miss that mood. He said: 'When the crowds at Murrayfield and Hampden sang "Flower of Scotland" so lustily, it became more than just an expression of pride in our rugby and football teams, it was an asser- tion of a national identity across the whole of Scottish society.'

McLetchie added later in the speech that the Tories had contrived to lose a generation of potential supporters. He said: 'This lost generation sees itself as Scottish and British, not British and Scottish, and we must see it that way too. From now on, in Scotland's first and oldest political party, we will be putting Scotland first. That will be at the heart of new Unionism. Labour tries to label the SNP as Tartan Tories as a badge of shame. But we must claim it as a

New politics, new Tories: William Hague and David McLetchie promise a new brand Scottish Conservative Party, Hampden Park, 29 January 1999. (Kindly supplied by *The Scotsman* Publications Ltd.)

badge of pride. We are the Tartan Tories – Scotland's other national party'.

McLetchie had a good Scottish election. He began it with persistent question marks over his leadership. He ended it winning praise on all sides for his gutsy determination and his powerful performance on the broadcast debates which are such a key feature of modern elections.

In truth, the Tories faced perhaps the least sustained targeting of the campaign, from rivals and the media. Most of the quizzical attention was on Labour and the SNP. The Liberal Democrats faced persistent challenges about their prospects under coalition. Nobody expected the Tories to win or even to share power. Naturally, the ever-vigilant BBC subjected their manifesto and policy pronouncements to searching scrutiny but, in general terms, it might be said that they had a relatively light election. Equally, I am sure it did not feel like that to the Tory participants.

McLetchie also had a relatively good start to his Scottish parliamentary career. For example, his attack upon the Labour/LibDem pact was sharp and cutting. At the very least, there is evidence of sentient, analytical thought on the Conservative benches. At best, they may be able to present a coherent, sustained, right-of-centre perspective.

None of which, of course, guarantees the Conservatives a return to their previous electoral position in Scotland or even a continued place in Scottish politics. Their fortunes are dependent on a range of other factors.

Firstly, despite their reaffirmed semi-autonomous status, they are inevitably affected by the performance of the party throughout Britain. If the Westminster Tories continue to bicker over their party's core beliefs, then the Scottish Tories will suffer.

Perhaps more directly, they are affected by the Westminster Tories' standpoint on Scotland's new Parliament and its place in the wider British constitutional settlement. The party in Scotland is fully alert to the need to accept devolution, to work with it. William Hague is similarly on board. Hague has privately warned senior colleagues that the Tories must not fall into the trap of becoming an English nationalist party, simply because they currently have no Westminster MPs from Scotland or Wales. Hague argues such a move would be counter-intuitive and politically catastrophic for the self-styled defenders of the Union.

However, the wider party at Westminster and throughout England has not yet got the message to the same degree. Every time a Westminster Tory spokesperson challenges devolution or talks slightingly about subsidies to Scotland, the party in Scotland utters a collective groan. This is not the same as questioning the implications of Scottish devolution for England, either in terms of finance or the balance of power at Westminster. As I shall examine later, these are completely legitimate areas for debate.

Rather, it is a question of tone. If the Conservative party at Westminster talks with a sneer about Scotland or the Scottish Parliament, then the Scottish electorate may feel entitled to think twice about the Scottish Tories' commitment to the new settlement. It may be unfair to the self-styled 'New Unionism' in Scotland but that is how it is.

The Scottish Tories are now indisputably a secondary opposition party. That may seem a trite statement of the obvious but it has taken a considerable period of time for the Scottish party to adjust to its true status. For decades, the Scottish Tories were a substantial party in their own right. For years, they governed on the basis of a British mandate. Scots Tories became used to being in government or on the verge of government. Now the challenge facing them is to act like a party which has to clamour to be heard.

There are a few in the party who believe that the Scottish Tories will only genuinely thrive under substantially enhanced devolution or even independence, that their economic policies would better fit a Parliament which had significant or even near-total financial autonomy – the flexibility, in other words, to allow a right-wing budgetary and fiscal package to be devised for Scotland.

Even if that analysis is accurate, it is not a development which lies in the hands of a relatively powerless Conservative group to deliver. For now, it also runs counter to the instincts of most Conservatives, which is to contain the devolved settlement.

To repeat: for the Scottish Conservatives, 1999 was a poorer performance than 1997. Their already depressed vote fell further. It was also far better. They ended up with seats, with elected, salaried Parliamentarians.

For the observer, their eagerness in the new Edinburgh Parliament is quite touching. Having performed the U-turn on devolution, they are now like repentant sinners, eagerly clutching one's arm to offer conviction that they have truly, truly changed. Their hope is that, over time, repentance will be accepted by the Scottish public and the voters will again consider their policies alongside the alternatives, rather than dismissing them out of hand because of the source.

Notes

1. *The Scottish Sun*, 28 January 1999.
2. Warner, G. (1988) *The Scottish Tory Party – A History*, London: Weidenfeld & Nicolson, p. 12.
3. Interview with Sir Malcolm Rifkind, February 1999.
4. Speech by David McLetchie, Glasgow, 29 January 1999.

12 The Scottish Liberal Democrats and Jim Wallace: a Profile

Jim Wallace was not a big fan of the Blair/Ashdown deal which brought his Liberal Democrat party to the antechambers of Westminster power. Jim Wallace was the leader who took his party into a coalition with Labour in the Scottish Parliament. Jim Wallace faces a conundrum.

The Liberal Democrats – or more accurately the Liberals – are much possessed by history. If a speaker at a party conference is seeking a burst of fervent applause, that speaker has only to evoke – preferably in sonorous tones – 'this great Liberal movement of ours'.

Self-evidently, the modern organisation is not remotely the same as the amalgam of Whigs, Peelites and Radicals which forged the Liberal Party on 6 June 1859 in opposition to the Conservatives. However, that sense of sustaining a proud tradition matters – and can have a direct impact on contemporary politics. Modern Liberals can never quite forget that their predecessor party dominated late nineteenth- and early twentieth-century Scottish politics to an extent that left them far more strongly entrenched than the Labour Party of recent history.

Liberal Democrat activists regularly claim ownership of the devolution movement. If our party conference speaker wants a second round of equally fervent applause, a guaranteed route is to remind supporters that 'for more than a century this great movement of ours has stood for Scottish Home Rule.' The subtle speaker will then remind the audience, with a defiant frown, that others have not shown such noble adherence to the cause.

I have long thought that this is decidedly a sword with two edges. On the one hand, it can be said to show political consistency. On the other hand, it is a reminder that for one hundred years the Liberals and their successors have been either unwilling or unable to do anything to implement Home Rule. It is an illustration of a party on the political margins, shorn of power.

However, that very contrast between self-image and harsh reality sums up the challenge which confronted the modern Liberal Democrats over their coalition decision in the Scottish Parliament. Some adhered to the first element: that the Liberal Democrats were the true believers, the pure flame of Scottish Home Rule. They argued, in essence although not in such terms, that their purity could only be corrupted by an arrangement with the Labour Party which history, that all-consuming sense of history, had taught them to mistrust as late, unconvincing converts to devolution.

Others, including Jim Wallace, laid stress on the second element of the Home Rule duality: that it would be perverse for the party to neglect an opportunity to join Scotland's devolved Government after a century of agitation for reform.

That, I believe, was the fundamental core within an argument which tended to coalesce around policy issues and in particular the remarkable debate over student tuition fees. Even with regard to this fundamental core, I would not want to give the impression that the balance of the argument lay indisputably in one direction. This was a tough call for the party leadership and activists.

Wallace, as I have said, was not instinctively a supporter of close links with the Labour Party. Although not a public opponent, he voiced fears privately and internally about the arrangement which saw Paddy Ashdown and other LibDems granted membership of a Blair Cabinet committee, initially to discuss areas of cooperation with regard to constitutional reform. He worried that his party might be damaged politically by being perceived as a subset of the Labour Party.

More generally, Scottish Liberal Democrats seemed anxious about the deal, owing to a variable perception of the Labour Party between

Scotland and Westminster. The Labour Party encountered by Ashdown was distinctly New, was Tony Blair, was the sprinkling of former Social Democrats surrounding the leader. The Labour Party encountered by many Scottish LibDems, particularly in their urban growth areas like Edinburgh, Aberdeen and the West of Scotland, often seemed rather different, a tangy blend of manipulative politics and municipal socialism.

To be blunt, there was also a class element to the inherent disparity between Labour and the Liberal Democrats at grassroots level in Scotland. The Liberal Democrats may not be entirely the sandal-wearing cyclists of mythology but they are decidedly middle-class. They are the party of the croissant rather than the bridie. Working-class politics is found in the Labour, Nationalist and smaller Socialist parties.

All these caveats help to explain why the deal between Labour and the Liberal Democrats caused such grief to the smaller party. It is equally true, however, that the coalition may be regarded as predestined.

Jim Wallace had a bad day on 28 April during the Scottish election campaign. The news agenda was dominated by claims in a biography of the former Trade Secretary Peter Mandelson that Blair and Ashdown had paved the way to a Scottish coalition over claret at Lord Irvine's West Hampstead home.[1] The talks, involving other senior Labour and LibDem figures, were said to have taken place, perhaps, early in 1996.

At a Labour news conference that same day, Donald Dewar stumbled a little over the nature of the talks – but firmly denied that they had involved any pact with regard to a Scottish Parliament. That was subsequently confirmed to me by Liberal Democrat sources who acknowledged that, in other respects, the account in the Mandelson biography was broadly correct, including the assertion that Labour and Liberal Democrat leaders had outlined ways to narrow the scope of the overt conflict between the two parties.

It was made clear by Labour that any talks which had taken place – and they declined to confirm either the venue or the refreshment served – had been based upon the emerging possibility of Westminster cooperation between the two parties in areas of mutual interest. This, it was said, paralleled the formal discussions on the Constitution led by Robin Cook for Labour and Robert Maclennan for the

Liberal Democrats. Labour sources pointed out that the party did not at that stage anticipate the Commons majority of 179 which the 1997 general election subsequently provided.

From an awkward start, the Labour spin gained momentum. Definitely no deal covering Scotland – merely a convivial chat among politicians who might need to be friends, within strictly defined limits of amicability, at Westminster.

If anything, the Liberal Democrat response was more hesitant. Party headquarters in Edinburgh appeared slightly bemused at first. Jim Wallace was on an election tour of the North-east and his immediate advisers seemed initially reluctant to facilitate a response from the leader. When a response did emerge, via a doorstep interview in Aberdeen as the leader paused during his tour, Wallace described the speculation about a pre-arranged pact as 'total rubbish'. He rather spoiled the effect of this comprehensive dismissal by disclosing that he had checked with Paddy Ashdown first.

I can accept that there was no formal Treaty of Hampstead which affected Scottish politics, eased by claret or any other wine. Both parties – eventually – pointed out that their Scottish spokespersons would have had to be on the guest list for any such conclusion to be reached. In any event, it was stressed that, in 1996, a Scottish parliamentary election was a relatively distant prospect, the other side of a general election.

Yet still, the claim gained credibility because the dynamic between the two parties at the highest level was all in the direction of the conclusion which ultimately emerged: a partnership government between Labour and the Liberal Democrats in Scotland.

The two parties had direct experience of cooperation in the Constitutional Convention. As I have discussed elsewhere, this was not a uniformly positive experience on either side. Several Liberal Democrats felt their party had suffered at the polls as a consequence. It did, however, provide a practical example of close working between the two parties and helped to build personal relationships which later proved valuable.

Further, the predisposition of leading Westminster Liberal Democrats, including Paddy Ashdown, was firmly towards Labour rather than the other potential partners, the Nationalists. In addition, the leadership of the party – in London and Scotland – was utterly opposed to granting the SNP their key demand, a referendum on possible independence for Scotland.

Strictly speaking, the Scottish LibDems were studiedly neutral about potential coalition partners. The party's campaign coordinator, Michael Moore, devised a tightly worded strategy which was endorsed by the executive of the Scottish party on 30 January 1999 at a meeting in Glasgow.

Michael Moore has blossomed – from victory in his Borders seat in 1997 as the constituency successor to David Steel – into an influential figure in the party. Good-humoured, disciplined and alert, he played a key role in the coalition talks, although not a Scottish Parliamentarian.

Moore's strategy paper had two key aims: to convince troubled party activists that the LibDems would not enter a coalition simply for the sake of power, and to head off persistent media questions about the party's possible partners. Each time we asked subsequently, we were advised to re-read the strategy paper.

This paper began by stressing that the Liberal Democrats were determined to win as many seats as possible and deliver as many of their policies as possible. However, moving swiftly on from that image of potentially limitless power, it addressed the possibility that the Liberal Democrats might not win the absolute approbation of the Scottish voters.

According to Moore's paper, the LibDems would talk first to the party with the largest number of seats in the Scottish Parliament – and would deal exhaustively with them, only moving to an alternative party if those initial talks failed. It was a simple but effective arithmetical formula which returned power to the electorate and allowed the LibDems, consistently, to deny that they had a preferred partner in mind.

To emphasise the point, Moore built informal contacts with the Nationalists to supplement the links with Labour which already existed through the Convention and other avenues. Moore was seen boldly lunching with John Swinney, the SNP's deputy leader and key strategist.

The LibDem strategy certainly slackened the fervour of the media questioning on the issue of coalitions or, more accurately, gave the LibDem leadership a consistent line to peddle in response.

The exchanges became almost formulaic. At news conferences during the election campaign, there would occasionally be welcome visitors, new blood in the media ranks, eager to demonstrate their incisiveness. 'Who', they would demand of the LibDems in tones that brooked no vacillation, 'are you going to work with in coalition?' Smugly, they would sit back, implying that they had instantly grasped the core of the contest which had eluded the resident Scottish hacks.

Back would come the reply: 'We want to win as many seats for Liberal Democracy as possible. If no party has a majority, we are prepared to work with the largest party. We are happy to leave this to the voters.' By the end of the campaign, we were able to repeat it along with them, like a nursery rhyme.

There was, of course, a flaw in this mantra. This was that the Liberal Democrats did not seriously envisage working with the Scottish National Party. They did not think the SNP would be the largest party, their Scottish and UK leadership completely opposed the idea of an independence referendum, their Westminster leadership in particular was adamantly hostile to advancing the cause of Nationalism in any form, their natural affinities at the upper reaches of politics were with the new Labour Party.

Within the Scottish Liberal Democrats there were individuals who tolerated or even favoured the idea of an accommodation with the SNP. Their liberal consciences glowed at the thought of a popular plebiscite on independence, on letting the people decide. Others, if forced to choose, narrowly preferred the Scottish patriotism of the SNP to the straightforward pragmatism of Labour. The vast majority, in their souls, simply wished the world was other than it was, that they were not confronted with such a choice.

Paddy Ashdown similarly wanted Liberal Democracy to thrive. However, he was in absolutely no doubt as to a choice between Labour and the SNP as potential partners. He actively preferred Labour and wanted nothing to do with the Nationalists, forcibly making plain his preference in private.

The Scottish LibDems held their 1999 conference in the Aberdeen Exhibition and Conference Centre, perched next to the North Sea at the Bridge of Don. Optimistically described as a spring conference, the event from 5 to 7 February was accompanied by biting winds and frequent snow. Blizzards closed the city's airport for a period.

Paddy Ashdown, however, offered an internal thaw with glowing private descriptions of Tony Blair and the project upon which, apparently, both leaders were embarked. He praised Blair's intellect and insight in remarkably fulsome terms.

Further, Ashdown stressed that the two parties – the Liberal Democrats and the remodelled Labour Party – were now occupying broadly the same territory. It was futile, he argued, to complain that the LibDems had been there first, that Labour was an interloper in the centre ground of moderate, free-market, reforming social democracy.

The proper response, according to Ashdown (at the time the federal leader of the LibDems), was to work with the grain of the new politics, to reconfigure the centre in a way that allowed social democratic ideals to flourish – and marginalised the alternatives of left-wing socialism or anti-European Toryism. His private audience inferred that he would have no intrinsic objection to a close accommodation between the two parties.

Indeed, in the run-up to the 1997 general election it is clear that Blair and Ashdown were actively contemplating the possibility of cooperation between the two parties in the event of a relatively close result. Both apparently felt it would be an opportunity to demonstrate in practical terms the reshaping of British politics, the regrouping of the centre Left and the marginalisation of the Tories. The size of the Labour majority ended any such prospect.

At the Aberdeen conference, consequently, Ashdown's strong views on possible Scottish cooperation with Labour were entirely consistent with the wider political project which he had begun with Blair. At precisely the same conference, remember, the Scottish Liberal Democrats were endorsing Michael Moore's paper – stating that they were formally neutral regarding their potential partners.

These two positions are not necessarily contradictory. It must be remembered that Paddy Ashdown, as federal leader, had no formal role in the Scottish coalition talks or in preparing the ground for the new Scottish politics.

The Liberal Democrats pride themselves on their federal set-up. The Scottish party is autonomous. Its leader at the time of the coalition talks was definitely Jim Wallace, not Paddy Ashdown.

However, Ashdown undoubtedly made his views known and his perspective would undoubtedly have been influential. Ashdown believed the Liberal Democrats were embarked on a joint project with Blair: a project which could self-evidently be advanced by cooperation in Scotland. Further, he disliked and distrusted the Nationalists.

There is another element, more directly connected to Jim Wallace. The leader of the Scottish Liberal Democrats is a thoroughly likeable individual: pleasant, well-mannered, bright and hard-working. He can also prove considerably tougher than his commonly smiling exterior would suggest. Wallace can be resolute, determined: to be blunt, stubborn.

During the run-up to the Scottish elections, he made perfectly clear that he would not endorse a referendum on independence. He took considerable care to ensure that this position was thoroughly understood – and endorsed – by the key decision-making centres within the Scottish party, including the executive. He got everyone on side.

There was room for moderation on certain policy issues. The pledge of a penny on Scottish income tax to fund education was, for example, hedged in by a statement that it would only be implemented 'if necessary'. It was quietly dumped in the coalition negotiations with Labour.

By contrast, however, Wallace could not have been plainer on the topic of a referendum. The people of Scotland could have independence if they voted for the SNP. If they did not vote for the SNP in sufficient numbers, the Liberal Democrats would not facilitate independence by the back door through the device of a referendum.

Scotland, according to Wallace, had endured enough constitutional navel-gazing. A little rich, perhaps, coming from the party of proportional representation and a century of agitation for Home Rule. Still, let that pass. Wallace made it abundantly clear. The Liberal Democrats would not endorse a coalition if it involved a referendum on independence.

The Nationalists, of course, knew that a deal with Labour was impossible. The two parties were declared enemies, historically, electorally and even occasionally at a personal level. The Tories had made plain that their votes in a Scottish Parliament would, in the last resort, be cast to prevent the SNP from thriving. The SNP needed to promote the possibility of a deal with the Liberal Democrats. Among potential Nationalist voters, they needed to foster the notion that an SNP vote would not be wasted, that it might lead to power by more than the simple route of an absolute majority.

Consequently, the Nationalists repeatedly attempted to blur the Liberal Democrat line on an independence referendum. They pointed to remarks by individuals like Donald Gorrie MP favouring a plebiscite and hinted repeatedly that there were many others who shared that view within the Liberal Democrats. They stressed that the referendum need not be within the first year of a Scottish Parliament. It could be deferred, possibly until the fourth year. They talked privately of assembling a coalition of Nationalists, quasi-Nationalist Labour MPs and dissident LibDems to bring about a referendum.

At no point did Jim Wallace give this talk any encouragement whatsoever. He simply repeated that he was against an independence referendum, that if the Nationalists wished to call such a ballot, they would have to win an outright majority or seek coalition partners elsewhere.

It is a facet of Wallace's character that he is – in his own quiet way – as staunch a Unionist as one would find in the Labour Party or even within the reformed Unionism of the Scottish Conservative Party. He believes strongly in the link with England. It is a belief that goes beyond the pragmatism one finds elsewhere on the centre Left in Scotland: the vague feeling that independence would be costly or that the process would be too much trouble. Wallace authentically backs the partnership with England.

Equally, however, he is a reformer. Ultimately, he would wish a federal structure for Britain. It is, he says, up to the people of England whether the English components of this federation are the entire nation as a unit or distinct regions. Put most simply, the Scottish Liberal Democrats suspended their federal ambitions in order to work with Labour, to advance the cause of devolution, the policy of another party.

Wallace told me that he believed Tony Blair's undoubted support for devolution was based on a pragmatic assessment of what Scotland required to sustain the Union.[2] Wallace said: 'I think Blair understands that devolution is right. I think still in his guts he just can't quite let go. Perhaps it's like the father of a son who's moving from adolescence to his twenties. He still wants to keep the tie there. I say: let's grow up. Let's grow up and still remain a member of the family.'

I would share this verdict on Blair – and also Wallace's further point that Blair's support for devolution is perhaps all the more remarkable given his inherent anxieties. This verdict upon the Prime Minister tallies with the evidence, which I have tracked earlier, that Blair has repeatedly sought to contain the scope of the devolution exercise.

There is, however, another dimension to Jim Wallace's remarks. He wants Scotland to remain, along with England, a member of the British family. Not a fellow member of an association of British states. Not a co-partner in the European union. Wallace positively wants firm ties with England in a reformed United Kingdom.

Take that personal perspective. Add the opposition to an independence referendum. Mix in Ashdown's views — and it is not hard to see that cooperation between the Liberal Democrats and the SNP was a virtual non-starter.

Up to and during the election campaign, it was valuable strategically for the Liberal Democrats to sustain the option of a deal with the SNP. It prevented the notion gaining further ground that they were simply in Labour's pocket, that a vote for the Liberal Democrats equated to a vote for Labour. No doubt the LibDems were sincere in endorsing Michael Moore's strategy paper on coalition tactics. In their hearts, however, they did not, could not truly envisage a pact with the Nationalists.

Even if talks had begun, they would in all probability have foundered on the question of an independence referendum. This would have been a fundamental issue: much bigger than the policy question of tuition fees which hindered the eventual deal with Labour. An independence referendum would have had the potential to alter the entire nature of Scotland's political settlement. Wallace argued that the SNP would have been canvassing for a Yes to independence while the Liberal Democrats, he firmly forecast, would have been lobbying for a No vote. What basis, he queried, would there have been for a coalition in such circumstances, with the partners split by definition on a fundamental issue?

Senior LibDems occasionally speculate with varying degrees of conviction that the Nationalists might have been prepared to water down their referendum demand. I think that is to misunderstand the nature of this issue for the SNP. It is their core reason for existence, not a transient policy pledge.

The Nationalist leadership was ready to defer the referendum but

I firmly believe they would have been in no position to surrender their demand entirely. Key activists within the SNP already suspected Alex Salmond of departing from the true cause of independence. The referendum was his key tool for convincing them otherwise. He could not have dropped it without splitting his party and putting his own leadership in jeopardy.

There were serious reasons, then, to question whether the Liberal Democrats could enter a coalition with the SNP. Labour knew that – and calculated consequently that they had a fall-back in the event of a hung parliament.

Donald Dewar, personally, had reservations about the prospect of a deal with the LibDems. Naturally, Labour's preference was for a full, working majority in the Scottish Parliament. Equally, Labour knew that the voting system – agreed with the LibDems in the Convention – made such a majority unlikely. The system, designed to broaden the appeal of devolution and prevent the Nationalists from snatching power on a minority vote, pointed towards a coalition.

Dewar, however, nurtured relatively troubled memories of his dealings with the Liberal Democrats in the Convention prior to 1992. From his own standpoint, he questioned whether they were reliable partners, although he appeared relatively comfortable with Wallace. While Labour was facing apparently adverse opinion polls during 1998, Dewar was even heard to mutter that the Tories might come to Labour's rescue in the event of a hung parliament.

Equally, there were strategic reasons for playing down the possibility of a deal with the Liberal Democrats. Labour sought to perpetuate its image as Scotland's most powerful party, even, occasionally, as Scotland's 'true' national party. It wanted nothing to confuse the voters, to muddy the simplicity of backing Labour.

At the same time, however, Labour strategists knew that the most likely outcome remained a Lib/Lab pact or accommodation of some form. Discreetly, low-level avenues of communication were maintained with the Liberal Democrats.

Indeed, one LibDem source indicated to me that these avenues of communication played an early role in the issue which was to become such a totem in the coalition talks: student tuition fees. In their manifesto for the Scottish parliamentary elections, the Liberal Democrats had made a precise pledge: they would scrap student tuition fees. They were an abhorrence, an abomination to be rejected by all right-thinking people.

Subsequently, more than one Liberal Democrat indicated to me that it might have been wiser to leave an escape route in this section. More than one Labour politician suggested to me that the Liberal Democrats should have pursued the question of maintenance grants for students, not tuition fees. Labour, it was claimed, had a relatively ready answer on fees: that they were not imposed on the poorest families.

There were a number of other potential stumbling blocks in the path of Labour and Liberal Democrat cooperation. The LibDems wanted more money for education – and were prepared to sanction an increase in Scottish income tax. The Liberal Democrats queried the impact of the Private Finance Initiative (building public works with private cash) upon the workforce and the community services involved.

None of these issues, however, subsequently threatened to jeopardise the coalition talks. Tuition fees became the totem of conflict for one unique reason. They were also opposed by the Nationalists – and, critically, by the Tories. The Conservatives' education spokesperson Brian Monteith volubly demanded the abolition of fees. As the election campaign progressed, it became apparent that there might be a potential majority against fees in the Parliament, that Nationalists, Tories and LibDems, combined, might be able to outvote Labour.

As one Liberal Democrat said to me later, perhaps the party should have been warned off when it found itself arguing the same standpoint as a right-winger like Brian Monteith. But, equally, most LibDem constituency hopes rested upon former Tory seats. Even if the abolition of fees amounted to a middle-class subsidy – as Labour alleged – the LibDems could not afford to be outbid by the Tories.

Labour had two problems with the demand to abolish fees. Firstly, they questioned what would replace them as a revenue earner within the Scottish budget. That struck me at the time as a relatively trivial point. The Scottish economy had survived before without tuition fees. It was not beyond the intellect of Scottish politicians to find a way of reallocating resources to accommodate the abolition of fees.

The second problem was far more grave. Westminster Cabinet Ministers with an eye to politics in England were bitterly opposed to the abolition of fees in Scotland. It was made abundantly plain to Donald Dewar that Scotland could not seriously offer free university education in direct competition with England – especially amid revived grumbling in the Commons at alleged 'subsidies' from England to Scotland.

On the one hand, as a detached observer, it was hugely amusing to watch the British Labour party wrestling with a direct practical consequence of Scottish Home Rule. What on earth did they think devolution was about if not the freedom for Scotland to pursue a different agenda and different policy priorities from England?

On the other hand, this was different from the range of varying policy priorities which might emerge now that a Scottish Parliament is up and running. Scottish Labour supported tuition fees. Few Labour activists were prepared to agitate for their abolition – as long as there was substantial provision to assist lower-income families.

Inevitably, during an election campaign, parties which may share many common aims will attempt to highlight their differences, to stress their areas of distinctive appeal to the electorate. From a Liberal Democrat perspective, the stance on tuition fees clearly differentiated their party from Labour.

It appeared to Labour strategists that the prospects for a coalition were being narrowed by an issue – tuition fees – to which their own activists attached little importance. According to my source, Labour let it be known informally to the Liberal Democrats that they would welcome a slackening of the party's line on student fees.

The Labour contact apparently questioned why the Liberal Democrats felt the need to be quite so firm on a relatively minor matter – minor, that is, in the context of the £15 billion budget available to the Scottish Executive. It is impossible to say whether this approach had high-level sanction or was simply a freelance effort by a Labour strategist concerned over an obstacle which appeared to be standing in the path of one route to power for his party. The latter seems more likely.

Apparently there was, however, a follow-up to this exchange. On BBC Scotland's 'Campaign 99' programme, Jim Wallace had caused a stir by indicating that the question of tuition fees might be 'on the table' for negotiation if there were to be talks with Labour. Wallace, it appeared from this remark, was also privately aware of the potential for conflict with Labour over this single issue.

The LibDem leader, however, came under subsequent pressure both from his own candidates who craved a simple, unvarnished line – and from Tory and Nationalist opponents who wanted to pin the LibDems down.

On Tuesday, 4 May – two days before the election – Wallace appeared on another BBC Scotland programme, 'From Here to Holyrood', alongside rival party leaders. Repeatedly pressed, Wallace now declared that the people of Scotland had made the issue of tuition fees 'non-negotiable'.

According to my source, the Labour strategist who had originally urged the LibDems to play down the issue of fees now commented sourly: 'That's the coalition buggered, then.'

As it turned out, the coalition was not in that particular position, although the talks were made much more difficult as a consequence.

Similar epithets have been applied, privately, by Liberal Democrat activists to their own party's prospects as a distinct entity now that they are in coalition. I must confess to finding that attitude a little puzzling, although I can appreciate the quandary which confronted the party over policy pledges delivered so firmly.

Surely the Liberal Democrats above all other parties should have been ready for the perils of coalition. They have, after all, preached PR and partnership politics for decades. They should perhaps have prepared the ground more carefully by including escape clauses in their manifesto. Perhaps the document should have been peppered with a few more 'if necessaries' and 'when practicables': the sort of get-out which accompanied the tax pledge. It is perhaps instructive that the tax pledge had only been delivered after detailed preparation.

That said, there were several in the party who seemed to have a fundamental objection to the particular coalition with Labour, quite apart from the arguments over individual policy issues.

Such activists, I believe, fear that their party is indeed in jeopardy of being subsumed or replaced by new Labour. That is not, I believe, an inevitable outcome. I understand that one element of the Blair/Ashdown talks was that Labour would not act like a predator, seeking to swallow up the Liberal Democrats.

It will, however, be important for Jim Wallace to demonstrate that he can gain practical advantages for his voters, for his party's own priorities, from the Scottish coalition. There were decidedly embarrassing moments for the Liberal Democrats in some of the early sessions of the new Parliament. Labour MSPs were asked by rivals, principally the Scottish Nationalists, to state what their party had conceded in the coalition negotiations. There ensued silence – followed by bluster. Jim Wallace knows that he needs to gather a list of concrete achievements, in line with his party's own aims, by the time of the next election.

At the time of writing, in the summer of 1999, it is not possible to predict the outcome of the coalition. It may thrive, stumble along or founder on policy differences.

At the very least, it will take careful handling by the Liberal Democrat leadership if a bitter irony is not to develop: that devolution, proportional representation and coalition politics – for which the Liberal Democrats have longed – end up presenting a substantial threat to the party's independent appeal to the voters.

Notes

1. Macintyre, D. (1999), Mandelson: the Biography, London: Harper Collins, pp. 342–3.
2. Interview with Jim Wallace, 7 December 1998.

13 A Question of Money

The former Secretary of State for Wales, Ron Davies, was fond of describing devolution as a process rather than an event. Davies, of course, had two targets in mind with this remark. He wanted to counter Plaid Cymru, the Welsh Nationalists, who were urging more extensive devolution of powers to Wales – and, equally, he wanted to warn those in his own party who distrusted devolution that the pace of reform, once begun, would accelerate rather than slow down.

This analysis, however, has wider application than in the particular circumstances of Wales, where sections of the Labour Party have been decidedly reluctant devolvers and where the scheme was only endorsed by the narrowest of margins in the Welsh referendum, held one week after the ballot in Scotland.

Devolution is structurally dynamic, not static. To some extent, that is true of all politics. Solutions emerge, positions change, often just when it appears that argument has been exhausted on all sides. Personalities play a part, as do shifting allegiances within parties.

Think of the European Union. Even as the bound copies of one Union treaty – such as Maastricht or Amsterdam – are being translated into a multitude of languages, the process of advancing the next stage of reform is under way. There is simply no fixed point which can sensibly be said to be the established political structure of Europe.

Similarly with Westminster. The decline in relative importance of the House of Commons cannot be traced to a single event, however much analysts may try to blame Tony Blair or over-powerful whips' offices or sycophantic backbenchers or the introduction of television or the development of non-partisan community politics or, indeed, devolution. Almost intangibly, however, the Commons is a lesser chamber.

Equally, it is absurd to assume that a Westminster government legislates for devolution – and that is it. Labour has been rather caught in a bind over this issue. To be fair to Donald Dewar, he has never pretended that there could not be further reform of the system. Indeed, he has pointed out that the package of powers might be altered in the light of experience or evident public demand. However, Labour has not been anxious to over-emphasise this element for fear of encouraging or appearing to encourage Nationalist ambition.

Consequently, each time the SNP leadership has spoken of devolution as a bridge to independence, Labour has tended to react by depicting devolution in relatively static terms, to talk of a 'settlement' as if the precise Parliament introduced by the Scotland Act were the final word.

To the detached observer, two things seem self-evident. The 'settlement' will be in a process of semi-permanent change. These may not be big changes such as the acquisition of further, specific powers. More probably, the relationship with Westminster or the intrinsic dynamic of the new Parliament itself will develop. Circumstances, which could not be envisaged at the time of the legislation, will forge the nature of the newly devolved structure.

Secondly, independence is not implicit in devolution. There is no guaranteed path from one to the other, no fixed route which one can track whereby a devolved Scotland definitely and finally breaks the Union with England. It may happen or it may not. The establishment of a devolved Parliament, however, is not a guarantee that independence will follow 'as night follows day', as the Tories used to claim before their conversion to accepting devolution.

In both cases – the development of devolution and the potential arrival of independence – there will be two interacting forces: the structural tensions which may arise within the UK's new constitutional set-up and the popular response to those tensions. It is important to note that neither force is purely in the hands of Westminster or the devolved Parliament.

Devolution is not simply the creature of Westminster. That is demonstrated by the very different nature of the packages advanced for Scotland, Wales and Northern Ireland. There is an attempt, admittedly, to impose some form of central order upon the three, to allow some cross-comparison. The differences, however, tend to outweigh the similarities.

For example, Wales has a power of secondary legislation to amend and refine the main statute laws which will still be laid down by Westminster. Scotland has primary legislative powers. So does the package laid down for Northern Ireland although, there, the areas of competence are substantially different from those set down for Scotland.

These evident differences – and there are many more – reflect the different nature of political reality and cultural identity in Scotland, Wales and Northern Ireland. Devolution is not centrally driven. It is a Westminster response, not an initiative. As a policy, devolution differs from Westminster's agenda with regard to education or health or defence in that Westminster would never have turned its attention to devolution without evident prompting. Again, let me stress that I intend no implicit criticism with such remarks. It can be thoroughly sensible politics to respond to powerful, identified popular pressure – although, of course, there will be partisan dispute about the nature and strength of the demand and the justice of the response.

Self-evidently, Westminster retains a substantial influence over the future dynamic of devolved politics in the UK. It would be decidedly over-simplistic to suggest that the future nature of the devolved bodies lies entirely in popular hands or under the control of politicians in the devolved organisations themselves. At the very basic level, any substantial alteration of the package of Scottish powers, for example, would require further Westminster legislation.

I would argue, however, that Westminster's role is now interactive, rather than pro-active. No longer will it be credible to maintain that the UK Government is all-powerful, however frequently the Scotland Act stresses the sovereignty of Westminster. Just as there have been shifts in the balance between the UK administration and the super-visory Commons, so in future there will be shifts in the balance of power between Westminster and the devolved bodies.

This will become more evident still when, with the passage of time, the politicians who are elected to the Parliament in Scotland owe their entire allegiance and have spent their entire career in devolved politics, rather than at Westminster. In practice, the shift was perceptible from the moment the referendum carried in September 1997. Those Westminster MPs who had declared for Holyrood started immediately to talk as if they were already Members of the Scottish Parliament.

For example, I recall the experience of Henry McLeish as Minister of State at the Scottish Office prior to devolution. He had declared his intention to pursue his career in the Scottish Parliament. Almost instantly, he told me, he found that he felt it rather odd to be at Westminster. In a curious way, he wondered what he was doing there when his political inclinations now tended towards Edinburgh.

I believe this is a tendency which will become still more marked. Politicians will become immersed in Scottish parliamentary politics. Their concerns, their style, their manner of address and, above all, the loyalties which shape their personal future will be different from the Westminster pattern, even for those who were previously members of the House of Commons. They will become institutionalised in the Scottish Parliament, owing their allegiance to that body.

Their political careers will depend solely on advancing Scotland's interests or at least on appearing to advance Scotland's interests. This may well bring them into explicit conflict with Westminster, including with members of their own political party at Westminster. This factor, I feel sure, will add to the structural tensions which are certain to exist within the new constitutional set-up.

By that analysis, I do not mean to imply that devolution is fatally flawed or dangerously unstable. It may be said, indeed, that all political structures are unstable in so far as they are all subject to change, often substantial change. The ambition of despots down the centuries has been to create 'stability' in the shape of their own entrenched, unchallenged rule. All, to date, have ultimately failed.

Similarly, there will always be tensions as long as one ambitious political person attempts to oust or thwart another ambitious political person. Provided they play reasonably fair, such a situation can be creative and productive. The key question is whether the tensions inherent in the new constitutional set-up can be harnessed to creative effect or whether they will tend towards political stalemate, friction or collapse.

Aside from the unpredictable events and incidents which will inevitably create difficulties between the various administrations within the UK, I believe there are three structural elements which may provoke tension: finance, Europe and the future governance of England. I intend to examine each in turn.

Firstly, finance. To recap, the Scottish Parliament receives a share of United Kingdom public expenditure from the UK Treasury. This is broadly in line with the previous block grant system for disbursing cash to the Scottish Office to enable it to carry out its task of administering Scotland on behalf of the UK.

In theory, the Scottish Parliament has complete freedom to determine its own spending priorities – although in practice that freedom is constrained by the obligation to provide statutory services such as education. The Parliament has a limited power to vary the standard rate of income tax, accruing additional revenue if it raises tax or returning cash to the Treasury if it lowers the rate.

The budget assigned to the Scottish Parliament and administration by the UK Treasury is regularly varied in accordance with a mechanism known as the Barnett formula. This takes the established, historic spending level in Scotland and alters it according to the change which has been affected in comparable spending departments for England alone or for England and Wales. The formula, consequently, governs only the changes in Scottish spending relative to England. Contrary to the impression fostered by some, it does not govern the base level of Scottish spending itself. That has been built up by historical precedent and past political haggling.

The Barnett formula is named after Joel Barnett, Labour's Chief Secretary at the Treasury in the late 1970s, who devised a funding mechanism to cope with the expected onset of devolution at that time. Devolution, of course, was frustrated by the 1979 referendum outcome but the formula survived.

Barnett conducted an assessment of the relative needs of areas of the UK. He wanted to find out whether the available money was fairly spread across the kingdom as a whole. This analysis disclosed that there was a spending bias in favour of Scotland and Wales – and, consequently, to the detriment of England.

Some contemporary Scottish politicians affect to regard the

Barnett formula as if it were Holy Writ. Any criticism of its operation, any suggestion that the Treasury might be looking on it with
disfavour is regarded as nothing less than treachery to Scotland. When
it was indicated, in the latter years of the previous Conservative
Government, that the Barnett formula was being called into question, politicians from across the party divide mounted a crusade to
preserve this magical elixir for the nation.

The Barnett formula, of course, is nothing of the sort. It is critical
to realise that, when it was first introduced by Joel Barnett, it was
firmly intended to narrow the gap in spending between Scotland
and England. Admittedly, it was envisaged that this gap would be
narrowed over an extended period of time but the intention was
clear: Barnett meant to rein back Scotland's cash lead over England.

Barnett was designed to introduce stability, certainly, but stability
which was predicated upon Scotland suffering a progressive disad-
vantage relative to England as each annual spending review came
into effect. The intention was to settle the topic of Scottish spending
on a relatively fixed basis and allow annual negotiations between
competing Ministers to focus on English spending departments: to
give the Treasury less to worry about, in other words.

Again, it is important to stress that Barnett does not dictate the
overall level of Scottish spending. That has developed historically.
Barnett only governs the annual or regular change in the total allo-
cated to Scotland. For example, if an English spending department
like Health gets a budgetary increase, a fixed proportion of that
sum – roughly a tenth – will be added to the Scottish block. Under
the rule of budgetary freedom, Scotland may spend that available
money according to choice. It does not have to be spent on health.

The comparison is only made with like-for-like departments: in
other words, with domestic spending departments like Education
where there is a comparable remit governing Scotland. Scottish
spending is not compared with departments like Defence or the
Foreign Office because there is no military or diplomatic remit
under Scottish devolution.

Barnett provides, consequently, for Scotland to get a fixed share
of the regular change in all the comparable Whitehall budgets.
Historically, consequently, those responsible for the Scottish Budget
– formerly the Scottish Secretary, now the First Minister – have had
an interest in supporting, where possible, those English domestic

spending Ministers seeking an increase in their budgets. If they can extract a big cake from the Treasury, Scotland gets an agreed slice.

There are one or two budgetary areas which are settled specifically for Scotland. For the most part, however, Scotland has not negotiated directly with the Treasury since Barnett was introduced in 1978. The change in Scotland's budget has depended, second-hand, on the change in comparable English departments like Education or Health – on the political clout of their Ministers in combating the Treasury, in other words.

The division of cash between Scotland, England and Wales was meant to be based upon population. When the Barnett formula was introduced, the percentages were set at Scotland 10 per cent, Wales 5 per cent and England 85 per cent. In other words, from every additional pound of public spending, 10p went to Scotland, 5p went to Wales and 85p went to England.

This arithmetical calculation was structurally more favourable to England than the historic division of cash between the territories. In other words, with each successive annual spending round, it was envisaged that England would do marginally better while Scotland and Wales retrenched fractionally. Over time, naturally, the gap between the territories would close. Again, for the avoidance of even the remotest shadow of doubt, this was not an accidental consequence of Barnett but its entire purpose.

However, for many years the formula did not achieve that purpose. Firstly, the population of Scotland continued to decline relative to England while the population-based formula remained unchanged. Spending per head in Scotland, consequently, stayed high because, simply, there were fewer heads upon which to lavish that spending.

Secondly, a key element of state spending is public sector pay. These pay settlements continued to be calculated and funded on a UK basis. That meant Scotland receiving every bit as much as England, per head, for pay when a strict application of the Barnett formula would have meant that precise equivalence should not have applied. As long as this happened, pay was effectively removed from the Barnett effect. Barnett was restricted to working on the non-wage element of public sector spending. In addition, other technical and political devices were found to bypass Barnett.

Steadily, however, these holes were plugged. In 1992, the

Conservative Government reconfigured the formula, tightening the calculation to reflect more accurately the relative population numbers. By 1996/97 – the last year of the Tory Government – Scotland was receiving 10.66 per cent of the cash available to purely English spending departments and 10.06 per cent of the money which went to services like law and order which covered both England and Wales.

Also, over a period of years, the Conservative Government obliged spending departments to fund certain key public sector pay rises – including local government – from 'efficiency savings'. This meant that Scotland's protection from the Barnett impact on pay had been severely eroded. Whitehall was no longer providing universal provision for pay, which meant that Scotland had to find the cash for pay rises from a budget which was now affected by a tighter Barnett deal. Finally, the Treasury steadily plugged the technical gaps in the formula.

Barnett, in short, began to bite. That impact – which was discernible in the final few years of the Conservative Government – has been substantially increased during the first few years of the Labour administration at Westminster.

The key decision, announced by the Treasury on 9 December 1997, was that the Barnett formula would in future be updated annually according to the changing population ratios and might be altered at other times to take account of technical changes. This radically altered the nature of Barnett, preventing its intended impact from being distorted or weakened. From 1999/2000, when this change took effect, Barnett applies strictly.

Barnett was tightened at the time of the Comprehensive Spending Review in July 1998 and again at the time of the Budget in March 1999. That Budget change left Scotland getting 10.39 per cent of the annual alteration in English spending and 9.81 per cent of the alteration in budgets affecting both England and Wales. Subsequently, Barnett will be further refined, based on a mid-year estimate of relative population numbers.

It is important to understand that this does not mean that Scotland's budget is being cut, as some of the less precise or politically motivated analysts would argue. Scotland will continue to receive a budget increase under normal circumstances, at least as long as English spending departments are receiving an increase. The difference is that – with Barnett biting – the percentage increase will be less than in England. This is inevitable – indeed, structural.

Scotland, historically, has received more in public spending than a strict population comparison with England would promote. This is arguably justified by higher spending needs – although the differential has been a cause of sharp political dispute. From now on, the annual changes in the Scottish and English budgets are to be determined strictly by population. That means Scotland's increase will now lag behind her historically high level of spending – while England, slowly but surely, catches up.

The spending gap is generally calculated by UK government analysts as around 20 per cent per head. In other words, Scottish spending has been a fifth more favourable than that applying to England. I am, of course, aware that these figures are estimates and are open to dispute. I have followed and analysed Nationalist claims, for example, that the calculation takes little account of hidden subsidies to the South-east of England through the disproportionate impact of, for example, defence spending and public sector jobs.

My purpose at this point is not to enter that fascinating, partisan debate. I do not intend in any way to belittle the argument between the Nationalists and the other parties over Scottish spending. It is in many ways critical to the future prospects of the various parties and, of course, to the future of Scotland. Equally, it can become somewhat sterile, with untested assumptions thrust into conflict with imponderable statistics.

Rather I intend to dwell for the moment upon another element: the spending challenge which will potentially face a Scottish administration of whatever political colour. If we work with the grain of the UK Government's calculations, it is clear that Scotland is now facing a relative squeeze, a Barnett squeeze.

Again, that does not imply instant penury. Indeed, most detached analysts confirm that the relatively high cash levels implied by the Chancellor's three-year Comprehensive Spending Review (CSR) should mean significant increases in spending for Scotland. As opposition politicians frequently point out, these increases follow two exceptionally tight years in which the Chancellor Gordon Brown adhered to Conservative spending plans and, indeed, contrived to produce an outcome tighter than the Tories had intended.

More generally, though, the point is a structural one rather than being based on an immediate – and possibly transient – assessment of Scottish spending. Scotland has received more money in the CSR – but England has received more still as a consequence of the new, tighter, fitter Barnett.

In years of stringency, that may have a sharp impact on Scotland. If, for example, England receives a spending increase at some future date which is calculated barely to cover the prevailing rate of inflation, then it is axiomatic that Scotland's increase will be below the inflation figure. Scotland could do little or nothing about that under the established rules.

This potential impact has been identified by economists. In April 1999, the respected Fraser of Allander Institute published an analysis of the UK Government's CSR spending plans for the period up to 2001/02 as they affected Scotland relative to the rest of the UK.

This report found that Scotland had indeed, as intended by Barnett, lagged behind England in the spending calculations.[1] Adjusting for price changes, the FAI report estimated that the Scottish budget would increase by some 6 per cent or 1.9 per cent per year – while the increase for the rest of the UK was 10.7 per cent or 3.4 per cent per year. The Scottish increase was less than half that scheduled for the remainder of the UK.

Again, to stress, this is not a cut in Scottish spending. Scotland is getting more money. The FAI report, however, noted: 'These comparisons imply that while Scotland is to receive an increase in public expenditure, the country fares much worse than the rest of the UK.'

This is simply a demonstration of new model Barnett in action. Scotland's increase is behind England's. For the future, it is envisaged that Scotland's increase will always lag behind England's. This is structural arithmetic – not political manipulation, although, of course, the arithmetic has a political origin. In years of relative generosity to England, there may not be an apparent problem for Scotland. In years of relative stringency for England, Scotland could face spending difficulties.

This potential for spending problems in Scotland was trenchantly analysed by Professor Neil Kay of Strathclyde University, writing in December 1998.[2] He argued that Scotland had received a relatively favourable deal on spending – because Barnett had been neglected over the preceding years. Now that Barnett was being implemented, he foresaw problems for the devolved Parliament in Edinburgh as a direct consequence.

Kay wrote: 'The corrosive effects of the Barnett squeeze on Scottish public spending could institutionalise a source of tension and conflict between Holyrood and Westminster.' It should be stressed once more that Kay envisages such a potential development over a long period as a result of the structural squeeze implicit in Barnett.

Equally, it should be stressed that there are other economists who believe that the potential impact of the Barnett squeeze is exaggerated. Professor Arthur Midwinter of Strathclyde University is an established and highly respected economic analyst, with a particular expertise on the funding of the Scottish public sector. He has been consulted repeatedly over the years by government and local authorities.

Professor Midwinter told me that he thought any Barnett squeeze would be 'minuscule'.[3] Further, he insisted that the Treasury's aim had never been to close the spending gap entirely between Scotland and England. Rather, they had nurtured a longstanding aim to narrow the gap and had tried to carry out that purpose over many years, under successive Westminster administrations.

There was, in short, a political element which would mitigate any technical Barnett squeeze. Professor Midwinter told me he had received private assurances from senior Ministers that Barnett would be renegotiated, should that technical prospect of convergence between Scotland and England come anywhere near completion.

In private conversations with Treasury sources, it has been similarly stressed to me that Barnett would not necessarily be applied rigidly at all points in the future. There might, for example, be distinctive and individual allocations of cash which benefited Scotland in percentage terms. An example suggested to me was the product of the windfall tax on the profits of the privatised utilities, introduced by the new Labour Government shortly after winning the 1997 election. This, arguably, was used substantially to benefit a jobs programme in Scotland, although relatively little of the cash had been raised from Scottish firms.

The point remains, however, that Barnett as it stands could have a substantial impact on Scotland over, admittedly, a long period. It is also far from guaranteed that any renegotiation of Barnett would necessarily be to Scotland's benefit. That might depend on the pre-vailing political climate and the developing attitude of Westminster towards Scottish spending.

One demand which is frequently heard is for a comprehensive assessment of spending needs: starting from scratch, in other words, with a full analysis of what the various territories of the UK actually need to meet the requirements of their citizenry, as opposed to what they have historically received.

This has an obvious logic of its own. It would, arguably, clarify matters. However, as the former Conservative Scottish Secretary Sir Michael Forsyth never tired of pointing out, such an approach could bring difficulties for Scotland. A needs assessment might simply hasten the spending convergence which Barnett is due to generate over time. The outcome of such an assessment would depend on the statistics and assumptions employed. Equally, it might depend on who had the final say. A Treasury-driven survey might not be especially favourable to Scotland, particularly with Scotland governed and administered by a distinctive Scottish Parliament which might have relatively little influence in Whitehall.

When the devolution White Paper was published, most attention in the financial area focused upon the promise that Barnett would be retained. As I have discussed, there was some comment upon the fact that the White Paper envisaged the formula being 'updated from time to time to take account of population and other technical changes'. There was relatively little attention paid to the sentence which follows.

That read: 'Any more substantial revision would need to be preceded by an in depth study of relative spending requirements and would be the subject of full consultation between the Scottish Executive and the UK Government.' This sentence postponed a full-scale needs assessment – but it did not preclude one entirely. Indeed, it might be argued that it raised the prospect.

For now, though, Scotland is likely to have to contend with the Barnett squeeze, with its potential impact, minor or substantial according to taste and economic analyst. The question of a more wide-ranging spending assessment has been set to one side, although not abandoned.

The Barnett squeeze is not simply an arcane debating point. It could have a direct effect on people. If, over a long period, the

Barnett squeeze were to have a substantial impact – or if it were to be felt by the Scottish population or by the political parties that Scotland was starting to slip in the spending stakes – then there could be pressure to use the Tartan Tax, the Parliament's power to vary the standard rate of income tax.

(I make no apology, incidentally, for using the phrase 'Tartan Tax'. I am aware that it was originally a pejorative term devised by the Tories. The word 'Tories' itself was also originally a pejorative term. Usage alters. Who now remembers the poll tax as the 'community charge'?)

There might be pressure, then, to use the Tartan Tax to refill an actual or perceived deficit in spending increases between Scotland and England. The Tartan Tax was designed to give the Parliament financial flexibility. It might reasonably be argued, particularly from a London standpoint, that – if Scotland wants to sustain historically high levels of expenditure – then Scotland has an available remedy in her own hands.

That is one reason why some Nationalists were unhappy with their party's pledge, during the Scottish parliamentary election campaign, to make use of the Tartan Tax if the SNP won. The SNP leadership offered to reverse for Scotland alone the Chancellor's planned cut of a penny off the standard rate of UK income tax.

The Nationalist case – advanced in a campaign styled 'Scotland's Penny' – was that the people of Scotland had the chance to reject what the party called a 'bribe' by Labour and to divert the product of the penny tax to productive public expenditure.

SNP leaders insist that this policy played well on the doorsteps in Scotland. They say people were open to the argument that they would not be paying more than at present in tax – because it was not a tax increase but rather the reversal of a planned tax cut. Equally, the SNP leadership says voters in Scotland were prepared to accept that they would end up paying more than comparable tax-payers in England in order to fund targeted spending on Scottish services.

One or two internal critics, however, feared that the SNP fell into a Unionist trap. By offering to use the very limited tax power of a devolved Parliament, it was argued, they gave London an excuse in future to trim the central budget made available to Scotland. Further, according to the critics, the SNP and the cause of independence more generally would become associated in the public mind with tax-raising.

I stress again that this analysis is sharply disputed by the Nationalist leadership – and certainly the party's tax plan was overwhelmingly endorsed by an SNP conference shortly before the Scottish elections. Perhaps, however, the circumstances of an impending political contest tended to narrow the scope of the debate. It was not likely that a leadership recommendation would be overturned at that stage.

Labour leaders were initially worried that the SNP would gain ground with their promise to spend more on health, education and housing. As the campaign progressed, however, Labour strategists claim they were able to contain this by, in effect, pointing out the inherent 'unfairness' of Scotland paying more than England in income tax. Labour insists that this argument applied purely in the circumstances of Gordon Brown's carefully balanced budget. However, as I have noted elsewhere, I believe Labour has created fundamental doubts about the nature and use of the Parliament's tax powers.

To return to the wider issue of Scotland's financial circumstances. Political argument in this field is not purely a matter of arithmetic. Scotland's future public spending will depend on political decisions, on political clout. Scotland can muster arguments against restricting spending – and, indeed, has had to muster these arguments repeatedly in the past when the Treasury or MPs from England have demanded answers.

Broadly, Scotland's case is: that spending needs are actually higher north of the Border with, for example, a relatively poor health record placing greater strain on hospital resources; that the public sector plays a larger part in Scottish life because of the low dependence on private provision in, for example, education; that the scattered population across a large land-mass places greater demands on spending in areas like transport; that there are sectors like the water industry which remain within public funding in Scotland while they are privately run elsewhere.

In addition, Scotland argues that comparisons are inevitably imprecise because there is relatively little all-England, all-service data with which to make comparisons. Scottish spending is grouped in a block while spending in England is dispersed across a range of departments and regions.

These are powerful and substantial arguments – which make the case for Scotland receiving more funding per head than England. They do not, however, make the case for that funding being at a particular level. Again, the disparity between the two territories might in future require to be established by an overall assessment of needs.

Labour and the Conservatives before them have faced a political dilemma over this question of Scottish spending. On the one hand, they want to vaunt the cash which Scotland receives, both for their own partisan credibility in Scotland and in an effort to undermine the SNP case for independence.

On the other hand, stressing Scotland's spending advantage has had the effect of prompting tough questions in the Commons and elsewhere, particularly from English MPs aggrieved that their areas are allegedly being sold short in order to featherbed the Scots. Nothing is more calculated to incense an MP from England – virtually regardless of party affiliation – than a reminder that more money per head goes to Scotland.

Despite this backlash, however, successive Secretaries of State for Scotland thought it right to publish detailed assessments of Scotland's claimed spending advantage. Ostensibly a statistical exercise, this became a political hammer with which to hit the SNP. Begun under the Tories, this initiative was pursued by Labour when they took office.

In November 1998, for example, Donald Dewar as Scottish Secretary published an analysis of Scottish spending relative to the rest of the UK.[4] This indicated that total government spending for Scotland in the year under scrutiny (1996/97) was £31.8 billion or 10.1 per cent of the UK total. That was broken down as £24.7 billion of identifiable cash spent specifically to benefit the residents of Scotland plus £3.1 billion of non-identifiable money, Scotland's estimated share of more general UK spending, and £4 billion of other expenditure including debt interest.

For the same year, government revenue in Scotland from tax and other sources – but excluding North Sea oil revenue – was put at £24.7 billion or 8.7 per cent of the UK total. The gap, supposedly filled by borrowing, was therefore put at £7.1 billion or 11.25

per cent of Scottish gross domestic product (GDP). For the same period, it was calculated that the UK's debt ratio was much lower, at 4.25 per cent.

Even including revenue from the North Sea in Scotland's budget, the report noted that there would be a deficit of £3.2 billion or 4 per cent of Scottish GDP. Under these circumstances, the UK debt ratio was said to be 3.25 per cent.

The report concludes, in short, that Scotland spends far more than she earns. The political interpretation placed upon this and similar earlier exercises by politicians who adhere to the Union was that Scotland would struggle under independence, that services would have to be cut or taxes would have to go up or both.

It is fair to say that this conclusion – and indeed the entire exercise – have been subject to challenge from the Nationalists and from some economists. Broadly, the SNP claim that the government exercise undervalues the extent of Scottish revenue and overplays the amount of spending. They note the admission by the report itself that the calculations are 'subject to inevitable imprecision' due to the need to use estimates.

At an earlier point, in January 1997, the SNP seized upon a Commons written answer from William Waldegrave, then the Tory Chief Secretary to the Treasury. Waldegrave had been asked by the SNP to show the relative financial position of Scotland and England from 1978 to 1995, assuming that 90 per cent of oil revenues had been attributed to Scotland. The Nationalists argued at the time that 90 per cent was a reasonable estimate based on international comparisons, although they used lower estimates for more detailed calculations during the Scottish election.

Waldegrave's answer suggested that, under these hypothetical circumstances, there would have been a net transfer of £27 billion from Scotland to England. That means, say the SNP, that Scotland subsidised England during that period. Sceptics say the outcome reflects the boom in the North Sea of the early 1980s and would not be a permanent feature of the spending relationship between Scotland and England.

Certain economists, notably Professor Andrew Hughes-Hallett of Strathclyde University, have argued that the whole method of analysing Scotland's independent financial position is misplaced. Professor Hughes-Hallett says there is a structural problem in that spending incurred entirely in England may be assumed, under the formula procedure, to have an automatically corresponding impact in Scotland although that may not truly be the case.

He argues further that the approach adopted by those politicians who place a dismal interpretation on the statistics is misdirected. They assume, he says, a static budget whereas Scotland might reorder priorities: for example, opting to reallocate her share of defence and diplomatic spending to other areas.

While recognising these significant challenges to the exercise and the outcome, it is also fair to say that many other analysts – and, of course, almost all non-Nationalist politicians – have tended to endorse the claim that Scotland's budget operates at a relatively significant deficit.

The point, they argue, is not that there is a deficit. The United Kingdom and most other established economies have regularly operated a deficit in the past, borrowing in order to finance expenditure or investment. The point is that Scotland's estimated deficit would appear to be disproportionately high: a structural deficit, in other words, rather than a temporary phenomenon dictated by prevailing economic circumstances.

This claim of a structural deficit is sharply contested by the Nationalists. During the Scottish election campaign, the SNP published their estimate of Scotland's budget under independence.[5] The essence of their argument is that Scotland is a rich country, potentially the seventh richest in the world. Far from a structural deficit, they argue that an independent Scotland could thrive and would be able to cut taxes or improve public services, according to political taste.

Most immediate interest in the publication, however, focused on two new policy developments from the Nationalists. Firstly, they indicated for the first time that an independent Scotland would retain sterling as the Scottish currency in the period before joining the single European currency, the Euro. The Nationalist case was that they expected a referendum on the Euro in 2003, and that it would make sense in terms of stability for Scotland to join on the same day and at the same rate as England. It would not make sense to the international currency markets, they argued, for Scotland to launch an entirely new currency for what would be a matter of months.

Critics pointed out, however, that this would mean Scotland's

interest rates continuing to be set by the Bank of England's monetary policy committee, at least in the interim. The Nationalists had
repeatedly argued in the past that the Bank committee's approach
took little account of the needs of Scotland.

There was further controversy over another element. After considerable media pressure at the news conference which launched
the document, the Nationalists eventually conceded that Scotland
might face an initial deficit under certain circumstances. These circumstances were broadly an insistence by the rest of the UK in the
negotiations leading to independence that Scotland must bear a
share of the UK national debt.

Under this 'worst case' scenario – incorporating that debt
cost – the Nationalists finally acknowledged that Scotland might
face a deficit of around £1.5 billion in 2000/01 – but it would
steadily shrink, they argued, and turn into a surplus.

However, in the 'worst case' section of their published document,
the SNP opted to publish only the figures for 2002/03 showing
Scotland virtually in balance – and for 2003/04, showing a projected
surplus of £1 billion: the rosier end of the picture, in other words.
Their argument was that they felt it right to publish the full picture
for the anticipated point of entry to the Euro. Further, they dis-
counted the prospect of this 'worst case' scenario coming to pass,
arguing that Scotland had already contributed her share of the UK
debt through North Sea oil in the 1980s.

The Nationalists also argued that any such 'worst case' deficit
would be less than for the UK – and would still easily be low enough
to enable Scotland to meet the Maastricht criteria for membership
of the Euro zone. They argued – in the main document – that their
'base case' showed a surplus for Scotland of £869 million in 2000/01,
rising to £3.3 billion in 2003/04. These figures excluded the UK
debt share estimate.

The exercise should perhaps be praised for its relative detail and
political courage so close to an election, but the Nationalists would
have helped their case substantially if they had been prepared to be
frank and to include all the deficit estimates in the main document.
Journalists, myself included, were obliged to pursue the issue with
the party's Treasury team of John Swinney and Andrew Wilson outside the news conference. As Swinney stood on the banks of the
Clyde outside the Moat House Hotel in Glasgow, he attempted to

answer our persistent queries with the use of a calculator borrowed from the *Financial Times* reporter. Eventually, Wilson produced a document with the figures listed.

This was not the SNP's finest moment. They were ready with arguments as to why the deficit was containable and not a source of concern. In which case, they should have had the courage to include the full figures in the published document. Privately, senior SNP strategists admit that they should have addressed this entire issue months or even years before the Scottish election, rather than allowing it to become a topic of contention days before polling.

Labour counter-attacked with a rebuttal news conference, chaired by the Chancellor. Among a series of claims, Labour argued that it would be ludicrous to attempt to exclude the UK debt from calculations, that the SNP had underestimated the independence costs of such matters as defence and social security and that the estimate of oil revenue was too high. The Nationalists, naturally, rebutted the rebuttals.

SNP strategists have long, privately, accepted that they cannot win the war of numbers outright. Their best hope, realistically, is to neutralise an extremely potent fear in the popular imagination, fostered by the SNP's rivals. The charge lodged by Labour and others is that independence would inevitably damage Scotland's economy. Like a defence advocate, the Nationalists hope they can plant a doubt in the public mind over this charge by offering an alternative explanation of events. They plead 'not guilty' in the hope of the charges being found 'not proven'.

One problem for the SNP is that at least part of their presentation rests upon the dynamics of independence itself, the claim that there would be an independence windfall, that Scotland might thrive in the same manner as the Irish economy in recent years.

Their critics attack these supposed future gains with arguments based on immediate problems: that claimed 'structural deficit' and the alleged cost of reconfiguring the relationship with England, dividing the UK public sector in areas like social security into two parts.

No matter how much either side attempts to argue that their economic claims are precise and defensible, the decision for the voters remains broadly an act of faith. Either they believe that Scotland is, broadly, better off in tandem with the rest of the UK or they believe that the economic advantage would lie in setting up an independent state or they believe that the advantages of independence outweigh any financial problems and they are prepared to take the risk.

That assessment is not purely an academic exercise. Naturally, it has an immediate impact in terms of the voters' view of devolution. To be precise, they may be more inclined to look favourably on the decisions of a devolved Parliament if they have firmly implanted in them the conviction that independence would be damaging. By contrast, if the Nationalists can gain the edge in the argument over the cost of independence, then the devolved settlement might come under question.

To conclude this chapter, let me revert to looking at the potential challenge which may confront Scottish spending under devolution: the Barnett squeeze.

When I discussed the matter with Donald Dewar, he described Barnett – in customarily cautious language – as 'a mixed blessing'.[6] On other occasions, he has been heard to suggest that there might come a time when the Scottish body politic begins to urge a rethink of the very formula it was once so keen to defend.

At the same time, of course, it is guaranteed that politicians from England will sustain the demand to cut Scottish spending and reallocate the money south of the Border. That demand will become more and more persistent – perhaps not immediately, but eventually. It is hard to escape the conclusion that – at some future date – there will have to be an overall assessment of the relative needs of the constituent parts of the UK.

That is not in the present thinking of the UK Government – but it could emerge at some future point, perhaps under a different Chancellor or in different economic circumstances.

Such a review could, as I have noted, present a further spending challenge to Scotland. However, there could be pressures in the other direction. As one senior Labour source cautioned me, one should never underestimate the desire of the British state to placate Scotland.

Notes

1. Paper by Professor Brian Ashcroft (April 1999), *Quarterly Economic Commentary*, Glasgow: Fraser of Allander Institute.

2. Professor Neil Kay (December 1998), *Quarterly Economic Commentary*, Glasgow: Fraser of Allander Institute.
3. Interview with Professor Arthur Midwinter, 24 March 1999.
4. November 1998, *Government Expenditure and Revenue in Scotland 1996/97*, Edinburgh: Scottish Office Statistics Division.
5. Scottish National Party (April 1999), *Taking Scotland into the Twenty-first Century: an Economic Strategy for Independence*.
6. Interview with Donald Dewar, 16 January 1998.

14 The European Question

Scotland is a marvellous place for mythology. Indeed, Scots have such a love of legend that they often seem capable of sustaining two mutually contradictory myths at one and the same time. At the most basic level, my fellow citizens can, simultaneously, remain alert to the realities of modern Scotland while painting a picture straight out of Ossian or Brigadoon for visitors. I have frequently done it myself. It is part of our charm.

In one breath, the Scot will praise the Scottish education system and laud the value of well-directed schooling. There may be hints that Scotland's system is superior to that of England or indeed the rest of the globe. The very next moment, scarcely pausing for a second breath, the Scot will talk cloyingly of our native intelligence, of those who display rare talent without the requirement to trouble the education system.

There will be much talk of Rabbie Burns. The scene will be unfolded whereby Burns tramps home from the field, casts aside his plough, scrapes the sharn off his calloused hands – and dashes off a perfect neo-Augustan mock-epic, devising his own verse form in the by-going.

Both self-images are, needless to say, economical with the truth. Burns absorbed as much classical education as was possible within the limited resources of his family circumstances. By dint of his own efforts, his reading was relatively extensive. An untutored ploughman poet he certainly was not. Equally, while Scotland's early establishment of a system of parish-based schooling is praiseworthy and her universities, ancient and modern, well worth defending, it may be self-deluding to categorise Scottish education as being of unquestioned international renown.

In the political field, there are several Scottish myths: some with a foundation in fact but often with an added varnish.

For example, we are frequently told that Scotland is inherently more egalitarian than England. Such assessments are often based on no more than a left-of-centre voting pattern, which may depend rather upon sociological make-up or historical loyalties or the decline of the Tories over the identity question. There are sporadic indications of a somewhat more collectivist approach in Scotland but the prevailing myth substantially overstates this factor.

Perhaps the most persistent contemporary myth is that Scotland is intrinsically pro-European while England is anti, that Scotland adores the European Union while England abhors it. Again, myth does not mean straightforward falsehood. This collective self-image has something of a basis in fact. Opinion polls have suggested, for example, that Scotland might be more amenable to the single European currency.

However, if you ask for evidence of Scotland's basic love of all things European, you may simply get vague references to the Auld Alliance with France and to long-distant trade with Belgium. In the last resort, you may even hear wild talk of the Hanseatic League. The untested presumption is that Scotland is, at bottom, internationalist and outward-looking while England is self-obsessed and isolationist.

Either way, fact or fiction, this self-image has a practical significance for modern Scottish politics. Myths matter. The wise political tactician will defer – at least overtly – to the conventional wisdom, as J. K. Galbraith called it. At the same time, our tactician may be attempting to bend public opinion in a different direction. You can generally spot such speeches. They will contain phrases like: 'While acknowledging that. . . .'

The European myth matters in Scottish politics because parties have had to factor it into their attitudes to self-government. One key test of the devolved Parliament – and rival schemes – has been its capacity to interact with European affairs, to give Scotland 'A

Voice in Europe': a phrase generally uttered as if in capital letters.

This has been particularly true since the SNP became pro-European. Since 1988, this previously Euro-sceptical party has definitively viewed sovereign Scottish membership of the European Union as a counterpoint to claims that Scotland would be breaking valuable collaborative links by sundering the Union with England. Scotland, it is argued, would leave the UK but join Europe as an independent nation. This is not, we are told, separation but reunion.

For the SNP, this stance has provoked a few awkward questions, initially from internal dissidents who regarded the switch as watering down the party's commitment to full Scottish sovereignty. What, they wondered, was the point of breaking with London only to hand power to Brussels? Subsequently, rival parties have challenged the SNP on European detail: for example, the party's commitment to Scottish membership of the single European currency. Such challenges became particularly acute after the SNP declared during the Scottish parliamentary election campaign that an independent Scotland would adhere to sterling during the transition to joining the Euro.

Despite such challenges, of varying intensity, the Nationalists have persisted with adherence to an emerging European ideal. The notion of Scotland in Europe is now built into the collective psyche of the SNP. It has become one of their core values.

For now, however, I am more concerned with the impact the European question has had on the wider Scottish political scene – and particularly the development of home rule. The SNP standpoint, in particular, has meant that advocates of devolution have been careful to stress the potential for the new Parliament to play a role in European affairs. Devolutionists could not allow their construction to be undermined by the suggestion that it would have minimal influence in the new European power-base.

The description of the role which a devolved Scotland could play in Europe has, however, varied sharply over the years.

In the first Convention document,[1] completed in 1990, there was warm approval for the concept of Scottish involvement in European affairs. It was argued that 'an effective Scottish voice in the EEC is a pressing priority.' The very phrase 'EEC' instantly dates the document but there are other elements which have also been overtaken.

The 1990 document, 'Convention One', stresses its devolutionary roots – repudiating independence with the remarkably confident assertion that Europe as a whole is abandoning such outdated notions as sovereignty. The document argues that Scotland should desist from 'struggling to re-establish a nation state at the very time Europe is moving away from this narrow concept'.

For now, we need not concern ourselves with this assertion which is, at the very least, arguable and open to qualification. It is the detail, later in the document, which provides more substance for analysis.

The document states that 'Scotland's Parliament should establish a representative office in Brussels to facilitate relations between itself and European Community institutions.' There has been little political dissent from this notion. Indeed, the previous Conservative Government – while preserving its opposition to devolution – backed the development of an office in Brussels to foster Scotland's trading and lobbying links, although an entertaining leak of a Scottish Office memo suggested that the concept was not universally popular among Ministers, with one voicing concern about subsidised junketing.

The more intriguing element lies in the further assertion in the 1990 Convention document that 'there should be a statutory entitlement for Scotland's Parliament and/or Executive to be represented in UK Ministerial delegations to the Council of Ministers.' By this, it is presumably meant that the legislation establishing a Scottish Parliament would guarantee that Scottish Ministers could cluster round the fabled 'top table' of European negotiations – and that the UK Government could not keep them away.

By the time of the 1995 Convention document,[2] the tone has changed somewhat. 'Great importance' is still attached to links with Europe. There is still support for a representative office in Brussels, although it is noted that the Scottish Parliament will 'undertake this through consultation and co-operation with other Scottish and UK organisations which operate European offices so as to maximise impact and provide co-ordination among agencies'.

While all this may be inherently sensible and even helpful, it is important to note that the independence of action of the Scottish Parliament's European operation has been qualified.

So too has that place at the 'top table'. Instead of the statutory representation offered in 1990, the 1995 document states that 'Scotland's Parliament will be represented in UK Ministerial delegations to the Council of Ministers *where appropriate* [my italics] and

Scottish Ministers will lead these UK delegations when the areas under discussion are of specific relevance to Scotland.' New links are also proposed: with the European Committee of the Regions and with the Economic and Social Committee (Ecosoc).

Again, this is a shift of emphasis, not the abandonment of a plan. There is, however, a clear distinction between a statutory right to attend talks and involvement 'where appropriate'. The key element, of course, is who decides when that involvement would be appropriate: Edinburgh or Whitehall, the Scottish Executive or the Foreign Office. The 1995 document does not make that point clear. However, the relatively firm forecast that Scottish Ministers will have the opportunity to lead UK delegations still leaves open the prospect of a significant European presence for the Scottish Parliament.

Any lingering doubts were cleared up after Labour took power at Westminster and produced its White Paper in 1997.[3] The chapter on relations with the European Union opens in unequivocal fashion: 'Relations with Europe are the responsibility of the United Kingdom Parliament and Government.' In mitigation, it adds, however: 'The Scottish Parliament will have an important role in those aspects of European Union business which affect devolved areas.'

Autonomy of action by the Scottish Parliament is clearly constrained. The picture painted is of the UK Government taking the lead – but drawing upon the expertise and advice of the Scottish Parliament and the other elements of the new 'regional government' structure emerging in the UK.

It is stressed that Scottish Ministers will be 'fully involved' in UK discussions about policy towards the EU – but equally it is stressed that there must be 'mutual respect for the confidentiality of those discussions and adherence to the resultant UK line'. No question, in other words, of the Scottish team pursuing a different approach. Self-evidently, this section is an attempt to reconstruct or replicate the concept of Cabinet collective responsibility which, as we have already discussed, is implicitly undermined by the existence of multiple legislatures and multiple executives.

Further, the White Paper proposes that Ministers and officials from the Scottish Executive should be able to play a role at relevant EU Council meetings. They are, it seems, potentially back at the top table. However, it is clear that their participation will be by invitation rather than as of right.

It is stressed that 'the UK lead Minister will retain overall responsibility for the negotiations and determine how best each member of the team can contribute to securing the agreed policy position so that, in appropriate cases, Scottish Executive Ministers could speak for the UK in Councils.' Their role, it is stressed, would be to 'support and advance the single UK negotiating line which they have played a part in developing'. Unlike the Convention documents drafted in opposition, there is no room for doubt here; the UK Government will set the rules for participation by the Scottish Executive in EU matters. Statutory representation is out.

While this is the kernel of the chapter, there are a range of other detailed provisions, including a requirement for the Scottish Parliament to implement EU obligations which cover devolved matters and proposals for the involvement of Scotland in the informal machinery of EU consultation.

Finally, the notion of a Scottish representative office in Brussels is restated – although it is argued that it should 'complement rather than cut across' UKREP, the formal diplomatic body which represents the views of the UK to European institutions. For the avoidance of any possible remaining doubt, the chapter concludes by stating that the 'guiding principle' should be the 'closest possible' cooperation between the UK Government and the Scottish Executive on EU affairs.

The legislation implementing devolution, the Scotland Act 1998, gives effect to that approach. It states that relations with the European Union are reserved to Westminster. Given that statement, there is very little detailed reference to Scotland's role. This, again, is entirely consistent; the Scottish Parliament's involvement in Europe is not statutory in the sense originally envisaged by the Convention, so there is no lengthy provision for it in the legislation. Schedule 5 of the Act provides a role for the new Parliament in 'assisting Ministers of the Crown' in relation to European matters.

This confirmation of a subsidiary position for the Scottish Parliament in Europe is, of course, entirely consistent with the overall approach of the White Paper and the Government's devolutionary measures more generally. As must be repeatedly stressed, the Labour Government's reforms are devolution within the United Kingdom, not a separation of Scotland and England.

From that perspective, the approach adopted within the White Paper and the subsequent legislation is not only consistent but inevitable. At the very least, however, it is instructive to note that the final approach in the legislation differs measurably from that promised or outlined in opposition. The early, eager ambition of the Convention has confronted the reality that a European member state must offer a united voice in negotiations, that there can be no room for disparity.

Again, I should stress that I am not remotely criticising the approach adopted in the legislation. Within the parameters of a devolutionary settlement, it is entirely reasonable to stress that the UK must take the lead role. Indeed, given the open scepticism of several Ministers and in sections of Whitehall, it is perhaps remarkable that anything has survived at all from the earlier plans to give the new Parliament a voice in Europe.

The inconsistency, if there is one, perhaps lies rather in the earlier Convention documents. As with the notion of 'entrenching' the devolved Parliament against future abolition, the Convention sought to promise what it could not deliver. It was never feasible that a devolved Parliament within a larger state – where state power persists – could have an autonomous or semi-autonomous role in Europe.

For one thing, common sense dictates that there must ultimately be a single member state position in European talks. European negotiations are difficult enough without the prospect of a multiple choice menu of policies emerging from a single member. For another, the apparent ambition for a semi-autonomous role in foreign affairs simply diverged from the core element of the scheme being mapped out for Scotland by the Convention. Given the challenge posed by the Nationalists, it is entirely understandable that the Conventioneers sought to highlight the possibility of a European voice.

But talk of a statutory role inevitably reflects full independence or the shared power of federalism, not devolution. If there is a single member state and a single state government, there must be a single voice, whatever formal consultations may precede the utterance of that voice.

I believe, however, that the contradiction between the early Convention approach and the final legislation reflects an inherent tension which may resurface. It is not difficult to envisage circumstances in which there could be an awkward dilemma.

Let us suppose that at some point in the future the European Union is considering a substantial revision of the rules governing fisheries. Perhaps the quota or the available fishing areas are to be altered. Let us suppose that the UK's interests in this matter are not uniform – that, for example, the Scottish fleet broadly wants one approach to be adopted while the fishing towns of the South-west of England favour another.

Negotiations are due to open in Brussels and the Scottish Executive, with its particular interest in this field, is invited to play its part in 'assisting Ministers of the Crown', as the Act provides. The relevant Scottish Minister duly attends preparatory talks to settle the single UK line which will be advanced at the European negotiations. But she faces a quandary.

It swiftly becomes clear that the demands of the Scottish fleet are out of step with the rest of the UK. A common UK position cannot be formulated around those demands. Further, the Scottish Minister suspects that the fisheries row may be used by the UK Government in a trade-off over another EU controversy, perhaps of more general relevance to the economy of the UK.

How, then, does our notional Scottish Minister proceed? She can argue strenuously for the Scottish position. In such circumstances, however, the fishing interests of Cornwall and Devon would be bound to complain, with some justification, that they are being thwarted by a Minister they did not elect from an Executive they cannot hold to account in a Scottish Parliament with which they have absolutely no connection. In any event, the UK Minister might well decide that the common state position runs contrary to the Scottish demands.

Alternatively, our Minister can hold her peace and sit placidly on the fringe of the eventual Brussels talks as a line perceived to be inimical to the interests of the Scottish fleet is advanced and agreed. In such circumstances, the Minister can expect a relatively warm reception from the Scottish Parliament – and the Scottish fleet – on her return.

I am aware that this is a deliberately extreme example where the interests are polarised. I am aware that most preparatory negotiations will involve an element of give and take. It is, however, by no means inconceivable that a Scottish Minister might be unable to square the apparent interests of her own backyard with the ultimate obligation to pursue a common UK line.

It will be argued that this quandary often confronted Ministers from the territorial departments under the pre-devolutionary system.

They frequently found that their 'regional' interest departed to some degree from the wider UK perspective.

Certainly that is true and it is arguable that matters will proceed smoothly by the customary system of trading off one demand against another – that Scotland, provided her Ministers are energetic and alert, should be able to chalk up as many, or more, successes than concessions. There is, however, I believe, something of a structural difference between the old system and the new.

The Scottish Parliament may be of a different political make-up from Westminster. The May 1999 elections, for example, left Scotland with a coalition in a hung parliament by contrast with the huge Labour majority at Westminster. The Scottish Parliament will certainly develop its own dynamic, command its own loyalty. In the past, territorial Ministers such as the Scottish Secretary were advancing their demands within a single Cabinet comprised of colleagues and were answerable to a common Parliament in which their party, by definition, could reasonably expect support from its own majority.

In the future, the First Minister from the Scottish executive will be haggling with UK Ministers from a different Parliament and, possibly, from a different party. The UK Ministers will be answerable to and influenced by one set of party political realities. The Scottish Ministers will be governed by another. Unlike Cabinet colleagues, the two sets of Ministers may have no over-riding partisan motivation for reaching an agreed deal, for preserving an appearance of unity. It may, indeed, be in their political interests to be seen to be standing up against the other side.

Further, this does not apply to Scotland alone. The European question may have become more sharply political in Scotland but Wales and Northern Ireland must be taken into account in any definition of the UK's developing constitutional structure. Certainly, the Foreign Office takes them into account.

While other Whitehall departments may have disregarded or played down the impact of devolutionary change, the Foreign Office has been alert to the potential challenge to the established order from the outset and was pro-active in preparing for the new set-up. Indeed, sources suggest that the Foreign Office Permanent Secretary Sir John Kerr was briefing internally to the effect that the advent of devolution was the single biggest structural issue facing the department.

In preparation for devolution, the Foreign Office set up a unit known as the Devolved Administrations Department – or DaD. Its civil service head – George Fergusson, an acute and intelligent Ayrshireman – is occasionally referred to, with mandarin wit, as Grandad. DaD's paternal duty towards his devolved offspring is to make sure that all is well within the family of nations and territories making up the reformed UK.

The object is to comply with the intentions of the devolution White Paper, that the views of Scotland – along with Wales and Northern Ireland, of course – are fed into the machinery of the UK Government with regard to foreign affairs and, particularly, European Union negotiations.

DaD works on three levels with regard to preparations for European negotiations. Officials will maintain informal contact between the administrations, on a daily basis if necessary. There may be formal talks in advance of important negotiations in order to establish the common UK line. Finally, if necessary, these preparatory talks may involve the full-scale Joint Ministerial Committee which has been established to bring together members of the various executives. A JMC covers each important area of governmental activity where there is crossover between Whitehall and the devolved administrations.

While it is stressed that this structure is designed to link Whitehall with all the devolved territories, it is tacitly recognised that Scotland may well seek to play a bigger role in European talks, given the nature of the Scottish Parliament and the history of political controversy over this issue in Scotland.

In many ways, of course, this structure simply replicates the previous arrangements for gathering and assessing the views of the territorial departments like the Scottish and Welsh Offices. Again, though, there is a clear structural difference.

The Foreign Office has diligently pursued the task of smoothing relations within the new administrative and political set-up. Its ultimate duty, however, is to Her Majesty's Government – and that means Westminster. Ministers from the devolved administrations receive briefing and guidance but not to the same degree as that available to Ministers from Westminster.

It has been decided within the Foreign Office that the briefing to devolved Ministers can only be strictly factual, an enhanced version of the information which might be made available, for example, to a British company or public sector organisation of recognised status. There can be no question of guiding devolved Ministers on policy or discussing strategic possibilities. The problem, again, is that the devolved Executives lie beyond the reach of the doctrine of collective responsibility which covers the Westminster Government. Further, the Foreign Office might find itself briefing political opponents of their Westminster bosses.

Two things seem clear from the Foreign Office perspective. Firstly, the department takes its obligations to consult and involve the devolved administrations extremely seriously – by contrast, occasionally, with the attitude elsewhere in Whitehall. Secondly, the Foreign Office is in no doubt where ultimate power lies.

Again from a Foreign Office perspective, it is taken as read from the legislation that UK Ministers will select, lead and guide the negotiating teams in European talks. Ministers from the devolved administrations may well be involved but within the ambit of an agreed UK line, as the White Paper made clear. Given the potential requirement to consult three devolved administrations, this seems – to the Foreign Office – to be simple common sense. As I have argued elsewhere, within the context of a devolved settlement, it is very hard indeed to disagree with that judgement, logically.

However, particularly in Scotland, there may well be dissent, polit-ically: either over the practical implications as they affect individual issues and Scottish grievances or over the principle of Westminster control. The Scottish Nationalists, understandably given their view-point, do not take kindly to DaD's supervisory role.

In a speech before the elections,[4] the SNP leader Alex Salmond made that concern explicit. He told the European Institute in Brussels that Scotland would not be satisfied with 'subsumed' involvement in EU matters. He warned: 'If the UK position is to be given in the Council of Ministers, it must never be given without either an assent from Scotland or a dissent from Scotland. Our democracy demands nothing less.'

Such an approach would be a clear breach of the approach spelled out in the White Paper and implemented by the Foreign Office. It would risk breaching the confidentiality rule governing preparatory talks and the establishment of a firm, single UK line. If applied rigorously, it might even give the Scottish Executive and Parliament an effective veto over UK proposals which it did not favour.

Self-evidently, such a veto would not be tolerated by the UK administration which must, as the member state, be able to advance its position with confidence. Equally self-evidently, the May 1999 elections did not give Mr Salmond a mandate to pursue this demand other than in opposition.

Donald Dewar has repeatedly sought to play down the potential for this issue to provoke friction. Delivering a lecture in January 1999,[5] he scorned the suggestion that Scotland might have distinctive interests which might diverge from those of the rest of the UK. Indeed, he listed key issues such as trade policy, the single market, agriculture, fisheries and regional policy – and declared, confidently, that 'in every case Scotland's interest and the interests of the rest of the UK are aligned.'

Mr Dewar went further in this lecture and sought to question the capacity of small member states to influence European decisions in their favour. He derided the claims surrounding the power of such small states as 'the tyranny of the tiny', plainly implying that its impact was overstated.

He added: 'The brute fact is that even in today's European Union, the big member states call the shots. Enlargement is likely to see voting power better balanced to share of population. More power to the big. Enlargement is likely to see an extension of majority voting. What use the Scottish veto?'

As I have noted elsewhere, I regard this line of argument as partially flawed. It may well be true that the accession of other states will alter the voting balance. It is incontestably true that a big state like Germany or the UK has more clout than a small state like Denmark or Ireland. Neither of these statements, however, has particular relevance for a sub-state nation like Scotland in determining its standpoint within Europe.

While it is true that the UK has more clout than Denmark, it may also be true that Denmark has more direct clout – as a member state with a place at that fabled 'top table' – than Scotland, whose views are filtered through UK membership. It depends on whether we accept Donald Dewar's assessment that the UK's interests and those of Scotland are always aligned.

If they are, then Scotland can rest easy, knowing that the muscle of the UK is flexing in her interests. If they are not – and I think it at least feasible they may occasionally diverge – then the potency of the UK may not be of much good to Scotland. Indeed, it is even technically possible that the UK's bargaining clout may be directed against the narrower interests of Scotland.

The key issue is the relative importance attached to individual demands. EU negotiations always involve a trade-off. Germany, for example, will moderate its demand for a reduction in its budgetary contributions provided France is willing to drop its objection to a trade liberalisation measure which the Germans are particularly anxious to secure.

In such circumstances, it is at least feasible that Scotland may attach particular importance to some sectoral interest such as fishing or transport – while UK negotiators may be keener to see movement on trade reform or EU expansion. It is, again, feasible that the UK negotiating team will be willing to drop issues which a Scottish team, from a different standpoint, would wish to pursue.

I am very far from asserting that there is an incontestable case for autonomous Scottish membership of the European Union. It may well be that Scotland benefits by being able to borrow a big stick from Westminster. It is arguable that an independent Scotland would be sidelined. Donald Dewar noted in his lecture that no European region has broken from its member state to assume sovereign membership of the EU. In passing, it might equally be noted, however, that there has scarcely been a rush of small nation states seeking to merge with their bigger neighbours to enjoy a share of their negotiating might.

It is not sufficient, I feel, simply to state that the UK carries weight – and that Scotland intrinsically benefits. This is an assertion which will require to be tested over a long period while the Scottish Parliament settles into its new role.

Meanwhile the Parliament can develop alliances at sub-state level. There is the Committee of the Regions (CoR), which was designed precisely to give a voice to such sub-state organisations as the new Parliament although, initially, Scotland was represented by local authority members.

It is amusing to recall that Scotland's membership of this Committee was once taken so seriously that the SNP members in the House of Commons were prepared to back the Tory Government in a key vote in return for an enhanced Scottish stake in the CoR. Looking back, it seems a triumph of expectation over reality.

I have attended meetings of the Committee of the Regions and I study its pronouncements with variable diligence. It has long struck me as resembling a street vagrant, clutching your arm and assuring you of his sincerity and concern for your welfare. You know that he means no harm but equally you know that he is overstating his powers and you would be better off free from his company. The Committee of the Regions is no doubt worthy – but is ignored by the powerful in the European institutions. It is not Scotland's entry to European decision-making.

Perhaps, then, Scotland might form relationships directly with other sub-state regions like the Spanish provinces or the German *Länder*. That would seem to me more productive than the institutional approach represented by the Committee of the Regions. It was the approach signalled by Donald Dewar when he announced the establishment of Scotland's lobbying office in Brussels, Scotland House.[6]

Dewar said that his officials had consulted some of the 150 or so regional organisations with offices already in Brussels. He cited the examples of Bavaria and Catalonia in arguing that Scotland would join them in becoming 'a more visible and more effective regional player on the European stage'.

There may, however, be a problem of mismatch. Britain's asymmetrical system of devolution differs from that of Spain – where there are provincial governments throughout the country with varying degrees of power – and is substantially different from the system in Germany where the *Länder* (or regional states) divide responsibilities with the Federal Government.

Ministers from the *Länder*, for example, will normally take the lead in European negotiations where the subject matter under discussion falls into their area of responsibility. In such cases, it will be a Minister from one of the sixteen *Länder* who will speak for Germany, nominated by the *Bundesrat*, the German upper parliamentary chamber which represents regional interests.

Further, the *Bundesrat* has considerable power within Germany to frustrate or delay the programme of the Federal Government if it does not like the direction advocated by Federal Ministers. Self-evidently, this clout gives the *Länder* a bargaining tool to obtain concessions, although it is a lever which is best used sparingly and in order to obtain an advance for the entire *Länder* sector rather than for a single Land.

Länder politicians are big league in Germany; Chancellor Gerhard Schröder was formerly the President of the *Bundesrat*. They can exercise power on the European stage; former Chancellor Helmut Kohl was obliged to reverse his stand on a proposed deal concerning immigration and justice matters at the European summit in Amsterdam following protests from the *Länder* who had responsibility for implementing part of the package.

It should be said, however, that there are influential German voices raised against the power of the *Länder*. It is claimed that the system is costly, cumbersome and bureaucratic. There is talk that the Federal Government – especially following its transfer to Berlin – may seek to re-establish the power of the centre at the expense of regional power. For now, though, it may be sufficient for our purposes to note that the Scottish Parliament's clout is likely to fall short of that available to the *Länder*.

It is entirely conceivable, however, that Scotland will be able to form a network of links with organisations and regional administrations in Brussels. At the very least, this network will act as a shared information system – an early warning for problems that could affect Scotland's interests. At best, Scotland may be able to cooperate with other sub-state governments in order to press for practical action such as amendments to proposed treaties.

As with so much in politics, it is impossible to be precise about Scotland's future role in Europe. We may benefit enormously from building new alliances across Europe. DaD from the Foreign Office may display a fatherly concern for our progress which produces genuine results. Alternatively, we may find the new structure frustrating and chafe at the constraints on our power.

Notes

1. Constitutional Convention report (November 1990), *Towards Scotland's Parliament*.
2. Constitutional Convention (November 1995), *Scotland's Parliament, Scotland's Right*.
3. Government White Paper (July 1997), *Scotland's Parliament*, Edinburgh: Scottish Office.
4. Lecture by Alex Salmond, European Institute, Brussels, February 1999.
5. Lothian European Lecture by Donald Dewar, Edinburgh, January 1999.
6. News release, Scottish Office, February 1999.

15 The English Question

Towards the end of the nineteenth century, Gladstone attempted to answer the Irish Question. The Parliament now established in Edinburgh is an attempt to address the Scottish Question. It is reasonable to argue that the great conundrum which has yet to be tackled seriously is the question of how to govern England under the reformed constitution which is emerging.

Perhaps I should start with a few trite truisms. The English Question is first and foremost for the people of England to address: that is, if they believe there is a problem at all. It affects Scotland only inasmuch as there may be a connected effort to alter Scotland's representation at Westminster. In reality, as opposed to perception, the governance of England has not been altered at all by Scottish devolution.

That last remark, I know, risks occasioning an outburst of spluttered indignation. Hasn't England been changed utterly by Scottish devolution? From outraged commentators, we hear tales of Celtic invaders insolently telling the English what to do. All the Scots ever do is whinge. Outrageous. Send them packing. If they want to run Scotland, good luck to them – but why should they run England as well?

For me as a Scottish journalist, the most intriguing and entertaining aspect of monitoring the English response to devolution has been that the sharpest, most horror-struck comments have come not from the Tory commentators, but from the liberal Left. I feel sure this has a partisan explanation. The Left fears its cause will suffer from the erosion – or disappearance – of the Scottish vote in UK politics.

Much of the right-wing comment has consisted of tedious similes from *Braveheart*, complete elision of the difference between devolution and independence and world-weary sorrow that the Scots are being misled. The finale is usually a thunderous warning to the people of England to wake up before it is too late.

Occasionally, there is a defiant, even jubilant note. Go, if you must, you Scots. England will be Tory forever! Certainly, Scotland's consistent contribution of large numbers of Labour MPs to the Commons adds a degree of force to such bravado from the Right – although the 1997 general election, when England also voted Labour in large numbers, is a rather inconvenient counterpoint. In general, though, Conservative commentators can comfort themselves with the notion that Scottish separation, as they invariably style it, might assist the Tory cause in England.

The Right, then, has spoken out. However, if you want real angst over the consequences of devolution, you must set aside *The Daily Telegraph* and turn to the pages of *The Guardian* or *The Observer*. In contrast with the underlying perspective of the Right, I believe the liberal Left fears that its project of reshaping England will be undermined if Scottish votes are withdrawn. It is a concern, consequently, not so much for Britain or England as for the sort of England which the centre Left wants to see.

Certainly, the extent of the concern has been wonderful to witness. Here's David Walker, providing an Analysis piece in *The Guardian*.[1] 'Even in the debate about daylight saving time, there's a new edge of English self-consciousness. Why should clocks be changed for the benefit of kids going to school in Glenrothes?'

Or Hugo Young – one of the most acute of contemporary commentators – also writing in *The Guardian*, before the general election.[2] He forecast then that the Tories in the Commons would fight to the last ditch over devolution; this proved to be wrong. He also claimed that Labour would have to play down elements of devolution like the financial subsidy of the Scots in order to get the package through. Then the apocalyptic warning: 'For the purposes of the election, Scotland has to be strung along in the belief that it can have the best of all worlds. But, after that, when the British wake up, it will be a different story.' Presumably by 'British' he means 'English', but the point is made.

Hugo Young again,[3] long after the general election, warning that the establishment of a Scottish Parliament has made it impossible in practical terms for senior Scots like Gordon Brown to advance their careers further at Westminster. 'The enormity of the price that Scotchness may yet exact must be intolerable to contemplate. It portends a systemic crisis for the working-out of modern Britishness, perhaps some kind of slow crack-up.'

On reading such remarks – and there are many more in similar vein – the casual observer, perhaps from overseas, would undoubtedly be intrigued. What kind of horror is it that has been imposed upon the poor, brave people of England? What are they being forced to endure?

The position is this. In future, now that devolution is in place, England will be governed exactly as she has been for centuries by a Parliament at Westminster where the vast majority of the MPs come from English seats. The only concrete difference is that, after the next shuffle of boundary constituencies, it is foreshadowed in legislation that there will be considerably fewer MPs from Scotland. It is also likely that several of the Scottish MPs who remain at Westminster, including the Nationalists, will voluntarily abstain on English issues. The arithmetic of the Commons will consequently be substantially tilted in favour of English interests. There will be no other change to the governance of English matters.

This is what is happening in practice – as opposed to what is frequently perceived to be taking place. England's control of her own domestic matters is growing proportionately stronger, not weaker. I thought it pertinent to state the genuine position presently confronting England before conceding that it is the perception which may well drive events.

There is talk again of the West Lothian question. In its original form – as advanced by the Labour MP Tam Dalyell whose constituency was formerly called West Lothian – the question was how it could be right that a Scottish MP at Westminster after devolution could vote upon matters such as education affecting English seats but that same MP could not vote on such matters affecting his own constituency because they would have been devolved to a Scottish Parliament.

Mr Dalyell intervened repeatedly during the debates over the 1970s devolution legislation to pose his question. As I recall, and I am aware that I am paraphrasing, he did so by summing up the impact upon communities in his area and similarly named areas in England. 'How could it be right', he would intone in that wonderfully penetrating voice, 'that I as the MP for West Lothian could vote upon schools in Blackburn, Lancashire, but not upon schools in Blackburn in my constituency?'

I have, incidentally, the greatest regard for Tam Dalyell as a parliamentarian. His persistence over such issues as the Lockerbie inquiry is to be commended. I particularly admire his style in asking supplementary questions. A Minister delivers the opening reply drafted for him by his civil servants and slumps on the front bench hoping for a lengthy and complicated supplementary to allow time to muster the next thought. Up pops Tam to boom simply 'Why?' or 'How much?' Much shuffling of front-bench papers ensues.

The clarity and simplicity of the Dalyell approach has been rather obscured over the passage of time with regard to the West Lothian question. It is now commonly expressed as challenging the right of Scottish MPs at Westminster to vote on English matters when English MPs cannot vote on Scottish affairs. In essence, it is now used as shorthand for the mood I have outlined above: English political resentment at unwarranted Scottish interference.

It has become a political cliché to say that there are no answers to the West Lothian question within a Union structure. There are, however, a series of potential rebuttals which mitigate or vary its force.

As noted above, it can be pointed out that the West Lothian question in its contemporary guise patently does not apply at present. England has voted Labour by a significant margin. It has applied very infrequently in the past. By my calculation, the political balance in England has only been upset by the addition of Scottish members twice in the post-war period.

In other words, England has twice elected more Conservative MPs than Labour ones – yet ended up governed by Labour. This applied to the Labour Government between 1964 and 1966 and to the administration which lasted from February to October 1974. Every other Labour Government has had a majority of seats in England as well as in Scotland.

By contrast, it might be noted that the other signatory of the Act of Union, Scotland, has regularly voted Labour only to end up governed by the Conservatives. This applied with perhaps the greatest force to the Conservative administrations of Margaret Thatcher, which applied a new ideological zeal to politics.

A second rebuttal to West Lothian, then, is to note that it has applied to Scotland – in reverse, if you like – more commonly than it has applied to England. This, I stress, can be advanced as no more than a plea in mitigation by those who would seek to tackle the West Lothian challenge. It does not address the concerns of England.

Thirdly, the Labour Government case is that Westminster has opted of its own free will to devolve power to Scotland – to activate the West Lothian question. It is argued therefore that West Lothian is not an unforeseen consequence but a tolerable and relatively minor anomaly created by the sovereign UK Parliament.

This has always struck me as a weak case. It ignores the fact that the 'sovereign Westminster Parliament' broadly does what it is told by the governing party, in effect by the executive. While it is true that Labour has the power to create whatever anomaly it likes, this is the negation of reasoned argument. It is almost tantamount to saying that the Government can do anything – however patently stupid or unfair.

Fourthly, it is pointed out that there has in the past been a parallel anomaly when Northern Ireland had its own assembly but continued to send members to Westminster. The particular sensitivities of Westminster tend to reduce the frequency with which this argument is deployed. Further, Northern Ireland sends far fewer MPs to Westminster than Scotland – and consequently has far less capacity to activate a form of West Lothian question.

Finally, there is the practical approach adopted by the Labour Government. This is to pave the way for a reduction in the numbers of MPs from Scotland sent to Westminster. For the general election after next, it is expected that a boundary review will cut the number from the present seventy-two to sixty or even fewer. This, of course, does not answer West Lothian. It will still be the case that Scottish MPs are free to vote upon English matters. It does, however, lessen the chances of Scottish votes outweighing England's political choice.

Each of these arguments, then, is a rebuttal, not an answer. The most common private reply to the West Lothian question, muttered by Ministers under their breath, is: 'So what?'

What difference does it truly make to England if Scotland has devolution? It is not a reply which a politically acute government will want to offer to the English people.

As I have argued above, English governance will experience no practical impact whatsoever from Scottish devolution. Indeed, Tony Blair's insistence that a Scottish Parliament be accompanied by a cut in Scottish representation at Westminster tilts the balance in England's favour.

Further, it seems to me that it is at the very least questionable that those Conservatives who most vigorously supported an unreformed Union can credibly argue now for further change. They fully backed the governance of Scotland and England by a United Kingdom Parliament. They were prepared to accept that a UK mandate might vary across the Border, that England might, infrequently, be governed by a party she did not directly elect and that Scotland might, more regularly, be governed against her apparent electoral wishes.

The Union mandate would apply to both. The Kingdom would be governed in a United fashion. From an undiluted Unionist perspective, this was an entirely consistent standpoint. What has happened now, under devolution, is that Scottish domestic matters will be governed according to a distinctly Scottish mandate, not a UK one. English domestic matters will continue to be governed in exactly the same way – with the exception that the Scottish input will ultimately be less.

Conservative critics of devolution were entirely content for England and Scotland to be governed by the established rules, disregarding a century of complaint from Scottish Home Rule activists. They argued, forcibly, that the system should not be changed. Why then, in logic, should they complain now? England's position has not been altered at all. English legislation will still be processed by the House of Commons, by a Parliament which in future will contain fewer Scottish MPs. England will still be governed by the UK mandate the Conservatives were seemingly so anxious to maintain for Scotland and England combined.

The answer to these questions, of course, is that political debate is not governed purely by logic. Psychologically, everything has changed. Democratic government operates by consent. If that consent is withdrawn or becomes grudging, then democratic government begins to stutter and fail.

This was the case, I would argue, in nineteenth-century Britain before the Reform Act of 1832. This was the case in late twentieth-century Scotland, particularly when the Conservatives continued to govern with shrinking Scottish support. It may become the case in England in the future.

There is, as I have said, no strictly logical reason why it should. Part of the potential for resentment is undoubtedly fostered by the miscomprehension of devolution, enhanced by commentators who confuse Labour's reforms, deliberately or otherwise, with independence for Scotland.

The impression is created in the public mind that Scotland has gone her own way entirely and yet continues to influence English politics. Scotland, of course, is still governed by the UK Parliament in key matters like defence, macro-economics and social security – and is consequently entitled to a democratic say in the formulation of decisions affecting those areas. Scottish MPs are entitled to be at Westminster.

One has only to turn to the issue of defence to negate any impression that devolution equals independence – and that Scottish MPs should, consequently, be sent packing from Westminster. Defence remains a matter reserved to Westminster. Scotland continues to house the Trident nuclear deterrent. Scottish service personnel are still sent into conflict on the orders of the United Kingdom Government. That will continue to be the case in the future under devolution – even if the party governing in London is different from the party governing in Edinburgh.

In the context of devolution, that is entirely justifiable and right. However much certain commentators and politicians may argue otherwise, devolution does not equal the separation of Scotland from the United Kingdom. There can be no question, therefore, under devolution of removing Scottish influence from the House of Commons entirely.

I am aware that I have rather laboured this point but it seems to me that so much comment on the topic of devolution is based upon a misconception of its true nature that it was worth pursuing the question. Under devolution, Scotland remains in the United Kingdom.

The only issue, then, in the developing political relationship between Scotland and England is whether English domestic matters should continue to be affected by Scottish votes. As with so much else in politics, those who address this question are often pursuing a range of issues rather than simply the core question of English governance.

Tory backbenchers in the Commons now routinely complain about Scottish involvement at Westminster. While sidelining demands for an English Parliament, William Hague has argued that MPs from Scotland should be excluded from votes on English matters.

Those Tories who pursue this issue are often motivated by their residual distaste for the entire devolution project rather than by concrete examples of any consequential problem for England. It is partly a question of a self-fulfilling prophecy. They forecast devolution would be a disaster and consequently have little motivation to play down their complaints now.

Equally, the complaints have become embroiled in a wider issue: the search for a renewed sense of English identity. This in turn is entwined with the arguments over the influence of the European Union. It is no accident – although a fraction ironic – that those who most vigorously condemn Europe's overweening power are also those who resent the transfer of power from Westminster to Edinburgh. They want nothing to alter England's status.

This is not purely a question of political structures. For the Tory critics – as for the originators of devolution – it is a question of identity. The quintessential English Tory feels threatened, a little uncertain. They see power and influence leaching away to Brussels on the one hand and to Edinburgh on the other. They wonder: where stands London, where stands England in this uncertain and changing world?

Several writers and commentators have bemoaned the lack of a clear English identity. The new Poet Laureate, Andrew Motion, has argued that it is an issue which requires to be addressed in the aftermath of the assertion of Scottish identity which the new Parliament in Edinburgh represents.

Philip Johnston, addressing this question in *The Daily Telegraph*, noted a problem of definition in that 'whereas Scots wave the Saltire with pride, the Cross of St George has become associated with lager louts, bigoted fringe nationalists and Morris dancing.'[4]

The Campaign for an English Parliament, a minor but zealous organisation, argues in its literature, distributed around party conferences, that 'the most important reason for creating an English Parliament is to help restore confidence and self-respect to the people of England.'

Others forecast that there may be something evil and demonic in a revival of English patriotism or nationalism. Writing in the *Daily Record*, Quentin Letts summoned up an image of an emotive political leader attempting to whip up English fervour.[5] In a bizarre and gruesome passage, he added: 'All it would take is a few killings of English children in Scotland. All it could take is an English Salmond to come along and appeal to the Lionheart Factor.'

Such outlandish sentiments, I would suggest, do not remotely represent the feelings of the English people. I lived happily in London for six years, making several close friendships in the process. I have not succumbed to the current Scottish affectation for finding London crowded and distasteful. Rather, I found it and still find it among the most exciting cities in the world. My elder son was born there. (I am uncomfortably aware that in the preceding paragraph I have begun to sound like the most irritating of visitors to Scotland who talk patronisingly of their vague Scottish connections.)

Living in the Surrey suburbs, I did not encounter an aggressively assertive people. I did not encounter any dislike of the Scots who made their living in the capital. Rather I found a pleasant, comfortable populace, perhaps rather insular by contrast with their counterparts among the educated Scottish middle classes who are accustomed to seeking their fortunes more widely. If they thought about their national status at all, they invariably described themselves as English or British interchangeably.

It seems unlikely to me that such a populace will easily be stirred into the vicious resentment forecast by some commentators. It is, however, possible over a longer period that constant repetition of the alleged unfairness of Scottish involvement in Westminster politics will begin to have an impact. Without being fully understood, this may well become part of the conventional wisdom.

As I noted earlier, the liberal Left has a different perspective. It was most succinctly described by the journalist and political analyst Will Hutton in a lecture reported by his newspaper, *The Observer*.[6] Hutton is a renowned advocate of the Third Way political philosophy of free-market, inclusive social democracy pursued by Tony Blair.

In his lecture, Hutton warned: 'Scottish independence would be the end of Britain and the end of any idea of constructing a federal Britain. It would also, I argue, gravely weaken the liberal social democratic Left in these islands just when it needs to build international alliances rather than balkanise into separate movements.'

At one level, this can be seen as a plea for the liberal Left in Scotland and England to conjoin in order to advance the reform agenda in both nations. Put more simply, however, that means that England could not be relied upon to continue to vote Labour (or Liberal Democrat) in sufficient numbers to sustain the Blairite project of building a near-permanent centre Left government.

At its crudest, this argument may be said to take the West Lothian question and elevate it to new heights. Scotland must stay in the Union – so that England can have a centre Left reforming government, presumably regardless of England's future voting pattern.

I stress again it is a question of perspective. From an English centre Left standpoint, it can be legitimate to argue for common effort. However, it is not in itself a particularly convincing argument to deploy against Scottish independence. A Scottish Nationalist is unlikely to be swayed by an appeal to abandon support for independence in order to protect England from Toryism. To be entirely fair to Hutton, he also voices other, economic anxieties about independence in his lecture.

A third strand of thought – to add to Conservative and liberal Left – has entered the debate about English identity. The Scottish Nationalists assert the sovereign right of the Scottish people to determine their own constitutional future. They are aware, however, that England must have a voice in this, if only because independence would require negotiations with London and legislation through Westminster.

The SNP leader Alex Salmond has attempted, consequently, to address the English Question. In a lecture,[7] he claimed that there was a 'crisis of identity' in England. As I have argued above, I believe this considerably overstates the true position and is, of course, advanced by Salmond primarily to create an impression that there may be UK-wide pressure for further reform in the direction of breaking the Union.

Salmond went on to say: 'We must aspire to a whole new concordat between the two nations, one which adds a new momentum to the process of discovering and securing the identity of both of these nations and defining the best future for both on this island that we share and this continent to which we are tied.'

Again this presupposes that there is any particular agitation in England for further reform. Even if there is, it assumes that any agitation will be more than ill-directed grumbling, that it will become a coherent campaign for reform. Salmond's contribution to the debate is, however, to be welcomed if only as a valuable externalisation of what can become a process of constitutional navel-gazing in Scotland.

What then, among these options, of the answer to the West Lothian question? There are, in reality, only two constitutional solutions which would answer – rather than mitigate – the question. These are independence or federalism. Neither of these solutions is presently being advanced by either the UK Government or principal opposition party.

Before addressing these two options, I should note that West Lothian is not remotely answered by English regionalism, however extensive. The UK Government has established an elected body for London and has set up regional development agencies around England which might mutate, according to demand, into regional assemblies.

Some argue that this addresses West Lothian, supplying an English counterbalance to the Scottish political structure. Certainly, such a regional dimension – if it could be established and if there were uniform demand for it – might help to mitigate such envy as exists towards Scottish autonomy. It would not, however, answer West Lothian unless it were proposed that these regional bodies should have law-making powers.

As long as the law for the East Midlands, for example, is laid down by Westminster – and as long as Scottish MPs participate in Westminster votes – then West Lothian applies. Establishing a regional development agency in Nottingham or even a full-scale assembly may be regarded as a valuable step in its own right but it has no impact whatsoever upon legislative politics and consequently upon the West Lothian question. Until Nottingham can legislate for the East Midlands – and such a development is utterly remote from government or popular thinking – then the regional dimension in

England will be, properly, a division of local government. It will not parallel the Scottish Parliament.

Firstly, West Lothian could self-evidently be answered by Scottish independence, by breaking the Union, by reducing the number of MPs from Scotland at Westminster to zero. That is steadfastly opposed by Labour, by the Liberal Democrats and by the Conservatives, apart from a handful of Tories who believe that it might advance the party's cause in England while allowing Scotland to adopt a zealously free-market approach, to become the Luxembourg of the British Isles.

Secondly, West Lothian could be answered by federalism: either a version incorporating English regional legislatures or, more probably, a system whereby Scotland, Wales, Northern Ireland and the whole of England become domestic self-governing units. Such an approach is broadly endorsed by the Liberal Democrats as a longer-term aim, although they have thrown their weight behind the devolution movement meantime.

There are two problems with federalism. Firstly, there is minimal evidence of a uniform demand in England for regional government – far less for full-scale regional federalism. Secondly, England as a whole would far outweigh the size of the other components in any new federal structure. Consider, for example, the prospect that Labour formed the federal government on the back of a UK mandate while the Conservatives could muster enough support to govern England.

Is it seriously suggested that a Labour federal Prime Minister might deal with defence and foreign affairs for the UK – while a Conservative English Prime Minister sorted out education, health and other domestic matters for England, for four-fifths of the UK population? Would they take turns in Downing Street? Would the two administrations take questions in the Commons on alternate days?

The federal solution which works in the United States and Germany – where no single state is completely dominant – would not easily translate to the UK, where one constituent nation has the vast majority of the population and the firmly established UK capital. The English Question – if it is subsequently posed with any vigour – may yet prove the toughest of Britain's constitutional conundrums to solve.

Notes

1. Article in *The Guardian*, 13 April 1999.
2. Article in *The Guardian*, 11 February 1997.
3. Article in *The Guardian*, 4 June 1998.
4. Article in *The Daily Telegraph*, 2 February 1999.
5. Article in the *Daily Record*, 23 April 1999.
6. John Mackintosh Lecture, Edinburgh University, 19 November 1998.
7. Lecture, London School of Economics, 25 February 1999.

Conclusion
A Look to the Future

In opposition, the former Labour leader John Smith described devolution as 'unfinished business'. With this phrase, he was reflecting partly upon his own role in attempting to steer reforms of the governance of Scotland through the Commons in the 1970s.

Equally, he was stressing Labour's determination to resume the task of devolving power to Scotland in the event that the party regained power. John Smith's early death, of course, robbed him of the opportunity to carry out that pledge personally.

Another phrase of Smith's with regard to devolution entered the established political vocabulary of Britain. He described the pressure for a system of Scottish government within the United Kingdom as the 'settled will of the Scottish people'.

By this, I believe John Smith meant no more than to argue that Labour was working with the grain of popular opinion in Scotland. His phrase encapsulated a more wide-ranging Labour ambition: to establish devolution firmly as the central position, marginalising by implication the Tories on the one hand and the SNP on the other.

As I have already noted, some have occasionally appeared to stretch Smith's phrase to imply that the specific scheme implemented by the UK Labour Government is close to the last word on the subject, that the governance of Scotland is now fixed.

By contrast, I do not believe that the 'settled will' of the people which prompted devolution is necessarily the final will. For the avoidance of any doubt whatsoever, I should stress again that I do not believe that Scottish independence is the guaranteed final destination. It may be. It may not.

For one thing, the definitions of sovereignty and independence may change in an increasingly interdependent continent. It is impossible to be precise about the United Kingdom's future relationship with the EU. Similarly, it is impossible to specify the developing role of the new devolved Scotland within the framework of that broader relationship.

What we would now understand as national independence – relative fiscal autonomy, a distinct defence force and separate foreign relations – may become less common if financial, military and diplomatic functions come increasingly to be shared within Europe or on a global basis.

For example, does Scotland truly need to set up a separate army, navy and air force – the full panoply of military might – to be considered 'independent', to establish the popular sovereignty which is the Nationalists' underlying aim? Looking into the future, I think it at least possible that the SNP may reconsider that element of their package.

Is sovereign independence negated by a shared currency, as some would argue? Can a country be 'independent' and join the Euro zone? If not, then Germany and France are no longer sovereign nations. It seems clear, again, that the definition of independence is changing, that sovereignty is pooled. Nationalist objectives, I believe, will tend to narrow to focus almost entirely upon securing a distinct voice for Scotland within the sovereignty pool that is the European Union.

More immediately, independence in the form prescribed by the SNP was turned down by the voters at the 1999 election. Given the choice, the people of Scotland indicated their preference for the various menus of shared governance within the United Kingdom set out by the other parties. Labour, the party with the largest share of the vote, made opposition to independence a central plank of its campaign. The other major parties were equally firm against breaking the Union.

For the immediate future, then, any changes which occur will be firmly within the devolved structure which has received popular support.

I believe there will be changes, although I think it likely that the pace of change will be relatively slow, at least at first. There is unlikely to be the political or public appetite in Scotland for substantial alteration to a structure so recently put together. Equally, Westminster would be extremely reluctant to sanction further significant devolution of powers so soon after the detailed negotiations which led to the present set-up.

However, devolution may become evolution. As Donald Dewar has been scrupulous in stressing, there is scope for the powers of the Parliament to alter if there is evident demand or evident need.

There may, of course, be change elsewhere in the United Kingdom. As I have discussed in the previous chapter, the English Question may ultimately need to be addressed. Certainly, there are strategic thinkers within the Labour Party who are beginning to formulate quasi-federalist answers to the question of how the UK should be governed, now that Scottish devolution is a reality.

Equally, for the reasons previously discussed, I do not presently

The scene inside the (temporary) Scottish Parliament in Edinburgh as the new Members are sworn in, 12 May 1999. (Kindly supplied by PA News Ltd.)

expect agitation for immediate change, despite the concerns voiced
by some politicians. Tory backbenchers may well have a point with
their variously voiced grievances about Scottish interference in
English politics – but I do not yet believe that there is among the
people of England a widespread sense of injustice, of a democratic
deficit. After all, it may be said that such a sense took 300 years to
incubate in Scotland.

Most of all, I think it likely that the dynamic of the new Scottish
Parliament itself will alter. I firmly believe – by contrast with those
who forecast that the new legislature would be 'Strathclyde Region
writ large' – that Scottish devolved politics will become big-league
politics. At the time of writing, in the summer of 1999, it is already
fairly clear that the Parliamentarians on the Mound see themselves
as players rather than observers, as participants rather than a state-
funded pressure group.

It may be that the people of Scotland – as the SNP hope – will
subsequently seek to extend their new devolved Parliament into
independence, however defined. It may be that devolution will
embed itself comfortably within a reformed United Kingdom. The
people will choose.

The Opening of the Parliament.
(Kindly supplied by *The Scotsman* Publications Ltd.)

Crowds line the Royal Mile for the Royal opening.
(Kindly supplied by *The Scotsman* Publications Ltd.)

Thumbs up for the new Parliament.
(Kindly supplied by *The Scotsman* Publications Ltd.)

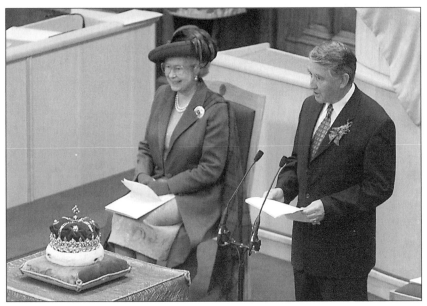

The Queen and Sir David Steel, the Presiding Officer, with the Scottish Crown at the formal opening of the Parliament on the 1st of July 1999.
(Kindly supplied by *The Scotsman* Publications Ltd.)

Index